T0366733

CICERO

XVb

LCL 507

CICERO

PHILIPPICS
7–14

EDITED AND TRANSLATED BY

D. R. SHACKLETON BAILEY

REVISED BY

JOHN T. RAMSEY
AND
GESINE MANUWALD

HARVARD UNIVERSITY PRESS

CAMBRIDGE, MASSACHUSETTS
LONDON, ENGLAND
2009

Library of Congress Control Number 2009930988
CIP data available from the Library of Congress

ISBN 978-0-674-99635-9

*Composed in ZephGreek and ZephText by
Technologies 'N Typography, Merrimac, Massachusetts.
Printed on acid-free paper and bound by
The Maple-Vail Book Manufacturing Group*

CONTENTS

LIST OF CICERO'S WORKS
SHOWING ARRANGEMENT
IN THIS EDITION

LIST OF CICERO'S WORKS

ABBREVIATIONS

Works by Cicero are referred to by title only, except in instances where confusion might arise. In the notes and introductions, where it is clear that references by speech number and section are to the *Philippics*, "*Phil.*" is generally omitted. Titles and names of ancient authors are abbreviated as in *OCD*[3].

The following abbreviations of modern works are employed in the introductions to the speeches and in the notes:

CIL	*Corpus Inscriptionum Latinarum.*
ILS	Dessau, H., ed. (1892–1916) *Inscriptiones Latinae Selectae*. Berlin.
MRR	Broughton, T. R. S. (1951–2, 1986) *The Magistrates of the Roman Republic*. 3 vols. Atlanta.
ORF	Malcovati, H., ed. (1976) *Oratorum Romanorum Fragmenta Liberae Rei Publicae*. 4th ed. Turin.
RE	Pauly, A. F. and Wissowa, G., edd. (1893–1980) *Real-Encyclopädie der klassischen Altertumswissenschaft*. Stuttgart.
SB, *Two Studies*[2]	Shackleton Bailey, D. R. (1991) *Two Studies in Roman Nomenclature*. 2nd ed. Atlanta.

PHILIPPIC 7

INTRODUCTION

While the senate awaited the return of the envoys, who had set off on 5 January 43 to meet with Antony (9.9), activities and discussions continued among the various factions in Rome. On the one hand, the senate decreed that one consul should set forth to war, and the other remain in Italy to begin preparations for war. The consuls distributed these tasks by drawing lots: A. Hirtius departed for the war in Cisalpine Gaul, and C. Vibius Pansa oversaw the preparations in Italy (7.11–13; 8.5–6; 10.16, 21; 11.21, 24; 14.4–5; *Fam.* 11.8.2; 12.5.2). On the other hand, Mark Antony's friends in Rome tried to influence public opinion by spreading rumors that Antony was willing to negotiate and by labeling Cicero a warmonger (7.2–5).

In view of this situation and of the fact that waiting for the return of the embassy imposed inactivity, Cicero took the opportunity to renew his call for a strict war policy against Antony when the senate met soon after the middle of January 43 to attend to some routine business (7.1, 27). Cicero could take up the topic of war because senators were not required to speak exclusively on the matter under debate but could introduce any topic they pleased. In the *Seventh Philippic* Cicero explains and justifies his war policy, expresses once again his disapproval of the embassy and of its consequences, and argues against peace with Antony. He points out that though he has been an advocate of

peace on other occasions, he is opposed to peace with Antony on the grounds that it will not be a true peace but a peace in name only, since true peace with Antony could not be achieved at present.

STRUCTURE

Exordium

(1) Confronting the threat posed by Antony is more important than dealing with routine business

Argumentatio

(2–7a) The political climate in Rome
    (2–5a) The pro-Antonian faction
    (5b–7a) Praise and encouragement of the consul Pansa
(7b–25) War, not peace, is the only response to Antony
    (7b–9a) Cicero, though a lover of peace, opposes peace
             with Antony because
        (9b–15) it is dishonorable
        (16–20) it is dangerous
        (21–25) it is impossible

Peroratio

(26–27a) Appeal for an appropriate reaction to the outcome of the embassy

Sententia

(27b) Cicero seconds the motion of Publius Servilius

M. TULLI CICERONIS
IN M. ANTONIUM
ORATIO PHILIPPICA SEPTIMA

1   [1] Parvis de rebus sed fortasse necessariis consulimur,
patres conscripti. De Appia via et de Moneta consul, de
Lupercis tribunus plebis refert. Quarum rerum etsi facilis
explicatio videtur, tamen animus aberrat a sententia sus-
pensus curis maioribus. Adducta est enim, patres conscripti, res in maximum periculum et in extremum paene
discrimen. Non sine causa legatorum istam missionem[1]
semper timui, numquam probavi: quorum reditus quid
sit adlaturus ignoro; exspectatio quidem quantum adferat
languoris animis quis non videt? Non enim se tenent ei qui
senatum dolent ad auctoritatis pristinae spem revirescere,
coniunctum huic ordini populum Romanum, conspiran-
tem Italiam, paratos exercitus, expeditos duces.

2   Iam nunc fingunt responsa Antoni eaque defendunt.
Alii postulare illum ut omnes exercitus dimittantur: scilicet

---

[1] *D*: legatorum missionem *V*

---

[1] Possibly repairs to the Via Appia and to the mint housed
in the Temple of Juno Moneta on the Capitoline Hill, as well as
some aspects of the regular business of the annual festival of the
Lupercalia, celebrated on 15 Feb.

MARCUS TULLIUS CICERO'S SEVENTH PHILIPPIC ORATION AGAINST MARCUS ANTONIUS

[1] We are being consulted, Members of the Senate, about minor but perhaps mandatory matters. The consul raises the issues of the Via Appia and the Mint; a tribune of the plebs raises the issue of the Luperci.¹ Dealing with these items seems to offer no difficulty, but the mind strays from a proposal, held in suspense by larger anxieties. For the situation has reached a peak of danger, Members of the Senate, and almost the ultimate crisis. It was not for nothing that I feared that mission of envoys, never approved of it: what their return will bring I do not know, but the great slackening of men's spirits which the waiting brings is plain to everyone. No effort is being spared by those who are sorry to see the senate reinvigorated in the hope of regaining its old authority, sorry to see the Roman people leagued with this body, Italy in unison, the armies prepared, the generals ready.

They are already inventing answers of Antonius and defending them. Some say he is demanding that all armies be

legatos ad eum misimus, non ut pareret et dicto audiens
esset huic ordini, sed ut condiciones ferret, leges impone-
ret, reserare nos exteris gentibus Italiam iuberet, se praesertim incolumi a quo maius periculum quam ab ullis
3   nationibus extimescendum est. Alii remittere eum nobis
Galliam citeriorem, illam ultimam postulare: praeclare, ex
qua non legiones solum sed etiam nationes ad urbem cone-
tur adducere. Alii nihil eum iam nisi modeste postulare
Macedoniam. Suam[2] vocat omnino, quoniam Gaius frater
est inde revocatus. Sed quae provincia est ex qua illa fax ex-
citare non possit incendium? Itaque idem quasi providi cives et senatores diligentes bellicum me cecinisse dicunt,
suscipiunt pacis patrocinium. Nonne sic disputant? "Irri-
tatum Antonium non oportuit: nequam est homo ille atque
confidens; multi praeterea improbi," quos quidem a se primum numerare possunt qui haec loquuntur; eos cavendos
esse denuntiant. Utrum igitur in nefariis civibus ulciscen-
di, cum possis, an pertimescendi diligentior cautio est?
4   [2] Atque haec ei loquuntur qui quondam propter levi-
tatem populares habebantur. Ex quo intellegi potest animo
illos abhorruisse semper ab optimo civitatis statu,[3] non voluntate fuisse populares. Qui enim evenit ut, qui in rebus
improbis populares fuerint, idem in re una maxime populari, quod eadem salutaris rei publicae sit, improbos se

---

[2] *Sternkopf*: Macedoniam, ‹quam› suam *Gruter, SB*
[3] statu, ‹casu› *add. SB*

---

[2] By a decree of the senate on 20 Dec. 44 (cf. 3.37–39). Earlier
in 44, Macedonia was to have been Antony's proconsular province, and so it is now free to be reclaimed by him according to this
scenario.   [3] Cf. 1.21, n. 42.

dismissed: I suppose we sent envoys to him, not for him to obey and bow to the will of this body, but to have him state terms, impose conditions, order us to open Italy to foreign peoples, while he himself, from whom there is worse to fear than from any tribes, keeps his position intact. Others 3 say he is turning over Hither Gaul to us and demanding that outer province: wonderful!—from where he can try to bring up not merely legions but tribes against the city. Others say his only demand now is the moderate one for Macedonia. He calls it absolutely his own, seeing that his brother Gaius has been recalled from it.[2] But what province is there from which such a firebrand cannot start a conflagration? And so these same people, posing as provident citizens and conscientious senators, say that I have blown the trumpet of war, and they set themselves up as advocates of peace. Does their line of argument not go like this? "Antonius should not have been provoked; he is a bad and self-assured man. And there are many criminals besides"—those who talk this way may as well begin the list with their own names—they warn us to beware of these. Well, when you are dealing with villainous citizens, which is the safer precaution, to take vengeance when you can or be frightened?

[2] And those who talk in this vein are the men who be- 4 cause of their fickleness used to be called "people's men."[3] Hence we can see that all along they disliked the best condition of the community, and that they were not "people's men" by inclination. How else does it happen that the same folk who were "people's men" in evil causes, prefer to be criminal rather than "popular" in the most popular cause that ever was, because it is also for the good of the

quam popularis esse malint? Me quidem semper, uti scitis,
adversarium multitudinis temeritati haec fecit praeclaris-
5 sima causa popularem. Et quidem dicuntur vel potius se
ipsi dicunt consularis: quo nomine dignus est nemo, nisi
qui tanti honoris onus[4] potest sustinere. Faveas tu hosti,
ille litteras ad te mittat de sua spe rerum secundarum,
eas tu laetus proferas, recites, describendas etiam des
improbis civibus, eorum augeas animos, bonorum spem
virtutemque debilites; et te consularem aut senatorem,
denique civem putes?

Accipiet in optimam partem C. Pansa, fortissimus
consul atque optimus; etenim dicam animo amicissimo:
hunc ipsum, mihi hominem familiarissimum, nisi talis
consul esset ut omnis vigilias, curas, cogitationes in rei
6 publicae salute defigeret, consulem non putarem. Quamquam nos ab ineunte illius aetate usus, consuetudo, stu-
diorum etiam honestissimorum societas similitudoque
devinxit, eiusdemque cura incredibilis in asperrimis belli
civilis periculis perspecta docuit non modo salutis sed
etiam dignitatis meae fuisse fautorem, tamen eundem, ut
dixi, nisi talis consul esset, negare esse consulem auderem:
idem non modo consulem esse dico sed memoria mea
praestantissimum atque optimum consulem, non quin pari
virtute et voluntate alii fuerint, sed tantam causam non habuerunt in qua et voluntatem suam et virtutem declara-
7 rent. Huius magnitudini animi, gravitati, sapientiae tem-

---

[4] *Cobet, SB*: nomen *codd*.

---

[4] Beyond a general aspect, addressing Q. Fufius Calenus (cf.
12.1–2).

[5] Pansa appears to have played a role in influencing Caesar to
permit Cicero to retain his position as an imperator (cf. *Lig.* 7).

Republic? As you know, I have always opposed the capriciousness of the crowd, but this splendid cause has made a "people's man" of me. And these men are called consulars, 5 or rather that is what they call themselves: nobody deserves that name unless he can support the burden of so great an honor. Are you,[4] sir, to back the enemy? Is he to send you letters about his hopes of success? Are you to produce them with a smile on your face, read them aloud, even give them to wicked citizens to copy, hearten such, sap the hope and courage of decent men? And then are you to regard yourself as a consular or a senator, or even a citizen?

Gaius Pansa, our most courageous and excellent consul, will take what I am about to say in very good part, for I shall speak in the friendliest spirit: even him, my intimate friend, I should not consider a consul if he were not a consul who concentrates all his watching, worrying, and thinking upon the safety of the Republic. Ever since his coming 6 of age, we have been linked by friendly intercourse and, furthermore, by our similarity and association in the most honorable pursuits. And in the most alarming situations during the civil war the unbelievable concern I saw on his part showed that he was anxious not only for my safety but for my dignity.[5] And yet, despite all this, as I said, I would not hesitate to declare him no consul at all, if he were not the consul he is. At the same time, I declare that he not only is a consul, but the most outstanding and excellent consul I can remember; not that others were not possessed of equal ability and goodwill, but they had no such great cause in which to demonstrate both their goodwill and their ability. Pansa's high-mindedness, responsibility, and 7

9

pestas est oblata formidolosissimi temporis. Tum autem illustratur consulatus, cum gubernat rem publicam, si non optabili, at necessario tempore. Magis autem necessarium, patres conscripti, nullum tempus umquam fuit.

[3] Itaque ego ille qui semper pacis auctor fui cuique pax, praesertim civilis, quamquam omnibus bonis, tamen in primis fuit optabilis—omne enim curriculum industriae nostrae in foro, in curia, in amicorum periculis propulsandis elaboratum est; hinc honores amplissimos, hinc mediocris opes, hinc dignitatem si quam habemus consecuti
8 sumus—ego igitur pacis, ut ita dicam, alumnus, qui quantuscumque sum (nihil enim mihi adrogo) sine pace civili certe non fuissem—periculose dico: quem ad modum accepturi, patres conscripti, sitis, horreo, sed pro mea perpetua cupiditate vestrae dignitatis retinendae et augendae quaeso oroque vos, patres conscripti, ut primo, etsi erit vel acerbum auditu vel incredibile a M. Cicerone esse dictum, accipiatis sine offensione quod dixero, neve id prius quam quale sit explicaro repudietis—ego ille, dicam saepius, pacis semper laudator, semper auctor, pacem cum M. Antonio esse nolo. Magna spe ingredior in reliquam orationem, patres conscripti, quoniam periculosissimum locum silen-
9 tio sum praetervectus. Cur igitur pacem nolo? Quia turpis est, quia periculosa, quia esse non potest. Quae tria dum explico, peto a vobis, patres conscripti, ut eadem benignitate qua soletis mea verba audiatis.

wisdom have been challenged by a political storm involving a most terrifying crisis. Now a consulship comes into the limelight when it guides the Republic, at a crucial, if undesired, juncture. But no juncture, Members of the Senate, has ever been more crucial than the present.

[3] Therefore, I am a man who has always been an advocate of peace, and although all decent men desire peace, especially peace between fellow countrymen, I have desired it more than most. My round of activity has always been worked out in the Forum, in the senate-house, in warding off danger from friends; that is how I have won the highest honors, moderate wealth, and any prestige I may enjoy. Therefore, I, a foster child of peace so to speak, who,   8
however great I am (I make no arrogant claims for myself), certainly should not have been what I am without peace in the community—I speak at my peril, Members of the Senate, and I tremble to think how you are going to receive this; but I beg and beseech you, Members of the Senate, bearing in mind my unflagging zeal for the maintenance and enhancement of your prestige, first of all to receive what I am about to say without offense and not to repudiate it until I have explained its meaning, even though the words grate upon your ears and you can scarcely believe they are Marcus Cicero's: I, a constant encomiast and advocate of peace (I shall state that repeatedly), am against peace with Marcus Antonius. I enter upon the rest of my speech with high hope, Members of the Senate, inasmuch as I have passed the most dangerous point without a sound of protest. Why, then, am I against peace? Because it is dis-   9
honorable, because it is dangerous, because it is impossible. And while I explain these three points, Members of the Senate, I ask you to listen to my words with your customary benevolence.

Quid est inconstantia, levitate, mobilitate cum singulis hominibus, tum vero universo senatui turpius? Quid porro inconstantius quam quem modo hostem non verbo sed re multis decretis iudicaritis, cum hoc subito pacem velle
10 coniungi? Nisi vero, cum C. Caesari meritos illi quidem honores et debitos, sed tamen singularis et immortalis decrevistis, unam ob causam quod contra M. Antonium exercitum comparavisset, non hostem tum Antonium iudicavistis, nec tum hostis est a vobis iudicatus Antonius cum laudati auctoritate vestra veterani milites qui C. Caesarem secuti essent, nec tum hostem Antonium iudicastis cum fortissimis legionibus, quod illum qui consul appellabatur, cum esset hostis, reliquissent, vacationes, pecunias, agros
11 spopondistis. [4] Quid? Cum Brutum omine quodam illius generis et nominis natum ad rem publicam liberandam exercitumque eius pro libertate populi Romani bellum gerentem cum Antonio provinciamque fidelissimam atque optimam, Galliam, laudibus amplissimis adfecistis, tum non hostem iudicastis Antonium? Quid? Cum decrevistis ut consules, alter ambove, ad bellum proficiscerentur,
12 quod erat bellum, si hostis Antonius non erat? Quid igitur? Profectus est vir fortissimus, meus collega et familiaris, A. Hirtius consul:[5] at qua imbecillitate, qua macie! Sed animi viris corporis infirmitas non retardavit. Aequum, credo, putavit vitam quam populi Romani votis retinuisset pro libertate populi Romani in discrimen adducere.

---

[5] *dist. Powell*: ad id igitur profectus est . . . consul. *SB*

---

[6] E.g. the decrees on 20 Dec. 44 and in Jan. 43.
[7] As augur.   [8] On A. Hirtius' illness and the prayers of the Roman people for his recovery cf. 1.37; 8.5; 10.16; 14.4.

Is anything more dishonorable not only to individuals but especially to the entire senate than inconsistency, irresponsibility, fickleness? And could anything be more inconsistent than suddenly to want peace made with a man whom in many recent decrees you have declared a public enemy, not in word but in substance?[6] Or did you not declare Antonius an enemy when you conferred upon Gaius Caesar honors that were, to be sure, his right and due, but nonetheless extraordinary and everlasting, solely in recognition of the fact he had raised an army against Marcus Antonius? And did you not declare Antonius an enemy when the veteran soldiers who had followed Gaius Caesar were commended by your authority? Did you not declare Antonius an enemy when you promised exemptions from military service, money, and lands to the very brave legions because they had abandoned him who was called a consul, while he was an enemy in fact? [4] Again, when in the most ample terms you commended Brutus, who was destined, as it were, by his family and name to be born to liberate the Republic, and commended his army, as they waged war against Antonius for the freedom of the Roman people, and commended the most faithful and loyal province of Gaul, did you not then declare Antonius an enemy? Or, again, when you decreed that the consuls, either or both, should set forth to war, what war was there if Antonius was not an enemy? What then? A very brave man, my colleague[7] and friend, the consul Aulus Hirtius, has set out: but how frail he was, how emaciated! Yet bodily infirmity did not retard the strength of his spirit. I imagine he thought it only fair to risk on behalf of the freedom of the Roman people a life saved by the Roman people's prayers.[8]

10

11

12

13

13 Quid? Cum dilectus haberi tota Italia iussistis, cum vacationes omnis sustulistis, tum ille hostis non est iudicatus? Armorum officinas in urbe videtis; milites cum gladiis sequuntur consulem; praesidio sunt specie consuli, re et veritate nobis; omnes sine ulla recusatione, summo etiam cum studio nomina dant, parent auctoritati vestrae: non est iudicatus hostis Antonius?

14 At legatos misimus. Heu, me miserum! Cur senatum cogor, quem laudavi semper, reprehendere? Quid? Vos censetis, patres conscripti, legatorum missionem populo Romano vos probavisse? Non intellegitis, non auditis meam sententiam flagitari? Cui cum pridie frequentes essetis adsensi, postridie ad spem estis inanem pacis devoluti. Quam turpe porro legiones ad senatum legatos mittere, senatum ad Antonium! Quamquam illa legatio non est, denuntiatio est paratum illi exitium, nisi paruerit huic ordini. Quid refert? Tamen opinio est gravis.[6] Missos enim legatos omnes vident; decreti nostri non omnes verba noverunt. [5] Retinenda est igitur nobis constantia, gravitas, perseverantia; repetenda vetus illa severitas, si quidem auctoritas senatus decus, honestatem, laudem dignitatemque desiderat, quibus rebus hic ordo caruit nimium diu. Sed erat tunc excusatio oppressis, misera illa quidem, sed tamen iusta: nunc nulla est. Liberati regio dominatu videbamur: multo postea gravius urgebamur armis domesticis. Ea ipsa

[6] *Pluygers, SB*: grui V^1: gravior V^2D

[9] Referring to the debates in the senate on 1–4 Jan. 43 (cf. 6.2–3).

[10] Nothing is known of these envoys.

[11] Under Caesar.

Again, when you ordered levies of troops to be held   13
throughout Italy and canceled all exemptions from military service, was Antonius not declared an enemy then?
You see arms factories in the city; soldiers follow the consul
sword in hand, outwardly for his protection, in truth and
reality for ours. Everyone is enlisting, without any excuses,
in fact with the greatest enthusiasm, obeying your authority. Has not Antonius been declared an enemy?

But we have sent envoys. Alas, dear me! Why am I   14
forced to find fault with the senate, which I have always
praised? I ask you: do you think, Members of the Senate,
you have won the Roman people's approval for the envoys'
mission? Do you not understand, do you not hear that they
are crying out for my proposal, which you flocked to support one day only to fall headlong the next into a state of an
empty hope for peace?[9] How dishonorable, furthermore,
that legions should send envoys to the senate[10] and the
senate send envoys to Antonius! True, that is not an embassy; it is rather a warning that he must expect to be destroyed if he does not obey this body. But what difference
does that make? The effect on public opinion is serious
all the same. For everyone sees that envoys have been
dispatched; but not everyone knows the wording of our
decree. [5] Therefore we must hold to our constancy, responsibility, and determination; we must get back to that
sternness of old, if the authority of the senate lacks honor,
respectability, credit, and dignity, things this body has too
long been without. Then,[11] however, there was some excuse, held down as we were; a sorry excuse, to be sure, but
a just one. There is none now. It looked as though we had
been freed from the rule of a monarch; later we were
pressed far harder by weapons in our midst. Those too we

15

depulimus nos quidem: extorquenda sunt. Quod si non
possumus facere—dicam quod dignum est et senatore et
15 Romano homine—moriamur. Quanta enim illa erit rei publicae turpitudo, quantum dedecus, quanta labes, dicere
in hoc ordine sententiam M. Antonium consulari loco!
cuius ut omittam innumerabilia scelera urbani consulatus,
in quo pecuniam publicam maximam dissipavit, exsules
sine lege restituit, vectigalia divendidit, provincias de populi Romani imperio sustulit, regna addixit pecunia, leges
civitati per vim imposuit, armis aut obsedit aut exclusit senatum: ut haec, inquam, omittam, ne hoc quidem cogita-
tis, eum qui Mutinam, coloniam populi Romani firmissi-
mam, oppugnarit, imperatorem populi Romani, consulem
designatum, obsederit, depopulatus agros sit, hunc in eum
ordinem recipi a quo totiens ob has ipsas causas hostis iudicatus sit quam foedum flagitiosumque sit?

16   Satis multa de turpitudine. Dicam deinceps, ut proposui, de periculo: quod etsi minus est fugiendum quam turpitudo, tamen offendit animos maioris partis hominum
magis. [6] Poteritis igitur exploratam habere pacem, cum
in civitate Antonium videbitis vel potius Antonios? Nisi
forte contemnitis Lucium: ego ne Gaium quidem. Sed, ut
video, dominabitur Lucius. Est enim patronus quinque et
triginta tribuum, quarum sua lege qua cum C. Caesare ma-
gistratus partitus est suffragium sustulit, patronus centu-
riarum equitum Romanorum quas item sine suffragio esse
voluit, patronus eorum qui tribuni militares fuerunt, pa-
17 tronus Iani Medii. Quis huius potentiam poterit sustinere?

---

¹² As tribune in 44, Lucius Antonius passed a law authorizing
Caesar to appoint half the magistrates, consuls excluded (cf. Suet.
Iul. 41.2; Nic. Dam. *Vit. Caes.* 67; 77; Cass. Dio 43.51.3).

¹³ For the basis of this claim cf. 6.12–15.

thrust off; now we must wrench them away. If we cannot do that—I shall speak as befits a senator and a Roman—let us die. For what a dishonor to the Republic, what a disgrace, what a blot it will be, if Marcus Antonius gives his opinion in this body among the ex-consuls! To say nothing of the countless misdeeds of his consulship in the city, during which he dissipated a vast sum of public money, brought back exiles without a law, sold off state revenues, removed provinces from the empire of the Roman people, granted kingdoms for money, imposed laws on the community by employing violence, beleaguered or excluded the senate with arms—to say nothing, I repeat, of all this, do you not even consider how foul a scandal it will be for the man who has laid siege to Mutina, one of the most staunch of the Roman people's colonies, blockaded an imperator of the Roman people and consul-elect, and devastated the territory, to be readmitted to this body, which has repeatedly declared him an enemy for these very reasons?

So much on the issue of dishonor. Next, as I proposed, I shall speak of danger: even though it is less to be shunned than dishonor, nevertheless it is more upsetting to the minds of the majority of people. [6] Well, then, will you be able to have any assurance of peace when you see Antonius, or rather the brothers Antonii, in the community? Perhaps you do not take Lucius seriously? I take even Gaius seriously. But, as I see it, Lucius will direct them. For he is patron of the thirty-five tribes, whose votes he took away by his law under which he shared out the magistracies with Gaius Caesar;[12] he is patron of the centuries of Roman knights, whom he likewise chose to disenfranchise, patron of the former military tribunes, patron of the Exchange.[13] Who will be able to stand up to his power, es-

15

16

17

Praesertim cum eosdem in agros etiam deduxerit. Quis
umquam omnis tribus, quis equites Romanos, quis tribunos militaris, ⟨quis Ianum Medium habuit clientis⟩?[7]
Gracchorum potentiam maiorem fuisse arbitramini quam
huius gladiatoris futura sit? Quem gladiatorem non ita appellavi ut interdum etiam M. Antonius gladiator appellari
solet, sed ut appellant qui plane et Latine loquuntur. Myrmillo in Asia depugnavit: cum ornasset Thraecidicis comitem et familiarem suum, illum miserum fugientem iugu-
lavit, luculentam tamen ipse plagam accepit, ut declarat
18   cicatrix. Qui familiarem iugularit, quid is occasione data
faciet inimico? Et qui illud animi causa fecerit, hunc
praedae causa quid facturum putatis? Non rursus improbos decuriabit, non sollicitabit rursus agrarios, non quere-
tur expulsos? M. vero Antonius non is erit ad quem omni
motu concursus fiat civium perditorum? Ut nemo sit alius
nisi ei qui una sunt et ei qui hic ei nunc aperte favent, parumne erunt multi, praesertim cum bonorum praesidia
discesserint, illi parati sint ad nutum futuri? Ego vero metuo, si hoc tempore consilio lapsi erimus, ne illi brevi tempore nimis multi nobis esse videantur.

19   Nec ego pacem nolo, sed pacis nomine bellum involu-
tum reformido. Qua re si pace frui volumus, bellum gerendum est; si bellum omittimus, pace numquam fruemur. [7]
Est autem vestri consili, patres conscripti, in posterum
quam longissime providere. Idcirco in hac custodia et tamquam specula collocati sumus uti vacuum metu popu-

---

7 *add.* SB

---

14 On L. Antonius' alleged gladiatorial past cf. 3.31, n. 38.

pecially when he has even settled those same people on lands? Who ever had all the tribes, the Roman knights, the military tribunes, the Exchange for clients? Do you imagine the Gracchi had greater power than this gladiator will have? And I do not call him a gladiator as Marcus Antonius too tends occasionally to be called a gladiator, but I do so like those who speak plain Latin. He put up a fight in Asia as a *myrmillo*: he equipped one of his followers, a personal friend, with the weapons of a Thracian gladiator and slaughtered the poor devil as he tried to get away; yet he himself received a heavy blow as proved by a scar.[14] Since   18
he slaughtered a comrade, what will he do to an enemy, if given the chance? And what do you think a fellow who did that to amuse himself will do for loot? Will he not organize troops of criminals yet again, stir up yet again people eager for a new distribution of land, and protest against evictions? As for Marcus Antonius, whenever there is trouble, will he not be the rallying point for desperate citizens? Even if these include only the people he has with him and those who are now openly supporting him here, will there not be enough of them, especially after the forces protecting decent men have gone off, while those people will be ready to move at a nod? For my part, I am afraid that if we make a mistake in our decisions now, we shall soon see there are too many of them.

I am not against peace, but I dread war camouflaged as   19
peace. Therefore, if we wish to enjoy peace, we must wage war; if we fail to wage war, peace we shall never enjoy. [7] Now it is the duty of your council, Members of the Senate, to look ahead as far as you can. Therefore we have been given this guardianship, placed as it were on a watchtower, in order that by our vigilance and foresight we might make

lum Romanum nostra vigilia et prospicientia redderemus.
Turpe est summo consilio orbis terrae, praesertim in re
20 tam perspicua, consilium intellegi defuisse. Eos consules
habemus, eam populi Romani alacritatem, eum consensum Italiae, eos duces, eos exercitus, ut nullam calamita-
tem res publica accipere possit sine culpa senatus. Equidem non deero: monebo, praedicam, denuntiabo, testabor
semper deos hominesque quid sentiam, nec solum fidem
meam, quod fortasse videatur satis esse, sed in principe
civi non est satis: curam, consilium vigilantiamque prae-
stabo.

21 [8] Dixi de periculo. Docebo ne coagmentari quidem
posse pacem; de tribus enim quae proposui hoc extremum
est. Quae potest pax esse M. Antonio primum cum senatu?
Quo ore vos ille poterit, quibus vicissim vos illum oculis in-
tueri? Quis vestrum illum, quem ille vestrum non oderit?
Age, vos ille solum et vos illum? Quid? Ei qui Mutinam cir-
cumsedent, qui in Gallia dilectus habent, qui in vestras
fortunas imminent amici umquam vobis erunt aut vos illis?
An equites Romanos amplectetur? Occulta enim fuit eorum voluntas iudiciumque de Antonio: qui frequentissimi
in gradibus Concordiae steterunt, qui nos ad libertatem
recuperandam excitaverunt, arma, saga, bellum flagitave-
runt, me una cum populo Romano in contionem vocave-
runt, hi Antonium diligent et cum his pacem servabit
22 Antonius? Nam quid ego de universo populo Romano dicam? Qui pleno ac referto foro bis me una mente atque

---

15 Probably when the senate met there on 2–4 Jan. 43.

the Roman people void of fear. It is a dishonor if the supreme council of the world is perceived to lack counsel, especially in so plain a case as this. Such are our consuls, such 20 is the ready spirit of the Roman people, such is the unanimous sentiment of Italy, such are our generals, such are our armies, that no calamity can befall the Republic without it being the fault of the senate. As for me, I shall not fail to do my part: I shall warn, I shall foretell, I shall give notice, I shall continually call gods and men to witness my sentiments; you will be able to count not only on my good faith, which may perhaps seem sufficient in itself but in a foremost citizen is not all that is required: you will be able to count as well on my care, counsel, and vigilance.

[8] I have spoken of danger. I shall show that it is not 21 even possible to patch up peace; for this is the last of my three propositions. What peace can exist between Marcus Antonius and, first, the senate? How will he be able to face you; how will you, in turn, be able to look upon him? Which of you will not hate him; which of you will he not hate? But come, will the hatred be confined to him and to you? Consider. What of the men who are besieging Mutina, levying troops in Gaul, reaching for your possessions: will they ever be your friends or you theirs? Further, will he grasp the hands of the Roman knights? To be sure, their sentiments and judgment concerning Antonius were a secret: they thronged the steps of the Temple of Concord,[15] they spurred us on to the recovery of freedom, demanded arms, military cloaks, war, they joined the Roman people in summoning me to a public meeting: will these men love Antonius, and will Antonius keep peace with them? As for the entire Roman people, what am I to say? 22 Twice they packed the Forum full to summon me to a pub-

voce in contionem vocavit declaravitque maximam libertatis recuperandae cupiditatem. Ita, quod erat optabile
antea ut populum Romanum comitem haberemus, nunc
habemus ducem. Quae est igitur spes, qui Mutinam cir-
cumsedent, imperatorem populi Romani exercitumque
23 oppugnant, eis pacem cum populo Romano esse posse? An
cum municipiis pax erit quorum tanta studia cognoscuntur
in decretis faciendis, militibus dandis, pecuniis pollicen-
dis, ut in singulis oppidis curiam populi Romani non desi-
deretis? Laudandi sunt ex huius ordinis sententia Firmani,
qui principes pecuniae pollicendae fuerunt. Respondendum honorifice est Marrucinis, qui ignominia notandos
censuerunt eos si qui militiam subterfugissent. Haec iam
tota Italia fiunt. Magna pax Antonio cum eis, his item cum
illo. Quae potest esse maior discordia? In discordia autem
pax civilis esse nullo pacto potest.

24   Ut omittam multitudinem, L. Visidio, equiti Romano,
homini in primis ornato atque honesto civique semper
egregio, cuius ego excubias et custodias mei capitis cognovi in consulatu meo, qui vicinos suos non cohortatus est
solum ut milites fierent sed etiam facultatibus suis subleva-
vit: huic, inquam, tali viro, quem nos senatus consulto col-
laudare debemus, poteritne esse pacatus Antonius? Quid
C. Caesari qui illum urbe, quid D. Bruto qui Gallia pro-
25 hibuit? Iam vero ipse[8] se placabit et leniet provinciae
Galliae, a qua exclusus et repudiatus est? Omnia videbitis,
patres conscripti, nisi prospicitis, plena odiorum, plena

8 *codd.*: ipsi *SB*

16 When Cicero delivered the *Fourth* and the *Sixth Philippics*.
17 Otherwise unknown.

lic meeting with one heart and voice, and they declared their passionate desire to regain freedom.[16] Hence, while formerly we could only pray to have the Roman people at our side, now we have them to lead us. So what hope exists that the men who are besieging Mutina, attacking an imperator of the Roman people and his army can be at peace with the Roman people? Will there be peace with the 23 towns of Italy, who have shown such great zeal in passing decrees, providing soldiers, and promising money that in no single town do you feel the absence of the Roman people's senate? The men of Firmum, who took the lead in promising money, should be commended by a resolution of this body. The Marrucini, who decreed that any dodgers of military service should be marked by public infamy, deserve an honorific acknowledgment. Such things are now happening throughout Italy. A fine peace Antonius will have with them and they with him! What strife can be sharper? And peace in the community cannot possibly exist amid strife.

To say nothing of the masses, take the Roman knight 24 Lucius Visidius, an eminently substantial and respectable person, always a model citizen;[17] I remember how he kept watch and vigil over my life when I was consul. He has urged his neighbors not only to enlist in the army but even given them subsidies of his own pocket. I say again: can Antonius be at peace with such a man as this, a man whom we ought to commend in a senatorial decree? Or can he be with Gaius Caesar, who banned him from the city, or Decimus Brutus, who banned him from Gaul? As for the 25 province of Gaul, which has excluded and repudiated him, will he himself calm and soothe his wrath toward it? Unless you take care, Members of the Senate, you will see every-

discordiarum, ex quibus oriuntur bella civilia. Nolite igitur id velle quod fieri non potest, et cavete, per deos immortalis, patres conscripti, ne spe praesentis pacis perpetuam pacem amittatis.

26   [9] Quorsum haec omnis spectat oratio? Quid enim legati egerint nondum scimus. At vero excitati, erecti, parati, armati animis iam esse debemus, ne blanda aut supplici oratione aut aequitatis simulatione fallamur. Omnia fecerit oportet quae interdicta et denuntiata sunt, prius quam aliquid postulet: Brutum exercitumque eius oppugnare, urbis et agros provinciae Galliae populari destiterit; ad Brutum adeundi legatis potestatem fecerit; exercitum citra flumen Rubiconem eduxerit, nec propius urbem milia passuum ducenta admoverit; fuerit et[9] in senatus et in populi Romani potestate. Haec si fecerit, erit integra potestas nobis deliberandi; si senatui non paruerit, non illi senatus, sed ille populo Romano bellum indixerit.

27   Sed vos moneo, patres conscripti: libertas agitur populi Romani, quae est commendata vobis; vita et fortunae optimi cuiusque, quo cupiditatem infinitam cum immani crudelitate iam pridem intendit Antonius; auctoritas vestra, quam nullam habebitis, nisi nunc tenueritis: taetram et pestiferam beluam ne inclusam et constrictam dimittatis cavete. Te ipsum, Pansa, moneo—quamquam non eges consilio, quo vales plurimum, tamen etiam summi gubernatores in magnis tempestatibus a vectoribus admoneri solent—hunc tantum tuum apparatum tamque praeclarum ne ad nihilum rec‹c›idere[10] patiare. Tempus habes tale

---

[9] *om.* D, SB
[10] *Zielinski, SB*: recidere *codd. (cf. 4.10)*

thing riddled with hatreds and with feuds, out of which arise civil wars. So do not wish for the impossible, and, by the immortal gods, Members of the Senate, beware of losing a lasting peace in the hope of an immediate peace.

[9] Where is this whole speech of mine leading? We do 26 not yet know what the envoys have achieved. But in spirit we should already be aroused, on the alert, ready, armed, so as not to be taken in by some soothing, pleading words or a pretense of fair play. He must have carried out all the restrictions and orders that have been imposed on him before he can make any request: given up attacking Brutus and his army and ravaging the towns and territory of the province of Gaul; allowed the envoys access to Brutus; withdrawn his army to this side of the river Rubicon and not have brought it within two hundred miles of the city; submitted to the control of both the senate and people of Rome. If he does these things, then we shall be free to deliberate; if he does not obey the senate, he will have declared war upon the Roman people, not the senate upon him.

But I warn you, Members of the Senate: what is at stake 27 is the freedom of the Roman people, which has been entrusted to your charge; likewise the lives and possessions of the very best men, long menaced by Antonius' insatiable greed combined with savage cruelty; and also your authority, which you will totally lose unless you hold it firmly now. Be sure you do not let this evil and destructive monster loose from the toils that confine him. Pansa, let me warn you personally—not that a man of your sagacity needs counsel, but even the best helmsmen are often advised by passengers in great tempests—do not let all the fine, extensive preparations you have made fall away to nothing.

quale nemo habuit umquam. Hac gravitate senatus, hoc studio equestris ordinis, hoc ardore populi Romani potes in perpetuum rem publicam metu et periculo liberare.

Quibus de rebus refers, P. Servilio adsentior.

You have an opportunity the like of which no man has ever had. With the support of a determined senate, an enthusiastic order of knights, and an ardent Roman people you can forever free the Republic from fear and danger.

On the business you have submitted for discussion, I agree with Publius Servilius.

PHILIPPIC 8

INTRODUCTION

Of the three envoys who set out on 5 January 43 to convey the senate's demands to Mark Antony (9.9), one, Ser. Sulpicius Rufus, died during the mission (cf. 8.22, 28; 9). The other two, L. Marcius Philippus and L. Calpurnius Piso Caesoninus, returned shortly before 2 February, accompanied by one of Antony's followers as his envoy, L. Varius Cotyla. Hence a meeting of the senate was held on 2 February 43. The envoys reported that Antony did not accept the conditions laid down by the senate, but instead made demands of his own (8.17, 24–28; 13.36–37; *Fam.* 12.4.1).

In the course of the debate on that day, three motions were put forward: Q. Fufius Calenus (probably) proposed a second embassy and issued another call to work out a peaceful settlement (8.11–13, 20). Cicero argued for an official declaration of war and urged that Antony be declared a public enemy (*hostis*) with whom there were to be no further relations (8.1, 32). A third position in between these extremes was taken up by Antony's uncle L. Iulius Caesar (8.1–2): he proposed softening Cicero's motion by substituting the term *tumultus* ("public emergency") for *bellum* ("war"), a compromise that was in harmony with the more cautious mood of the senate (cf. 12.17; 14.20). Accordingly, the senate accepted Caesar's motion, probably be-

cause it received the support of the consul Pansa (8.1): it declared a state of *tumultus* and ordered the people to put on their military cloaks (*saga*) from 4 February onwards (8.1–2, 6, 32; 10.19; 12.12, 16; 13.23; 14.1–3; *Ad Caes. iun.* fr. 16).

At about this same time, a report arrived in Rome from the consul A. Hirtius concerning military operations in northern Italy (8.6). On 3 February 43, the consul Pansa convened a meeting of the senate (8.1) at which he read out his colleague's report (8.6) and probably put before the senate a petition by the Massilians (8.18–19; 13.32). At that meeting, Cicero delivered the *Eighth Philippic*, in which he adduced Hirtius' report as proof that a state of war already existed, even though the senate had hesitated to make it official, and he criticized the decree of a *tumultus* on the previous day as too weak. He particularly faulted Calenus for his hostility towards the Massilians and for his desire to make peace with Antony. Cicero went on to lament the tepid response of the consulars in general, and he held up to scorn Antony's counter-demands.

Cicero ended his speech with a motion (8.33) that appears to have been adopted by the senate (*Ad Caes. iun.* fr. 1; App. *B Civ.* 3.63.258; Cass. Dio 46.31.2). He proposed that those who defected from Antony by 15 March should be exempt from punishment, while any who joined Antony after the passage of the decree (with the exception of Cotyla[1]) were to be regarded as committing treason. The consuls were to arrange for a discussion of rewards in the senate for any of Antony's followers who performed a mer-

[1] In this, Cicero had modified his motion, yielding to objections of other senators on the preceding day (cf. 8.32).

itorious service (such as, presumably betraying or even killing Antony, or otherwise hindering his operations).

STRUCTURE

Exordium

(1–2a) Assessment of the senate meeting on the previous day

Propositio

(2b–10) A state of war (*bellum*) exists in fact, if not in word
    (2b–4a) The term *"tumultus"* (decreed the previous day) contrasted with *"bellum"*
    (4b–6) Indications that war is already a reality
    (7–10) Singularity of the present war

Refutatio

(11–19) Criticism of the consular Q. Fufius Calenus
    (11–13a) Peace as aimed at by Calenus means slavery
    (13b–16a) Wishing *all* people to survive is harmful to the community
    (16b–19) Cicero's opposition to Calenus is not accompanied by anger but by mental anguish

Argumentatio

(20–32a) Discussion of the attitude of the other consulars
    (20–22) Inappropriateness of a second embassy and effect of the first embassy

M. TULLI CICERONIS
IN M. ANTONIUM
ORATIO PHILIPPICA OCTAVA

1   [1] Confusius hesterno die est acta res, C. Pansa, quam postulabat institutum consulatus tui. Parum mihi visus es eos quibus cedere non soles sustinere. Nam cum senatus ea virtus fuisset quae solet, et cum re viderent omnes esse bellum quidamque id verbum removendum arbitrarentur, tua voluntas in discessione fuit ad lenitatem propensior. Victa est igitur propter verbi asperitatem te auctore nostra sententia: vicit L. Caesaris, amplissimi viri, qui verbi atrocitate dempta oratione fuit quam sententia lenior. Quamquam is quidem, ante quam sententiam diceret, propinquitatem excusavit. Idem fecerat me consule in sororis viro quod hoc tempore in sororis filio fecit, ut et luctu soro-
2 ris moveretur et saluti populi Romani provideret. Atque ipse tamen Caesar praecepit vobis quodam modo, patres conscripti, ne sibi adsentiremini, cum ita dixit, aliam se sententiam dicturum fuisse eamque se ac re publica dig-

---

1 L. Iulius Caesar's sister Iulia was Antony's mother. On her husband cf. 2.14 and n. 14.

MARCUS TULLIUS CICERO'S
EIGHTH PHILIPPIC ORATION
AGAINST MARCUS ANTONIUS

[1] The transaction of business yesterday, Gaius Pansa, was vaguer than the normal practice under your consulship called for. It seemed to me that you did not take a firm enough stand against persons to whom you do not generally give way. For when the senate showed its usual courage, and everyone saw that war existed in fact, while there were some who wanted the term "war" removed, your wishes inclined to mildness in taking the vote. So because of the harshness of the word, my proposal was defeated at your instance, and that of Lucius Caesar, a very distinguished gentleman, won the day; in withdrawing the frightful word, he was milder in the language than in the actual proposal. To be sure, he pleaded the excuse of a family relationship before he put forward his proposal. When I was consul, he acted in the case of his sister's husband as he has acted now in that of his sister's son: he was both affected by his sister's sorrow and attentive to the welfare of the Roman people.[1] And yet, Members of the Senate, Caesar himself after a fashion advised you not to follow him, when he said that he would have have put forward a different proposal, one worthy of himself and the Repub-

nam, nisi propinquitate impediretur. Ergo ille avunculus:
num etiam vos avunculi qui illi estis adsensi?

At in quo fuit controversia? Belli nomen ponendum
quidam in sententia non putabant: tumultum appellare
malebant, ignari non modo rerum sed etiam verborum:
potest enim esse bellum ut tumultus non sit, tumultus au-
3 tem esse[1] sine bello non potest. Quid est enim aliud tumultus nisi perturbatio tanta ut maior timor oriatur? Unde
etiam nomen ductum est tumultus. Itaque maiores nostri
tumultum Italicum quod erat domesticus, tumultum Gal-
licum quod erat Italiae finitimus, praeterea nullum nomi-
nabant. Gravius autem tumultum esse quam bellum hinc
intellegi potest quod bello [Italico][2] vacationes valent, tumultu non valent. Ita fit, quem ad modum dixi, ut bellum
sine tumultu possit, tumultus sine bello esse non possit.
4 Etenim cum inter bellum et pacem medium nihil sit, necesse est tumultum, si belli non sit, pacis esse: quo quid ab-
surdius dici aut existimari potest? Sed nimis multa de verbo. Rem potius videamus, patres conscripti, quam quidem
intellego verbo fieri interdum deteriorem solere.

[2] Nolumus hoc bellum videri. Quam igitur municipiis
et coloniis ad excludendum Antonium auctoritatem da-

---

[1] *Isidorus*: ut tumultus esse V[1]: sine tumultu tumultus (ut
tumultus V[2]) esse (esse *post* bello *b*) DV[2]

[2] *del. Faërnus*: in bello *Isidorus*: bello italico V: bello gallico D

---

[2] Actually *tumultus* is connected etymologically with *tumor*
("a swelling"), not "fear" (*timor*), as Cicero asserts according to ancient etymology.

[3] Cf. 5.53.

lic, if he had not been hampered by family ties. Very good, he is the uncle. What about you who supported him: are you uncles too?

But what was the argument about? Certain persons thought that the name of war ought not to be used in the motion: they preferred to use the term "public emergency," showing their ignorance not only of facts but also of terminology. For while a war can exist without a public emergency, a public emergency cannot exist without a war. For what else is a public emergency but a disturbance so 3 serious that fear beyond the ordinary arises from it? And it is from this fact that the word "public emergency" has its origin.[2] Accordingly, our ancestors spoke of a "public emergency in Italy" (because it took place within our borders) and a "public emergency in Gaul" (because it was next door to Italy), but of no other public emergency besides. And that a public emergency is something more serious than a war can be inferred from the fact that exemptions from military service are valid in a war but are not valid in a public emergency.[3] Hence, as I have just observed, war can exist without a public emergency, but a public emergency cannot exist without war. After all, since 4 there is no halfway house between war and peace, if a public emergency does not come under the heading of war, it must come under the heading of peace. And what more absurd than this can be said or thought? But I have dwelt too long upon terminology. Let us rather look at substance, Members of the Senate, which indeed I realize is sometimes apt to be made worse by terminology.

[2] We do not want this to be seen as a war. Then what authority do we give to the municipalities and colonies to refuse Antonius admission? What authority to enlist as

37

mus? Quam ut milites fiant sine vi, sine multa, studio, voluntate? Quam ut pecunias in rem publicam polliceantur? Si enim belli nomen tolletur, municipiorum studia tollentur; consensus populi Romani, qui iam descendit in causam, si nos languescimus, debilitetur necesse est. Sed quid plura? D. Brutus oppugnatur: non est bellum. Mutina obsidetur: ne hoc quidem bellum est. Gallia vastatur: quae pax potest esse certior? Illud vero quis potest bellum esse dicere quo consulem, fortissimum virum, cum exercitu misimus? Qui, cum esset infirmus ex gravi diuturnoque morbo, nullam sibi putavit excusationem esse oportere, cum ad rei publicae praesidium vocaretur. C. quidem Caesar non exspectavit vestra decreta, praesertim cum illud esset aetatis: bellum contra Antonium sua sponte suscepit. Decernendi enim tempus nondum erat; bellum autem gerendi tempus si praetermisisset, videbat re publica oppressa nihil posse decerni. Ergo illi nunc et eorum exercitus in pace versantur. Non est hostis is cuius praesidium Claterna deiecit Hirtius; non est hostis qui consuli armatus obsistit, designatum consulem oppugnat, nec illa hostilia verba nec bellica quae paulo ante ex collegae litteris Pansa recitavit: "Deieci praesidium; Claterna potitus sum; fugati equites; proelium commissum; occisi aliquot." Quae pax potest esse maior? Dilectus tota Italia decreti sublatis vacationibus; saga cras sumentur; consul se cum praesidio descensurum esse dixit.

4 Cf. 1.37; 7.12; 10.16; 14.4.
5 These quotations purport to reproduce the main points from Hirtius' dispatch.

soldiers without compulsion or fines but from spontaneous zeal? What authority to promise financial resources in aid of the Republic? If the name of war is removed, the zeal of the municipalities will be removed as well; the united impulse of the Roman people, who have already come down on our side, must inevitably be weakened if we falter. But why waste words? Decimus Brutus is under attack: but it is not a war! Mutina is under siege: but not even that is a war! Gaul is being laid waste: can any peace be more assured? Who can indeed call that action a war to which we have dispatched a consul, a very brave man, at the head of an army? Ill as he was from a serious and longstanding ailment,[4] he thought there should be no excuse for him when summoned to defend the Republic. Gaius Caesar did not wait for your decrees, even though he was so young: he went to war with Antonius of his own accord. The time for decrees had not yet arrived; but he saw that if he let the time for military action pass, the Republic would be crushed and nothing could be decreed. Well, those commanders and their armies are now at peace. It is no enemy whose garrison was thrown out of Claterna by Hirtius; it is no enemy who is in armed opposition to a consul, attacking a consul-elect. Those were not hostile or warlike words that Pansa has just read out from his colleague's dispatch: "I threw out the garrison; I took possession of Claterna; the cavalry was put to flight; battle was joined; some were killed."[5] What peace can be greater? Levies have been decreed throughout the whole of Italy with the cancellation of exemptions from military service; military cloaks will be donned tomorrow; the consul has stated that he will appear in public with an armed escort.

5

6

7   Utrum hoc bellum non est, an etiam[3] tantum bellum
quantum numquam fuit? Ceteris enim bellis maximeque
civilibus contentionem rei publicae causa faciebat: ‹con-
tendebat›[4] Sulla cum Sulpicio de iure legum quas per vim
[con. Sulla][5] latas esse dicebat; Cinna cum Octavio de no-
vorum civium suffragiis; rursus cum Mario et Carbone
Sulla ne dominarentur indigni et ut clarissimorum hominum crudelissimam puniretur necem. Horum omnium
bellorum causae ex rei publicae contentione natae sunt.
De proximo bello civili non libet dicere: ignoro causam,
8   detestor exitum. [3] Hoc bellum quintum civile geritur—
atque omnia in nostram aetatem inciderunt—primum non
modo non in dissensione et discordia civium sed in maxima consensione incredibilique concordia. Omnes idem
volunt, idem defendunt, idem sentiunt. Cum omnis dico,
eos excipio quos nemo civitate dignos putat. Quae est igitur in medio belli causa posita? Nos deorum immortalium
templa, nos muros, nos domicilia sedesque populi Romani, aras, focos, sepulcra maiorum; nos leges, iudicia, libertatem, coniuges, liberos, patriam defendimus: contra M.
Antonius id molitur, id pugnat ut haec omnia perturbet,
evertat, praedam rei publicae causam belli putet, fortunas
nostras partim dissipet, partim dispertiat parricidis.

3 an etiam *D*: etiam *V*: an est *C. F. W. Müller, SB*
4 *add. Sternkopf*: faciebat. Sulla *SB*   5 *del. Fedeli*

6 Italians recently made Roman citizens in 90–89 as a consequence of the Social War.
7 Killed in the proscriptions under Marius and Cinna in 87/86.
Carbo's consular colleague in 82, Marius, was the son of the elder
Marius. Sulla returned to Italy in 83, after concluding the Mith-

Is this not a war, or even a war on a scale such as never   7
before existed? In other wars, and particularly civil wars,
the conflict originated from a political issue: Sulla fought
Sulpicius about the validity of laws which according to
Sulla had been passed by violence. Cinna fought Octavius
about voting rights for the new citizens.[6] Sulla again fought
Marius and Carbo to put an end to the rule of the unworthy
and to avenge the terribly cruel deaths of illustrious men.[7]
All these wars had their origins in political disputes. As for
the last civil war,[8] I would rather not speak of it: I do not
know its cause, and I abominate its outcome. [3] The fifth   8
civil war is now being fought—and they all occurred in my
lifetime—, and for the first time there is no division or dis-
cord among citizens, but on the contrary the utmost consensus and extraordinary unity. All men have one desire,
one cause, one sentiment. When I say "all," I mean all but
those whom nobody thinks worthy to be citizens. What
then is the avowed reason for this war? We are defending the temples of the immortal gods, the city walls, the
dwellings and houses of the Roman people, the altars, the
hearths, the tombs of our ancestors; we are defending
laws, courts of law, freedom, wives, children, and our native land. Marcus Antonius, on the contrary, is devising
and fighting to throw into confusion and overturn everything I have just mentioned, to regard the plunder of the
Republic as a cause for war, to squander one part of our
possessions and to parcel out the other among traitors.

ridatic War in Asia Minor, and overthrew his political enemies,
who had been in power since late 87.

[8] Between Caesar and first Pompey, and later Pompey's successors, in 49–45.

9   In hac tam dispari ratione belli miserrimum illud est
quod ille latronibus suis pollicetur primum domos—urbem enim divisurum se confirmat—deinde omnibus portis quo velint deducturum. Omnes Cafones, omnes Saxae
ceteraeque pestes quae sequuntur Antonium aedis sibi op-
timas, hortos, Tusculana, Albana definiunt. Atque etiam
homines agrestes, si homines illi ac non pecudes potius,
inani spe ad aquas usque et Puteolos pervehuntur. Ergo
habet Antonius quod suis polliceatur. Quid nos? Num quid
tale habemus? Di meliora! Id enim ipsum agimus ne quis
posthac quicquam eius modi possit polliceri. Invitus dico,
sed dicendum est: hasta Caesaris, patres conscripti, multis
improbis et spem adfert et audaciam. Viderunt enim ex
mendicis fieri repente divites; itaque semper hastam videre cupiunt ei qui nostris bonis imminent, quibus omnia

10   pollicetur Antonius. Quid nos? Nostris exercitibus quid
pollicemur? Multo meliora atque maiora. Scelerum enim
promissio et eis qui exspectant perniciosa est et eis qui pro-
mittunt. Nos libertatem nostris militibus, leges, iura, iudicia, imperium orbis terrae, dignitatem, pacem, otium pollicemur. Antoni igitur promissa cruenta, taetra, scelerata,
dis hominibusque invisa, nec diuturna neque salutaria:
nostra contra honesta, integra, gloriosa, plena laetitiae,
plena pietatis.

11   [4] Hic mihi etiam Q. Fufius, vir fortis ac strenuus, amicus meus, pacis commoda commemorat—quasi vero, si
laudanda pax esset, ego id aeque commode facere non pos-

---

9 Probably the town of Baiae on the Bay of Naples, famous for
its volcanic hot springs, which made it a fashionable spa.

10 Cf. 2.64, n. 72, and 4.9, n. 3.

In this quite different conception of war by the two   9
sides, the most deplorable aspect is the promises he is
making to his cutthroats: first our town houses—for he as-
sures them that he will divide up the city—then that he will
lead them out of all the city gates and settle them wherever
they wish. Cafo, Saxa, and their kind, all the evil creatures
in Antonius' train, are earmarking the best houses,
suburban estates, and properties at Tusculum and Alba.
And these uncouth fellows, if they are human beings and
not rather cattle, even let their idle hopes carry them as far
as the Waters[9] and Puteoli. Well, Antonius has something
to promise his followers. What about us? Do we have anything of the sort? May the gods forbid it! Our purpose is
precisely to make sure that nobody can promise anything
of this kind in the future. I say it with reluctance, but say it
I must: Caesar's lance,[10] Members of the Senate, brings
both hope and daring to many a criminal. For they saw
beggars suddenly become rich; and so those who menace
our property, to whom Antonius is promising everything,
are always eager to see such a lance. What about us? What   10
do we promise our armies? Far better and greater things.
The promise of crimes spells ruin both for those who
expect and for those who promise. We promise our soldiers freedom, laws, justice, law courts, dominion over the
world, dignity, peace, and tranquillity. Antonius' promises
are bloody, sinister, criminal, hateful to gods and men; they
will not last nor bring any good. Ours by contrast are honorable, fair, glorious, full of joy, and full of patriotism.

[4] But here is Quintus Fufius, a courageous and ener-   11
getic man, a friend of mine, actually reminding me of the
blessings of peace—as though, if peace needed praising, I
could not do it as well as himself. Have I defended peace

sem. Semel enim pacem defendi? Non semper otio stu-
dui? Quod cum omnibus bonis utile est, tum praecipue
mihi. Quem enim cursum industria mea tenere potuisset
sine forensibus causis, sine legibus, sine iudiciis? Quae
12   esse non possunt civili pace sublata. Sed quaeso, Calene,
quid tu? Servitutem pacem vocas? Maiores quidem nostri
non modo ut liberi essent sed etiam ut imperarent arma
capiebant: tu arma abicienda censes ut serviamus? Quae
causa iustior est belli gerendi quam servitutis depulsio? In
qua etiam si non sit molestus dominus, tamen est miserrimum posse, si velit. Immo aliae causae iustae, haec necessaria est. Nisi forte ad te hoc non putas pertinere quod
te socium fore speras dominationis Antoni. In quo bis labe-
ris: primum quod tuas rationes communibus interponis;
deinde quod quicquam stabile aut iucundum in regno pu-
13   tas. Non, si tibi antea profuit, semper proderit. Quin etiam
de illo homine queri solebas: quid te facturum de belua
putas?

Atque ais eum te esse qui semper pacem optaris, semper omnis civis volueris salvos. Honesta oratio, sed ita si
bonos et utilis et e re publica civis: sin eos qui natura cives
sunt, voluntate hostes, salvos velis, quid tandem intersit inter te et illos? Pater tuus quidem, quo utebar sene auctore
adulescens, homo severus et prudens, primas omnium ci-

***

[11] Alludes to the advancement Calenus enjoyed under Caesar.

only once? Have I not always favored tranquillity? Peace is advantageous for all decent men, but particularly for me. Where would my activity have found scope without court cases, without laws, without law courts? These cannot exist if internal peace is taken away. But I ask you, Calenus, 12 what do *you* say: do you call slavery peace? Our ancestors took up arms not only to be free but also to rule. Do you think we should throw our arms away in order to be slaves? Is there any more justifiable reason for waging war than to ward off slavery? In slavery, even if the master is not oppressive, the sorry thing still is that he can be if he wishes. Indeed, other reasons are justifiable, but this one is compelling. Or do you think perhaps that this does not concern you because you expect to be a partner in Antonius' despotism? You make two mistakes there: first, because you mix up your personal interests with the interests of the community; second, because you think that anything can be stable or agreeable in a tyranny. Even if it may have worked to your advantage previously,[11] it will not always work to your advantage. After all, you were accustomed to grum- 13 ble about that person, a human being; what do you think you will you do in reaction to a monster?

And you describe yourself as one who has always wished for peace, always wanted all citizens to survive. That is an honorable sentiment, but only if you mean decent citizens, men of use and benefit to the Republic. But should you want the survival of people who are citizens by birth but public enemies by choice, where, I ask, would be the difference between you and them? Your father, at any rate, a strict and wise man, who was a model for me when I was young and he was old, was in the habit of giving the place of honor among all citizens to Publius

vium P. Nasicae, qui Ti. Gracchum interfecit, dare solebat:
eius virtute, consilio, magnitudine animi liberatam rem
14 publicam arbitrabatur. Quid? Nos a patribus num aliter accepimus? Ergo is tibi civis, si temporibus illis fuisses, non
probaretur, quia non omnis salvos esse voluisset. "Quod L.
Opimius consul verba fecit de re publica, de ea re ita censuerunt uti L. Opimius consul rem publicam defenderet."
Senatus haec verbis, Opimius armis. Num igitur eum, si
tum esses, temerarium civem aut crudelem putares, aut
Q. Metellum, cuius quattuor filii consulares, P. Lentulum,
principem senatus, compluris alios summos viros qui cum
Opimio consule armati ⟨C.⟩⁶ Gracchum in Aventinum
persecuti sunt? Quo in proelio Lentulus grave volnus accepit, interfectus est Gracchus et M. Fulvius consularis,
eiusque duo adulescentuli filii. Illi igitur viri vituperandi:
non enim omnis civis salvos esse voluerunt.
15   [5] Ad propiora veniamus. C. Mario L. Valerio consulibus senatus rem publicam defendendam dedit; L. Saturninus tribunus plebis, C. Glaucia praetor est interfectus.
Omnes illo die Scauri, Metelli, Claudii, Catuli, Scaevolae,
Crassi arma sumpserunt. Num aut consules illos aut clarissimos viros vituperandos putas? Ego Catilinam perire
volui. Num tu qui omnis salvos vis Catilinam salvum esse
voluisti? Hoc interest, Calene, inter meam sententiam et
tuam: ego nolo quemquam civem committere ut morte

⁶ add. SB

12 By using the traditional wording, Cicero refers to the first
instance of the so-called *senatus consultum ultimum* (cf. 2.51, n.
56), which empowered the consul Opimius in 121 to crush the ex-
tribune Gaius Gracchus and his supporters.

Nasica, who killed Tiberius Gracchus, holding the view that Nasica's courage, judgment, and greatness of spirit had brought freedom to the Republic. Well? Surely we 14 have not heard any differently from our fathers? So, if you had been alive in those days, you would not have approved of Nasica as a citizen because, in your view, he had not wanted everyone to survive. "Whereas the consul Lucius Opimius spoke concerning the Republic, the senate decreed on this matter that the consul Lucius Opimius should defend the Republic."[12] So did the senate intervene with words, Opimius with weapons. Would you have deemed him a rash or cruel citizen, if you had lived then, and held the same view of Quintus Metellus, who had four consular sons, or Publius Lentulus, leader of the senate, or a number of other eminent men who chased Gaius Gracchus to the Aventine with weapons in their hands along with the consul Opimius? In that battle Lentulus was seriously wounded, Gracchus was killed, as was the consular Marcus Fulvius and his two young sons. So, those men ought to be censured, for they did not want all citizens to survive.

[5] Let us come to events closer to our own time. The 15 senate committed the defense of the Republic to the consuls Gaius Marius and Lucius Valerius; the tribune of the plebs Lucius Saturninus and the praetor Gaius Glaucia were killed. That day all the Scauri, Metelli, Claudii, Catuli, Scaevolae, and Crassi took up arms. Surely you do not think that either those consuls or those illustrious men ought to be censured? I wanted Catilina destroyed. Surely you, who want everyone to survive, did not want Catilina to survive? The difference between my professed view and yours, Calenus, is this: I want no citizen to act in such a way

47

multandus sit; tu, etiam si commiserit, conservandum putas. In corpore si quid eius modi est quod reliquo corpori noceat, id uri secarique patimur, ut membrum aliquod potius quam totum corpus intereat. Sic in rei publicae corpore, ut totum salvum sit, quicquid est pestiferum amputetur. Dura vox! Multo illa durior: "Salvi sint improbi, scelerati, impii; deleantur innocentes, honesti, boni, tota res publica!" Uno in homine, Q. Fufi, fateor te vidisse plus quam me: ego P. Clodium arbitrabar perniciosum civem, sceleratum, libidinosum, impium, audacem, facinerosum; tu contra sanctum, temperantem, innocentem, modestum, retinendum civem et optandum. In hoc uno te plurimum vidisse, me multum errasse concedo.

16

Nam quod me tecum iracunde agere dixisti solere, non est ita. Vehementer me agere fateor, iracunde nego. Omnino irasci amicis non temere soleo, ne si merentur quidem. Itaque sine verborum contumelia a te dissentire possum, sine animi summo dolore non possum. Parva est enim mihi tecum aut parva de re dissensio? Ego huic faveo, tu illi? Immo vero ego D. Bruto faveo, tu M. Antonio: ego conservari coloniam populi Romani cupio, tu expugnari studes. [6] An hoc negare potes, qui omnis moras interponas quibus infirmetur Brutus, melior fiat Antonius? Quo usque enim dices pacem velle te? Res geritur; conductae vineae[7]

17

---

[7] conductae *suspectum: edd. varia coni., velut* conductae ⟨copiae, actae⟩ vineae *Sternkopf* | vineae *ed. Veneta:* liniae *V:* lineae *D*

---

[13] Ponderous irony: as tribune of the plebs in 61, Calenus helped bring about the acquittal of Clodius on a charge of sacrilege, despite Cicero's incriminating evidence (*Att.* 1.14.5). Clodius then drove Cicero into exile in 58.

that he has to be punished with death; you think a citizen should be preserved even if he has so acted. If something in the body is of the sort to cause harm to the rest, we allow it to be cauterized or cut so that this or that part may perish rather than the whole body. Likewise in the body politic: let whatever is noxious be amputated so that the whole may be saved. A harsh saying! This one is far 16 harsher: "Let the criminals, the wicked, the traitors be saved; let the innocent, the respectable, the decent, the entire Republic be wiped out!" I do admit, Quintus Fufius, that in the case of one person your perception was better than mine: I used to think Publius Clodius a pernicious citizen, criminal, lustful, unpatriotic, insolent, villainous; you on the contrary regarded him as blameless, moderate, innocent, and unassuming, a valuable and desirable citizen. In this one instance I acknowledge your keen perspicacity and my own grave error.[13]

As for your claim that I am apt to take an angry tone with you, that is not so. I admit to vehemence, but anger I deny. In general it is not my habit to grow angry easily with my friends for no good reason, even if they deserve it. Accordingly, I can differ from you without using offensive expressions, though not without mental anguish. For is it a minor disagreement I have with you; is it about a minor issue, a matter of my backing this man and your backing that one? No, it is a matter of my backing Decimus Brutus and your backing Marcus Antonius: I am anxious to see a Roman colony saved, you are eager for it to be taken by storm. [6] Can you deny as much, when you are putting up all manner of delays to make Brutus weaker and Antonius better off? How much longer will you say that you want peace? War is in progress; siege-works have been assem-

sunt; pugnatur acerrime. Qui intercurrerent, misimus tris principes civitatis. Hos contempsit, reiecit, repudiavit Antonius: tu tamen permanes constantissimus defensor
18 Antoni. Et quidem, quo melior senator videatur, negat se illi amicum esse debere: cum suo magno esset beneficio, venisse eum contra se. Vide⟨te⟩[8] quanta caritas sit patriae: cum homini sit iratus, tamen rei publicae causa defendit Antonium!

Ego te, cum in Massiliensis tam es acerbus, Q. Fufi, non animo aequo audio. Quo usque enim Massiliam oppugnabis? Ne triumphus quidem finem fecit belli, per quem lata est urbs ea sine qua numquam ex Transalpinis gentibus maiores nostri triumpharunt? Quo quidem tempore populus Romanus ingemuit: quamquam proprios dolores suarum rerum omnes habebant, tamen huius civitatis fidelissimae miserias nemo erat civis qui a se alienas arbitraretur.
19 Caesar ipse, qui illis fuerat iratissimus, tamen propter singularem eius civitatis gravitatem et fidem cotidie aliquid iracundiae remittebat: te nulla sua calamitate civitas satiare tam fidelis potest? Rursus iam me irasci fortasse dices. Ego autem sine iracundia dico omnia nec tamen sine dolore animi: neminem illi civitati inimicum esse arbitror qui amicus huic sit civitati. Excogitare quae tua ratio sit, Calene, non possum: antea deterrere te ne popularis esses

[8] *add. Manutius, SB*

---

[14] Cicero switches from addressing Calenus directly in the second person to speaking about him.

[15] A representation of the town of Massilia, which had been compelled to surrender to Caesar during the Civil War (49), was

bled; there is bitter fighting. We sent three leading men of the community to intervene. Antonius has despised, rejected, and repudiated them: and yet you still remain Antonius' most resolute defender. And what is more, to make himself appear a more conscientious senator, he says he has no call to be Antonius' friend, seeing that Antonius appeared against him in court though owing him a great favor.[14] See how great a love he has for his native land: although he has a personal grievance against the man, nonetheless, for the sake of the Republic he defends Antonius!

I find it hard to listen with patience, Quintus Fufius, to your bitter language against the Massilians. How long are you going to attack Massilia? Did not even the triumph bring the war to an end, a triumph in which that city was borne in effigy,[15] a city without which our ancestors never triumphed over the nations beyond the Alps? At that time the Roman people groaned: though all had their own personal griefs, there was not a citizen who did not feel the sufferings of this most faithful community as his own. Caesar himself, terribly furious though he had been with them, abated something of his anger every day because of the extraordinary dignity and faithfulness of that community. Can so faithful a community not content you with any measure of calamity? Perhaps you will say that I am now getting angry again. Yet I say everything without anger, though not without mental anguish. I do not think any man who is an enemy of that community is a friend of this one. I cannot make out, Calenus, what your rationale is: previously we could not deter you from being a "peo-

18

19

displayed in Caesar's triumphal procession in 46, celebrating his conquest of Gaul (58–50).

non poteramus; exorare nunc ut sis popularis non possumus. Satis multa cum Fufio ac sine odio omnia, nihil sine dolore. Credo autem, qui generi querelam moderate ferat, aequo animo laturum amici.

20   [7] Venio ad reliquos consularis, quorum nemo est—iure hoc meo dico—quin mecum habeat aliquam coniunctionem gratiae, alii maximam, alii mediocrem, nemo nullam. Quam hesternus dies nobis, consularibus dico, turpis illuxit! Iterum legatos? Quasi⁹ ille faceret indutias? Ante os oculosque legatorum tormentis Mutinam verberavit; opus ostendebat munitionemque legatis; ne punctum quidem temporis, cum legati adessent, oppugnatio respiravit. Ad hunc legatos? Cur? An ut eorum reditu vehementius pertimescatis? Equidem cum ante legatos decerni non censuissem, hoc me tamen consolabar, [quod]¹⁰ cum illi ab Antonio contempti et reiecti revertissent renuntiavissentque senatui non modo illum de Gallia non discessisse, uti censuissemus, sed ne a Mutina quidem recessisse, potestatem sibi D. Bruti conveniendi non fuisse, fore ut omnes inflammati odio, excitati dolore, armis, equis, viris D. Bruto subveniremus. Nos etiam languidiores postea facti sumus quam M. Antoni non solum audaciam et scelus sed etiam

21

22 insolentiam superbiamque perspeximus. Utinam L. Caesar valeret, Ser. Sulpicius viveret! Multo melius haec causa

---

⁹ *Clark*: quid si *C. F. W. Müller, SB*: qui si *V*: quod si *bt*: quid *nsυ*   ¹⁰ *del. Lambinus*

---

16 On the different meanings of *popularis* cf. 1.21, n. 42.

17 The consul Pansa.

18 According to Cicero, poor health prevented L. Iulius Caesar from attending all meetings of the senate (cf. *Fam.* 12.2.3). Ser. Sulpicius Rufus died on the embassy to Antony.

ple's man"; now we cannot beg you into being a "people's man."[16] I have dealt long enough with Fufius—all without anger, nothing without distress. And I believe that since he bears with restraint the complaint of his son-in-law,[17] he will calmly bear that of a friend.

[7] I come now to the other consulars, among whom there is no one—I am entitled to say this—who does not have some personal tie with me, very close in some cases, not so close in others, but in every case something. What a day of dishonor yesterday dawned for us, I mean, for us consulars! Envoys once again? As if that man were entering into a truce? But he pounded Mutina with his artillery before the envoys' very eyes; he showed the envoys his works and fortifications; there was not a moment's respite in the assault while the envoys were present. Envoys to him? Why? To make you even more frightened than ever upon their return? Although previously I had opposed authorizing envoys, nevertheless I had this consolation, that when they returned despised and rejected by Antonius, when they reported to the senate that not merely had Antonius failed to evacuate Gaul, as we had decreed, but he had not even withdrawn from Mutina, and that they had not been permitted to meet Decimus Brutus—after such reports, all of us would be aflame with hatred, spurred by indignation, and would go with weapons, cavalry, and infantry to Decimus Brutus' assistance. But we have become even more languid, now that we have seen not only the insolent wickedness of Marcus Antonius but also his arrogant audacity. If only Lucius Caesar were well and Servius Sulpicius were alive![18] This cause would be much better

20

21

22

ageretur a tribus quam nunc agitur ab uno. Dolenter hoc dicam potius quam contumeliose: deserti, deserti, in- quam, sumus, patres conscripti, a principibus. Sed—saepe iam dixi—omnes in tanto periculo qui recte et fortiter sen- tient erunt consulares. Animum nobis adferre legati de- buerunt: timorem attulerunt—quamquam mihi quidem nullum—quamvis de illo ad quem missi sunt bene existi- ment: a quo etiam mandata acceperunt.

23   [8] Pro di immortales! Ubi est ille mos virtusque maio- rum? C. Popilius apud maiores nostros cum ad Antiochum regem legatus missus esset et verbis senatus nuntiasset ut ab Alexandria discederet, quam obsidebat, cum tempus ille differret, virgula stantem circumscripsit dixitque se renuntiaturum senatui, nisi prius sibi respondisset quid facturus esset quam ex illa circumscriptione exisset. Prae- clare! Senatus enim faciem secum attulerat auctorita- temque [r.p.];[11] cui qui non paret, non ab eo mandata acci- 24 pienda sunt, sed ipse est potius repudiandus. An ego ab eo mandata acciperem qui senatus mandata contemneret? Aut ei cum senatu quicquam commune iudicarem qui im- peratorem populi Romani senatu prohibente obsideret? At quae mandata! Qua adrogantia, quo stupore, quo spiri- tu! Cur autem ea legatis nostris dabat, cum ad nos Cotylam mitteret, ornamentum atque arcem amicorum suorum, hominem aedilicium, si vero tum fuit aedilis cum eum ius- su Antoni in convivio servi publici loris ceciderunt?

11 *del. Sternkopf*

19 In 168, to force the Syrian king Antiochus IV Epiphanes to withdraw from his invasion of Egypt.

pleaded by three than it is now being pleaded by one. I shall say this in sorrow rather than with any wish to cause offense: we are deserted, I repeat, deserted, Members of the Senate, by the leading men. But—I have often said it already—in so dangerous a situation all right-minded and courageous persons will be consulars. The envoys ought to have brought us courage, but instead, they brought alarm—though none to me for sure—, however much they entertain a favorable opinion of the person to whom they were sent, from whom they even accepted instructions.

[8] By the immortal gods! Where is that customary 23 courage of our ancestors? In the days of our ancestors, when Gaius Popilius was sent as envoy to king Antiochus[19] and conveyed verbatim the senate's demand that the king retire from Alexandria, which he was besieging, when the king kept introducing delays, Popilius used a stick to draw a line around him where he stood, and said he would convey a negative report back to the senate unless the king gave him an answer as to his intentions before he left that circle. Admirable! He had brought with him the appearance and authority of the senate, and if a man does not obey it, no directives should be accepted from him, but he himself should be repudiated. Or was I to accept directives 24 from one who was defying the senate's instructions? Was I to think that a man who was besieging an imperator of the Roman people against the senate's orders had anything in common with the senate? And what directives! What arrogance, what obtuseness, what haughtiness they show! And why was he giving them to our envoys when he was sending us Cotyla, an ornament and strong refuge of his friends, an ex-aedile—if indeed he *was* an aedile on that occasion when public slaves beat him with leather straps at a dinner party on Antonius' orders?

25 At quam modesta mandata! Ferrei sumus, patres conscripti, qui quicquam huic negemus. "Utramque provinciam," inquit, "remitto; exercitum depono; privatus esse
non recuso." Haec sunt enim verba. Redire ad se videtur.
"Omnia obliviscor, in gratiam redeo." Sed quid adiungit?
"Si legionibus meis sex, si equitibus, si cohorti praetoriae
praemia[12] agrumque dederitis." Eis etiam praemia postulat quibus ut ignoscatur si postulet, impudentissimus iudicetur. Addit praeterea ut, quos ipse cum Dolabella dederit,
26 agros, teneant ei quibus dati sint. Hic est Campanus ager
et Leontinus, quae duo maiores nostri annonae perfugia
ducebant. [9] Cavet mimis, aleatoribus, lenonibus; Cafoni
etiam et Saxae cavet, quos centuriones pugnacis et lacertosos inter mimorum et mimarum greges collocavit. Postulat
praeterea ut chirographorum sua et commentariorum[13]
collegaeque sui decreta maneant. Quid laborat ut habeat
quod quisque mercatus est, si quod accepit habet qui vendidit? Et ne tangantur rationes ad Opis; id est, ne septiens
miliens recuperetur. Ne fraudi sit septemviris quod egissent. Nucula hoc, credo, admonuit;[14] verebatur fortasse ne

12 *Ernesti*: praedam *VD* (praeda *v*): praedia *Clark*

13 V: chirographorum et commentariorum *del. Kayser,
Schelle, SB*: chirographorum (-aphum *s¹v*) et commentariorum
(-atorum *v*) sua *D*

14 admonuit ‹vel potius Lucius frater› *SB dub. in app.*

20 Most probably Hither Gaul and Outer Gaul.
21 For these settlements cf. 2.43, 101.
22 I.e. Antony's consular colleague Dolabella.
23 The seller must be Antony, who, in exchange for bribes, produced forged decrees and laws supposedly found in Caesar's
archives.

56

But what modest directives they are! We must have   25
hearts of stone, Members of the Senate, to refuse this man
anything. "I resign both provinces,"[20] he says. "I lay down
my army; I am willing to become a private citizen." These
are his words. He seems to be coming to his senses. "I forget all that has happened, am ready for a reconciliation."
But what comes next? "If you will give bounties and land to
my six legions, my cavalry, and my praetorian cohort." He
actually demands bounties for men for whom, if he were to
demand a pardon, he would be considered grossly impu-
dent. On top of that, he demands that lands granted by
himself and Dolabella be retained by those to whom they
were given.[21] This means the Campanian and Leontine   26
territories, both looked upon by our ancestors as the ultimate reserves of the corn supply. [9] He is looking out for
the interests of actors, gamblers, pimps; he also safeguards
the interests of Cafo and Saxa, those pugnacious, brawny
centurions whom he settled among the droves of male and
female mimes. He further demands that his own and his
colleague's[22] decrees concerning memoranda and hand-
written documents remain valid. Why is he concerned that
every buyer keep what he bought, so long as the seller
keeps what he received?[23] And he demands that the accounts in the Temple of Ops be left as they are; that is to
say, that the seven hundred million not be recovered.[24]
That no penalty attach to the Board of Seven on account of
their actions:[25] I take this to be Nucula's suggestion; per-

[24] Cf. 1.17 (and n. 34); 5.11 (and n. 10), 15.
[25] On the *Lex Antonia agraria* and the Board of Seven cf. 5.7
(and n. 4); 6.14.

amitteret tantas clientelas. Caveri etiam vult eis qui secum
sint quicquid contra leges commiserint. Mustelae et Tironi
27   prospicit; de se nihil laborat. Quid enim commisit umquam? Num aut pecuniam publicam attigit aut hominem
occidit aut secum habuit armatos? Sed quid est quod de
eis laboret? Postulat enim ne sua iudiciaria lex abrogetur.
Quo impetrato quid est quod metuat? An ne suorum aliquis a Cyda, Lysiade, Curio condemnetur? Neque tamen
nos urget mandatis pluribus; remittit aliquantum et re-
laxat. "Galliam," inquit, "togatam remitto, comatam pos-
tulo"—otiosus videlicet esse mavolt[15]—"cum sex legionibus," inquit, "eisque suppletis ex D. Bruti exercitu," non
modo ex dilectu suo, tam diuque ut obtineat dum M.
Brutus C. Cassius consules prove consulibus provincias
obtinebunt. Huius comitiis Gaius frater—eius est enim
28   annus—iam[16] repulsam tulit. "Ipse autem ut quinquen-

[15] V: non vult *SB*: malo *bnsv*: mavolo *t*

[16] *D*: enim iam annus ut V: enim etiam annus iam *SB dub. in
app.*

---

26 Followers whom he had won by distributing land according
to their wishes.

27 On Antony's judiciary law and these men cf. 5.12–16.

28 Presumably, Antony put forward the demand taken up next
by Cicero as an alternative to the one mentioned first, at the beginning of §25, since the two are mutually exclusive and come
with different concomitant conditions. Cicero, however, tries to
obscure this fact in order to present Antony as an irresponsible
and devious bargainer.

29 Cicero's ironic comment implies two aspects: "at ease" (1) in
that Antony offered to limit himself to just one province, and (2) in

haps he was afraid of losing such a vast clientele.[26] Also
Antonius wants to protect those who are with him, as to any
breach of law they have committed. He is looking out for
Mustela and Tiro; he has no concern on his own account.
After all, what law did he ever break? Did he lay hands on   27
public funds or kill somebody or have armed men about
him? But why should he be concerned about these things,
since he demands that his judiciary law not be repealed? If
he gets that, what has he to fear? That one of his associates
be found guilty by Cydas, Lysiades, and Curius?[27] However, he does not press us with too many directives, but
yields a little and gives way.[28] "I resign Gallia Togata," he
says. "I ask for Gallia Comata"—obviously he prefers to
be at ease[29]—"with six legions," says he; "and these to be
brought up to strength out of Decimus Brutus' army," not
just from his own levy; and he demands tenure as long as
Marcus Brutus and Gaius Cassius hold provinces as consuls or proconsuls. In the elections, as he pictures them,
his brother Gaius—for it is Gaius' year—has already been
defeated.[30] "Provided," he says, "that I myself have tenure   28

that Antony would free himself from the exertions of besieging D.
Brutus in Mutina (in Hither Gaul). Elsewhere (5.37; 7.3; cf. 12.13;
13.37), however, Cicero had commented on the danger of Outer
(*comata*) Gaul serving as a base for waging war against the Roman
people, and the emphasis on Antony's request for an army here
recalls this warning.

[30] According to Cicero, Antony accepts that M. Brutus and C.
Cassius will be elected consuls for 41, which will mean a defeat for
Antony's brother Gaius, who was praetor with Brutus and Cassius
in 44 and so eligible to stand for the consulship in the same year.

nium," inquit, "obtineam." At istud vetat lex Caesaris, et tu
acta Caesaris defendis.

[10] Haec tu mandata, L. Piso, et tu, L. Philippe, principes civitatis, non dico animo ferre verum auribus accipere
potuistis? Sed, ut suspicor, terror erat quidam: nec vos ut
legati apud illum fuistis nec ut consulares, nec vos vestram
nec rei publicae dignitatem tenere potuistis. Et tamen nescio quo pacto sapientia quadam, credo, quod ego non possem, non nimis irati revertistis. Vobis M. Antonius nihil tribuit, clarissimis viris, legatis populi Romani: nos quid non
legato M. Antoni Cotylae concessimus? Cui portas huius
urbis patere ius non erat, huic hoc templum patuit; huic
aditus in senatum fuit; hic hesterno die sententias vestras
in codicillos et omnia verba referebat; huic se etiam sum-
mis honoribus usi contra suam dignitatem venditabant.

29   O di immortales! Quam magnum est personam in re
publica tueri principis! Quae non animis solum debet sed
etiam oculis servire civium. Domum recipere legatum
hostium, in cubiculum admittere, etiam seducere hominis
est nihil de dignitate, nimium de periculo cogitantis. Quod
autem est periculum? Nam si maximum[17] in discrimen ve-
nitur, aut libertas parata victori est aut mors proposita vic-

17 *codd.*: maxime *Faërnus, SB*

31 For the period 43–39 (in inclusive reckoning), i.e. as long as
M. Brutus and C. Cassius remain in power; for if consuls in 41 (see
preceding note), they would go on to govern provinces for two
years (cf. 1.19).

32 Because Caesar's law permitted governors only a two-year
term after their consulship (1.19).   33 Perhaps a sarcastic
allusion to Piso's well-known Epicureanism.

for five years."[31] But this demand of yours is forbidden under Caesar's law,[32] and you are defending Caesar's acts.

[10] As to these directives, could you, Lucius Piso, and you, Lucius Philippus, leaders of the community, I do not say put up with them but even listen to them? But I suspect there was some intimidation: you did not stand in his presence as envoys or as consulars, nor could you maintain your own dignity and that of the Republic. And yet, somehow or other, by some sort of philosophy[33] as I imagine (something I could not have done myself), you were not too angry when you came back. Marcus Antonius did you no courtesies, illustrious men as you were, envoys of the Roman people: what courtesies have we not extended to Marcus Antonius' envoy Cotyla? It was not right for the gates of this city to stand open to him, and yet this temple was open to him; he was given access to the senate; yesterday, he took down in his notebooks the expressions of your views and your speeches, every word; persons who had filled the highest offices made themselves agreeable to him to the detriment of their own dignity.

By the immortal gods! How hard it is to sustain the role 29 of a leader in the Republic! That role demands concern not only about what the public thinks but also about what it sees. To receive an envoy of the enemy into one's house, to admit him to one's private chamber, even draw him aside —that is the conduct of a man who thinks nothing of dignity and too much of danger. But what is the danger? For if the situation reaches the ultimate crisis, the outcome will be either freedom for the winner or death for the loser, the

to; quorum alterum optabile est, alterum effugere nemo
potest. Turpis autem fuga mortis omni est morte peior.
30 Nam illud quidem non adducor ut credam, esse quosdam
qui invideant alicuius constantiae, qui labori, qui eius[18]
perpetuam in re publica adiuvanda voluntatem et senatui
et populo Romano probari moleste ferant. Omnes id quidem facere debebamus, eaque erat non modo apud maiores nostros sed etiam nuper summa laus consularium vigi-
lare [cogitare],[19] adesse animo, semper aliquid pro re
31 publica aut cogitare aut facere aut dicere. Ego, patres
conscripti, Q. Scaevolam augurem memoria teneo bello
Marsico, cum esset summa senectute et perdita valetu-
dine, cotidie simul atque luceret facere omnibus conveniendi potestatem sui; nec eum quisquam illo bello vidit in
lecto, senexque et debilis primus veniebat in curiam.
Huius industriam maxime equidem vellem ut imitarentur
ei quos oportebat; secundo autem loco ne alterius labori
inviderent.

32   [11] Etenim, patres conscripti, cum in spem libertatis
sexennio post sumus ingressi diutiusque servitutem per-
pessi quam captivi servi frugi[20] et diligentes solent, quas
vigilias, quas sollicitudines, quos labores liberandi populi
Romani causa recusare debemus? Equidem, patres conscripti, quamquam hoc honore usi togati solent esse cum

---

18 *King*: labori eius *V*: laboribus qui eius *n*: labori eius (huius *s*)
qui eius *bs*: alicui, ‹qui ei›us constantiam, qui laborem, qui *SB*
19 *del. Faërnus*
20 *V*², *SB*: captivi frugi *D*: captivi servi fruget *V*¹

---

34 I.e. Cicero's (or of men like him).
35 Another term for the Social War of 91–88.

first of which is prayed for, while the second can be escaped by no one. Worse than any death is a dishonorable flight from death. For I cannot bring myself to believe that there are certain people who are jealous of someone's constancy and hard work,[34] who are displeased that his unremitting desire to aid the Republic meets with approval from both the senate and the people of Rome. All of us ought to have done that; and not only in the days of our ancestors but quite recently as well, the highest glory of consulars was to be watchful and alert, to be always thinking or doing or saying something in the interest of the Republic. Members of the Senate, I recall that Quintus Scaevola the augur, at the time of the Marsic War,[35] although he was very old and broken in health, gave admittance to everyone every day, as soon as it grew light. And nobody during that war ever saw him in bed: old and feeble though he was, he was the first to arrive at the senate-house. I would have greatly wished that those who ought to have done so were following his conscientious example; or failing that, that they were not jealous of someone else's toil.

[11] Indeed, Members of the Senate, now that after six years[36] we have begun to entertain the hope of liberty, after enduring servitude longer than enslaved prisoners of war customarily do if they are well behaved and conscientious, we must decline no vigils, no anxieties, no labors in the cause of the freedom of the Roman people. For my part, Members of the Senate, although persons of this rank by custom retain their togas when the community is in mil-

30

31

32

[36] Reckoned inclusively from the outbreak of the Civil War in Jan. 49.

est in sagis civitas, statui tamen a vobis ceterisque civibus
in tanta atrocitate temporis tantaque perturbatione rei publicae non differre vestitu. Non enim ita gerimus nos hoc
bello consulares ut aequo animo populus Romanus visurus
sit nostri honoris insignia, cum partim e nobis ita timidi
sint ut omnem populi Romani beneficiorum memoriam
abiecerint, partim ita a re publica aversi ut se hosti favere
prae se ferant, legatos nostros ab Antonio despectos et irri-
sos facile patiantur, legatum Antoni sublevatum velint.

Hunc enim reditu ad Antonium prohiberi negabant
oportere et in eodem excipiendo sententiam meam corri-
gebant. Quibus geram morem. Redeat ad imperatorem
suum Varius, sed ea lege ne umquam Romam revertatur.
Ceteris autem, si errorem suum deposuerint et cum re publica in gratiam redierint, veniam et impunitatem dandam
puto.

33   Quas ob res ita censeo: "Eorum qui cum M. Antonio
sunt, qui ab armis discesserint et aut ad C. Pansam consulem aut ad A. Hirtium consulem[21] aut ad D. Brutum imperatorem, consulem designatum, aut ad C. Caesarem pro
praetore ante Idus Martias primas[22] adierint, eis fraudi ne
sit quod cum M. Antonio fuerint. Si quis eorum qui cum
M. Antonio sunt fecerit quod honore praemiove dignum
esse videatur, uti C. Pansa A. Hirtius consules, alter ambove, si eis videbitur, de eius honore praemiove primo

---

[21] *SB, praeeunte Halm*: ad c. pansam consul aut ad hirtium
V: ad (*om. sv*) c. pansam aut ad (*om. nstv*) a. hirtium coñs.
[consulem *v*] D

[22] *D*: proximas *SB*: *om. V*

itary cloaks, I have decided not to dress differently from you and the rest of the community in so dire a situation and with the Republic in such a state of turmoil. For in this war we consulars are not conducting ourselves in such a way that the Roman people are likely to view the outward signs of our rank with complacency since some of us are so faint-hearted that they have cast away all recollection of the Roman people's favors, while others are so averse to the Republic that they openly admit to supporting the enemy, are quite happy to see our envoys despised and ridiculed by Antonius, want to ease matters for Antonius' envoy.

They said he should not be prevented from rejoining Antonius and wished to correct my proposal by making an exception of him. I shall humor them. Let Varius go back to his imperator, but on condition that he never return to Rome. As for the rest, if they put their error aside and are reconciled with the Republic, my view is that they should be granted pardon and immunity.

Therefore I propose as follows: "That of the persons now with Marcus Antonius, those who leave his army and go over to either the consul Gaius Pansa, or the consul Aulus Hirtius, or the imperator and consul-elect Decimus Brutus, or to the propraetor Gaius Caesar, before this fifteenth of March,[37] shall suffer no penalty because they were with Marcus Antonius. Further that if anyone of those now with Marcus Antonius performs some action deemed worthy of honor or reward, that the consuls Gaius Pansa and Aulus Hirtius, either or both, if they see fit, shall consult the senate concerning an honor or reward for that

33

[37] In Cicero's motion on 1 Jan., the proposed deadline was 1 Feb. (5.34).

quoque die ad senatum referant. Si quis post hoc senatus consultum ad Antonium profectus esset praeter L. Varium, senatum existimaturum eum contra rem publicam fecisse."

person on the first day possible. And finally, that if any person joins Antonius after this decree of the senate, Lucius Varius excepted, the senate will deem him to have acted against the Republic."

PHILIPPIC 9

INTRODUCTION

On 2 February 43, the senate received a report from the envoys sent to Antony and declared not war, but a "state of public emergency" (*tumultus*). Then, at a meeting of the senate on the following day, Cicero delivered his *Eighth Philippic* in which he criticized Antony's failure to obey the senate and the senate's failure to react to his disobedience more decisively. Soon afterwards, probably on 4 February, the consul C. Vibius Pansa again convened the senate, this time to discuss honors for Ser. Sulpicius Rufus, an envoy who had died during the mission (9.3).

Several other proposals of how best to honor Sulpicius had been brought forward during this meeting before Cicero spoke: the consul Pansa delivered an introductory speech full of praise, and he seems to have suggested erecting a statue, perhaps a gilt equestrian one (9.3, 13). By contrast, P. Servilius Isauricus, who spoke after the consul and before Cicero (9.3), argued against a statue, since Sulpicius had died of illness, not a violent death, which was a precondition for an envoy to be honored with a statue according to Servilius' interpretation of the traditional Roman custom. Servilius did, however, propose the honor of a public tomb (9.3, 14).

In the *Ninth Philippic*, Cicero countered Servilius' objections to a statue by pointing out that Sulpicius' death

71

was brought about by his participation in the embassy and could even have been foreseen in advance because he was in such poor health at the time of his departure that he could not have been expected to return (9.2). So, in effect, as the embassy had only become necessary because of Antony, there was no essential difference between Sulpicius and any other ambassador who was literally killed at the hands of the enemy (9.7). Accordingly, Cicero proposed that Sulpicius be honored with a bronze, pedestrian statue, a public tomb, and a state funeral (9.15–17). This proposal was passed by the senate (cf. Pompon. *Dig.* 1.2.2.43; Hieron. *Ab Abr.* 1873 [p. 157e Helm]).

Although the *Ninth Philippic* deals with a narrow issue not directly involving Antony, Cicero still used the debate to further his fight against him by interpreting both Sulpicius' efforts and the senate's reaction in a way that suited his policy: Cicero argued that the erection of a statue to honor a Roman citizen who perished while serving the Republic and was in effect murdered by Antony provided a clear, public, and permanent indication of the senate's negative judgment on Antony's conduct (9.7, 15). In addition, it indirectly implied the declaration of Antony as a public enemy and defined the present situation as a state of war (9.7, 15). At the same time, Cicero depicted Sulpicius as an eminent jurist, an exceptional statesman, and an ideal politician of the type Cicero expected and demanded the senior consulars to be. Sulpicius even sacrificed his life in the service of his country. Thus Cicero was able to hold up for praise qualities that he himself laid claim to and to contrast them by innuendo with those of Antony and of other consulars who showed a lack of resolve and support for the Republic.

INTRODUCTION TO PHILIPPIC 9

STRUCTURE

Exordium

(1–2) Tribute to Sulpicius' active service as an envoy

Argumentatio

(3–10a) Sulpicius died as an envoy and deserves public honor
  (3–5a) Precedents for honoring envoys who laid down their lives
  (5b–10a) Sulpicius' death an immediate consequence of the embassy

Confirmatio

(10b–12) Accomplishments of Sulpicius

Propositio

(13–15a) Statue and public tomb for Sulpicius
  (13) Bronze, pedestrian statue best suits Sulpicius
  (14–15a) Further honor of a public tomb (proposed by P. Servilius) also deserved

Sententia

(15b–17) Statue, state funeral, and public tomb for Sulpicius

M. TULLI CICERONIS
IN M. ANTONIUM
ORATIO PHILIPPICA NONA

1   [1] Vellem di immortales fecissent, patres conscripti, ut
vivo potius Ser. Sulpicio gratias ageremus quam honores
mortuo quaereremus. Nec vero dubito quin, si ille vir legationem renuntiare potuisset, reditus eius et vobis gratus
fuerit et rei publicae salutaris futurus, non quo L. Philippo
et L. Pisoni aut studium aut cura defuerit in tanto officio
tantoque munere, sed cum Ser. Sulpicius aetate illis ante-
iret, sapientia omnibus, subito ereptus e causa totam lega-
2   tionem orbam et debilitatam reliquit. Quod si cuiquam
iustus honos habitus est in morte legato, in nullo iustior
quam in Ser. Sulpicio reperietur.[1] Ceteri qui in legatione
mortem obierunt ad incertum vitae periculum sine ullo
mortis metu profecti sunt: Ser. Sulpicius cum aliqua perve-
niendi ad M. Antonium spe profectus est, nulla revertendi.
Qui cum ita adfectus esset ut, si ad gravem valetudinem la-
bor accessisset, sibi ipse diffideret, non recusavit quo mi-

----

[1] V²D: quam in Ser. Sulpicio re- om. V¹

----

[1] To win the support of his audience, Cicero here gives a posi-
tive assessment of the two other envoys, which is quite different
from what he said about them in the preceding speech (8.28).

MARCUS TULLIUS CICERO'S
NINTH PHILIPPIC ORATION
AGAINST MARCUS ANTONIUS

[1] I only wish that the immortal gods had made it pos- 1
sible for us, Members of the Senate, to thank Servius Sulpicius in life rather than seek ways of honoring him in
death. Nor do I doubt that if that great man could have reported on the mission, his return would have been both
welcome to you and beneficial to the Republic; I say this
not because Lucius Philippus and Lucius Piso lacked either zeal or diligence in so important a duty and charge,[1]
but since Servius Sulpicius surpassed them in age and all of
us in wisdom, his sudden loss left the whole embassy bereft
and enfeebled. Now if ever an honor was properly ac- 2
corded to an envoy in death, no case will be found more
deserving than that of Servius Sulpicius. Others who met
their deaths on an embassy set out in face of an uncertain
risk to life but without any fear of death: Servius Sulpicius
set out with some hope of reaching Marcus Antonius, but
none of returning. Although he was in such poor health
that he himself lacked confidence in his stamina if exertion
should be added to grave illness, nevertheless he did not

nus vel extremo spiritu, si quam opem rei publicae ferre posset, experiretur. Itaque non illum vis hiemis, non nives, non longitudo itineris, non asperitas viarum, non morbus ingravescens retardavit, cumque iam ad congressum colloquiumque eius pervenisset ad quem erat missus, in ipsa cura ac meditatione obeundi sui muneris excessit e vita.

3   Ut igitur alia, sic hoc, C. Pansa, praeclare, quod et nos ad honorandum Ser. Sulpicium cohortatus es et ipse multa copiose de illius laude dixisti. Quibus a te dictis nihil praeter sententiam dicerem, nisi P. Servilio, clarissimo viro, respondendum putarem, qui hunc honorem statuae nemini tribuendum censuit nisi ei qui ferro esset in legatione interfectus. Ego autem, patres conscripti, sic interpretor sensisse maiores nostros ut causam mortis censuerint, non genus esse quaerendum. Etenim cui legatio ipsa morti fuisset, eius monumentum exstare voluerunt, ut in bellis periculosis obirent homines legationis munus audacius. Non igitur exempla maiorum quaerenda, sed consilium est eorum a quo ipsa exempla nata sunt explicandum.

4   [2] Lars Tolumnius, rex Veientium, quattuor legatos populi Romani Fidenis interemit, quorum statuae steterunt usque ad meam memoriam in rostris. Iustus honos: eis enim maiores nostri qui ob rem publicam mortem obierant pro brevi vita diuturnam memoriam reddiderunt. Cn. Octavi, clari viri et magni, qui primus in eam familiam

---

2 In 438, when the Latin town of Fidenae defected from Rome to the Etruscan town of Veii.

3 Leader of an embassy to Syria in 163/162.

decline to attempt with even his last breath whether he could render any service to the Republic. So not winter's violence, nor snow, nor the length of the journey, nor the roughness of the roads, nor his worsening illness held him back; and when finally he reached the point of meeting and speaking with the person to whom he had been sent, just as he was pondering and preparing to execute his charge, he departed this life.

In this as in other respects, Gaius Pansa, you have acted 3 outstandingly in that you both urged us to honor Servius Sulpicius and yourself eulogized him at abundant length. After what you have said, I should do no more than present a motion, were it not that I feel some answer should be given to Publius Servilius, an illustrious gentleman, who has given it as his opinion that this honor of a statue ought to be conferred only on an envoy killed by the sword in the course of his mission. Now I, Members of the Senate, interpret our ancestors' intention to have been that the cause of death be examined, not the manner of it. They wanted there to be a monument to an envoy whose actual mission had cost him his life, so that in dangerous wars people should undertake such missions more boldly. So we should not just look for precedents of our ancestors, but make plain their design out of which those very precedents arose.

[2] Lars Tolumnius, king of Veii, killed four envoys of 4 the Roman people at Fidenae,[2] and within my own recollection their statues continued to stand on the Rostra. An honor rightly so bestowed: to those who had met their deaths in the service of the Republic our ancestors gave long-lasting memory in return for brief life. We see on the Rostra the statue of Gnaeus Octavius,[3] a great and famous

CICERO

quae postea viris fortissimis floruit attulit consulatum, statuam videmus in rostris. Nemo tum novitati invidebat; nemo virtutem non honorabat. At ea fuit legatio Octavi in qua periculi suspicio non subesset. Nam cum esset missus a senatu ad animos regum perspiciendos liberorumque populorum, maximeque, ut nepotem regis Antiochi, eius qui cum maioribus nostris bellum gesserat, classis habere, elephantos alere prohiberet, Laudiceae in gymnasio a quodam Leptine est interfectus. Reddita est ei tum a maioribus statua pro vita quae multos per annos progeniem eius honestaret, nunc ad tantae familiae memoriam sola resta[re]t.[2] Atqui et huic et Tullo Cluilio et L. Roscio et Sp. Antio et C. Fulcinio, qui a Veientium rege caesi sunt, non sanguis qui est profusus in morte, sed ipsa mors ob rem publicam obita honori fuit.

[3] Itaque, patres conscripti, si Ser. Sulpicio casus mortem attulisset, dolerem equidem tanto rei publicae vulnere, mortem vero eius non monumento, sed luctu publico esse ornandam putarem. Nunc autem quis dubitat quin ei vitam abstulerit ipsa legatio? Secum enim ille mortem extulit quam, si nobiscum remansisset, sua cura, optimi fili fidelissimaeque coniugis diligentia vitare potuisset. At ille cum videret, si vestrae auctoritati non paruisset, dissimilem se futurum sui, sin paruisset, munus sibi illud pro re publica susceptum vitae finem fore, maluit in maximo rei

[2] del. Ernesti, SB

[4] Cn. Octavius was the first in his family to hold the consulship (in 165), thereby ennobling it. Cicero implies that such "new men" (men without noble ancestors) were better treated in the past.

78

gentleman, who first brought the consulship into this family, which later could be proud of its very courageous men. Nobody in those days looked with ill will upon the lack of noble ancestry;[4] nobody did not respect worth. But Octavius' mission was one in which lay no suspicion of danger. For when he was sent by the senate to observe the dispositions of monarchs and free states, and more particularly to forbid the grandson of that king Antiochus who had waged war with our ancestors to maintain fleets and keep elephants, he was assassinated at Laodicea by one Leptines in the gymnasium. In return for his life, a statue was then 5 granted him by our ancestors, which was to honor his descendants throughout many years, and it is now the sole memorial of so great a family. And yet both in his case and in that of the victims of the king of Veii, namely Tullus Cluilius, Lucius Roscius, Spurius Antius, and Gaius Fulcinius, it was not the blood they shed as they died which brought them the honor but the death itself incurred in the service of the Republic.

[3] So, Members of the Senate, if Servius Sulpicius' death had been caused by an accident, I would indeed be grieving at so heavy a loss for the Republic, but I would think that his death should be honored not by a monument, but rather by public mourning. But as matters stand, who doubts that it was the embassy itself that took his life? For he set off carrying his death with him, a death that, had he remained with us, he might have avoided by his own care and the diligence of an excellent son and a very devoted wife. But when he saw that he would not be true to 6 his nature if he did not obey your authority, whereas if he did obey, that charge undertaken for the sake of the Republic would be the end of his life, he preferred at the time

publicae discrimine emori quam minus quam potuisset videri rei publicae profuisse. Multis illi in urbibus iter qua faciebat reficiendi se et curandi potestas fuit. Aderat et hospitum invitatio liberalis pro dignitate summi viri et eorum hortatio qui una erant missi ad requiescendum et vitae suae consulendum. At ille properans, festinans, mandata vestra conficere cupiens, in hac constantia morbo adversante perseveravit.

7   Cuius cum adventu maxime perturbatus esset Antonius, quod ea quae sibi iussu vestro denuntiarentur auctoritate erant et sententia Ser. Sulpici constituta, declaravit quam odisset senatum cum auctorem senatus exstinctum laete atque insolenter tulit. Non igitur magis Leptines Octavium nec Veientium rex eos quos modo nominavi quam Ser. Sulpicium occidit Antonius: is enim profecto mortem attulit qui causa mortis fuit. Quocirca etiam ad posteritatis memoriam pertinere arbitror exstare quod fuerit de hoc bello iudicium senatus. Erit enim statua ipsa testis bellum tam grave fuisse ut legati interitus honoris memoriam consecutus sit.

8   [4] Quod si excusationem Ser. Sulpici, patres conscripti, legationis obeundae recordari volueritis, nulla dubitatio relinquetur quin honore mortui quam vivo iniuriam fecimus sarciamus. Vos enim, patres conscripti—grave dictu est sed dicendum tamen—vos, inquam, Ser. Sulpicium vita privastis: quem cum videretis re magis morbum quam oratione excusantem, non vos quidem crudeles fuistis—

of a severe crisis of the Republic to die outright rather than to appear to have done less for the Republic than he might have done. In many towns through which he passed he had opportunity for refreshment and looking after himself. There were invitations from friends, liberal as befitted the dignity of a person so eminent, and encouragement from his fellow envoys to rest and take thought for his life. But hastening, hurrying, eager to discharge your commission, he held to his resolve in the face of illness.

His arrival threw Antonius into great consternation, for 7 the commands presented to him on your orders had been drawn up on the authority and motion of Servius Sulpicius; Antonius made plain how much he hated the senate by his insolent delight at the demise of the senate's guiding counselor. Therefore, Leptines did not kill Octavius, nor the king of Veii those whose names I have just mentioned, more certainly than Antonius killed Servius Sulpicius: for obviously he who was the cause of death is responsible for it. Accordingly, I think it also relevant to the way in which posterity will remember these events that the judgment of the senate concerning this war should stand recorded. The statue itself will bear witness that the war was so formidable that the death of an envoy received an honorable memorial.

[4] If you are willing to recall, Members of the Senate, 8 Servius Sulpicius' plea to be excused from undertaking the mission, no doubt will remain about our obligation to repair the injury we did him in life by honoring him in death. For you, Members of the Senate—it is a hard thing to say, but still, it has to be said—you, I repeat, took Servius Sulpicius' life: seeing him offer the excuse of illness, not in words so much as in actuality, I will not say you were

81

quid enim minus in hunc ordinem convenit?—sed cum
speraretis nihil esse quod non illius auctoritate et sapientia effici posset, vehementius excusationi obstitistis atque
eum qui semper vestrum consensum gravissimum iudica-
9   visset de sententia deiecistis. Ut vero Pansae consulis accessit cohortatio gravior quam aures Ser. Sulpici ferre didi-
cissent, tum vero denique filium meque seduxit atque ita
locutus est ut auctoritatem vestram vitae suae se diceret
anteferre. Cuius nos virtutem admirati non ausi sumus ad-
versari voluntati. Movebatur singulari pietate filius; non
multum eius perturbationi meus dolor concedebat. Sed
uterque nostrum cedere cogebatur magnitudini animi ora-
tionisque gravitati, cum quidem ille maxima laude et gratulatione omnium vestrum pollicitus est se quod velletis
esse facturum, neque eius sententiae periculum vitaturum
cuius ipse auctor fuisset. Quem exsequi mandata vestra
properantem mane postridie prosecuti sumus; qui quidem
discedens mecum ita locutus est ut eius oratio omen fati vi-
10 deretur. [5] Reddite igitur, patres conscripti, ei vitam cui
ademistis. Vita enim mortuorum in memoria est posita vi-
vorum. Perficite ut is quem vos inscii ad mortem misistis
immortalitatem habeat a vobis. Cui si statuam in rostris decreto vestro statueritis, nulla eius legationem posteritatis
obscurabit oblivio.

Nam reliqua Ser. Sulpici vita multis erit praeclarisque
monumentis ad omnem memoriam commendata: semper
illius gravitatem, constantiam, fidem, praestantem in re
publica tuenda curam atque prudentiam omnium mortalium fama celebrabit. Nec vero silebitur admirabilis quae-

cruel—what would be more unlike this body?—, but in
your hope that nothing was beyond his authority and wisdom to accomplish, you quite strenuously opposed his excuse and made him change his mind; for in his judgment
your united will always weighed most heavily. But when   9
the consul Pansa added an exhortation in terms more
pressing than Servius Sulpicius' ears had learned to tolerate, then eventually he drew his son and me aside and said
in effect that he put your authority before his own life. Ad-
miring his courage, we did not venture to oppose his will.
His son, in his extraordinary devotion, was deeply moved;
my sorrow almost matched his distress. But we were both
forced to yield to the nobility of his spirit and the authority
of his words when, to enthusiastic applause and joyful expressions of gratitude from all of you, he promised to do as
you wished and not to shun the danger arising from a decree that he himself had sponsored. Early the following
day we saw him off, eager to execute your commission, and
as he departed, he spoke to me in words which seemed an
omen of his doom. [5] Therefore, Members of the Senate,   10
restore life to him from whom you took it away. For the life
of the dead resides in the memory of the living. Let him
whom you sent to his death unknowingly gain immortality
at your hands. If by your decree you set up a statue for him
on the Rostra, no forgetfulness of generations to come
shall dim the memory of his mission.

The rest of Servius Sulpicius' life will be handed down
to everlasting recollection by many shining memorials: his
gravity, steadfastness, loyalty, exceptional diligence, and
wisdom in guarding the Republic will ever be on the lips of
all mankind. Nor will posterity have nothing to say about
that particular amazing, unbelievable, almost superhuman

dam et incredibilis ac paene divina eius in legibus inter-
pretandis, aequitate explicanda scientia. Omnes ex omni
aetate qui in hac civitate intellegentiam iuris habuerunt si
unum in locum conferantur, cum Ser. Sulpicio non sint
comparandi. Nec enim ille magis iuris consultus quam
11 iustitiae fuit. Ita ea quae proficiscebantur a legibus et ab
iure civili semper ad facilitatem aequitatemque referebat;
neque instituere litium actiones malebat quam controver-
sias tollere. Ergo hoc statuae monumento non eget; habet
alia maiora. Haec enim statua mortis honestae testis erit,
illa memoria vitae gloriosae, ut hoc magis monumentum
grati senatus quam clari viri futurum sit.
12 Multum etiam valuisse ad patris honorem pietas fili videbitur; qui quamquam adflictus luctu non adest, tamen
sic animati esse debetis ut si ille adesset. Est autem ita adfectus ut nemo umquam unici fili mortem magis doluerit
quam ille maeret patris. Et quidem etiam ad famam Ser.
Sulpici fili arbitror pertinere ut videatur honorem debitum
patri praestitisse. Quamquam nullum monumentum cla-
rius Ser. Sulpicius relinquere potuit quam effigiem morum
suorum, virtutis, constantiae, pietatis, ingeni filium, cuius
luctus aut hoc honore vestro aut nullo solacio levari potest.
13 [6] Mihi autem recordanti Ser. Sulpici multos in nostra
familiaritate sermones gratior illi videtur, si qui est sensus
in morte, aenea statua futura et ea pedestris quam inaurata

expertise of his in the interpretation of our laws and the unfolding of equity. If all who at any period have had understanding of jurisprudence in this community were brought together in one place, there would be no comparing them with Servius Sulpicius. For he was an expert in justice no less than in jurisprudence. To the interpretations of statutes and the civil law he always brought flexibility and a sense of fair play; he was not fonder of setting up processes of litigation than of clearing away disputes. Therefore he does not need the monument of a statue; he has other and greater ones. For this statue will testify to an honorable death, while those accomplishments of his will be reminders of a glorious life, with the result that this monument will be one of a grateful senate rather than of an illustrious man. 11

Moreover the devotion of his son will appear to have counted for much in the honor paid to the father, and although he is too heavily stricken with grief to be here today, you should feel in your hearts as if he were present. Such is his distress that no man ever grieved more for the death of an only son than he mourns the death of his father. Indeed I think it concerns the reputation of Servius Sulpicius junior that he should appear to have presented his father with the honor owed to him. To be sure, Servius Sulpicius could have left no finer memorial than a son in his own likeness—the likeness of his character, courage, steadfastness, devotion, and intellect—whose grief can be comforted by this honor from you or in no way at all. 12

[6] As I recall my many conversations with Servius Sulpicius in the course of our friendship, I have the feeling that if consciousness exists after death, he will prefer a statue of bronze and on foot to a gilt equestrian statue such 13

equestris, qualis L. Sullae primum statu⟨t⟩a[3] est. Mirifice enim Servius maiorum continentiam diligebat, huius saeculi insolentiam vituperabat. Ut igitur si ipsum consulam quid velit, sic pedestrem ex aere statuam tamquam ex eius auctoritate et voluntate decerno; quae quidem magnum civium dolorem et desiderium honore monumenti minuet et leniet.

14 Atque hanc meam sententiam, patres conscripti, P. Servili sententia comprobari necesse est: qui sepulcrum publice decernendum Ser. Sulpicio censuit, statuam non censuit. Nam si mors legati sine caede atque ferro nullum honorem desiderat, cur decernit honorem sepulturae,[4] qui maximus haberi potest mortuo? Sin id tribuit Ser. Sulpicio, quod non est datum Cn. Octavio, cur quod illi datum est huic dandum esse non censet? Maiores quidem nostri statuas multis decreverunt, sepulcra paucis. Sed statuae intereunt tempestate, vi, vetustate, sepulcrorum autem sanctitas in ipso solo est, quod nulla vi moveri neque deleri potest, atque, ut cetera exstinguuntur, sic sepulcra sanctio-

15 ra fiunt vetustate. Augeatur igitur isto honore etiam is vir cui nullus honos tribui non debitus potest; grati simus in eius morte decoranda cui nullam iam aliam gratiam referre possumus. Notetur etiam M. Antoni nefarium bellum gerentis scelerata audacia. His enim honoribus habitis Ser. Sulpicio repudiatae reiectaeque legationis ab Antonio manebit testificatio sempiterna.

[3] *corr. Graevius*
[4] *post* sepulturae *fort.* publicae *addendum SB in app.*

as was first erected for Lucius Sulla. For Servius had an extraordinary love for the modesty of our ancestors and used to criticize the extravagances of the present epoch. It is therefore by his authority and desire as it were, just as if he were here for me to ask his wishes, that I propose a bronze statue on foot; and it will lessen and ease our countrymen's deep grief and sense of loss by the honor of a memorial.

And this proposal of mine, Members of the Senate, 14 must necessarily find support in the motion of Publius Servilius, who proposed that Servius Sulpicius be voted a public tomb, but argued against a statue. For if the death of an envoy without bloodshed and weapons calls for no honor, why does he propose the honor of public burial, the greatest honor that can be conferred upon a dead man? But if he grants Servius Sulpicius something not given to Gnaeus Octavius, why is he opposed to giving the former what was given to the latter? Our ancestors decreed statues for many, but public tombs only for a few. But statues perish by weather, physical force, or age, whereas the sanctity of tombs is inherent in the soil itself, which no physical force can remove or obliterate; and while other things are destroyed by the lapse of time, tombs only grow more sacred. Therefore, let this man, on whom no honor can be 15 conferred beyond his deserving, be glorified by this honor also; let us show ourselves grateful in distinguishing the death of one to whom we can now make no other return. Also let there be branded the criminal audacity of Marcus Antonius as he wages a wicked war. For in these honors paid to Servius Sulpicius there will remain for all time a testimony to Antonius' repudiation and rejection of the mission.

[7] Quas ob res ita censeo: "Cum Ser. Sulpicius Q. f. Lemonia Rufus difficillimo rei publicae tempore, gravi peri-
culosoque morbo adfectus, auctoritatem senatus, salutem
rei publicae vitae suae praeposuerit contraque vim gravi-
tatemque morbi contenderit, ut in castra M. Antoni quo
senatus eum miserat perveniret, isque, cum iam prope castra venisset, vi morbi oppressus vitam amiserit maximo rei
publicae tempore, eiusque mors consentanea vitae fuerit
sanctissime honestissimeque actae, in qua saepe magno
usui rei publicae Ser. Sulpicius et privatus et in magistrati-
16 bus fuerit: cum talis vir ob rem publicam in legatione mortem obierit, senatui placere Ser. Sulpicio statuam pedestrem aeneam in rostris ex huius ordinis sententia statui,
circumque eam statuam locum ludis gladiatoribusque liberos posterosque eius quoquo versus pedes quinque habere, quod is ob rem publicam mortem obierit, eamque
causam in basi inscribi;[5] utique C. Pansa A. Hirtius consules, alter ambove, si eis videatur, quaestoribus urb‹an›is[6]
imperent ut eam basim statuamque faciendam et in rostris statuendam locent, quantique locaverint, tantam pecuniam redemptori attribuendam solvendamque curent.
Cumque antea senatus auctoritatem suam in virorum fortium funeribus ornamentisque ostenderit, placere eum
17 quam amplissime supremo suo die efferri. Et cum Ser.

---

[5] *codd.*: eamque causam in basi inscribi quod is ob rem publicam mortem obierit *Clark, SB*   [6] *corr. Ferrarius*

---

[5] I.e. a square of ten Roman feet per side or a circle with a
radius of five Roman feet, with the statue in the center.

[6] Magistrates responsible for administering the treasury (cf.
14.38).

[7] For which reasons I make the following motion: "Whereas Servius Sulpicius Rufus, son of Quintus, of the tribe Lemonia, in a situation of utmost difficulty for the Republic, being afflicted by a severe and dangerous malady, set the authority of the senate and the welfare of the Republic before his own life and struggled against the strength and severity of his illness in order to reach the camp of Marcus Antonius, whither the senate had sent him; and whereas, having almost arrived at the said camp, overborne by the strength of his illness he lost his life at a juncture most serious for the Republic; and whereas his death was in harmony with a most upright and honorable life, in the course of which Servius Sulpicius was often of great service to the Republic both as a private citizen and in public offices; since such a man has met his death while 16 an envoy in the service of the Republic: that it is resolved by the senate that a statue, on foot and made of bronze, be erected to Servius Sulpicius on the Rostra by resolution of this body; further that his children and descendants be entitled to a space of five feet in any direction around the said statue[5] to view games and gladiatorial shows, because he met his death in the service of the Republic, and that this reason be inscribed upon the pedestal; further that the consuls Gaius Pansa and Aulus Hirtius, either or both, if they see fit, direct the city quaestors[6] to let a contract for the construction and placement on the Rostra of the said pedestal and statue and see to it that the sum agreed be allocated and paid to the contractor. And whereas in the past the senate has shown its will in dignifying the funerals of brave men, that it is resolved that on his very last day he be borne to burial with all possible ceremony. And whereas 17

Sulpicius Q. f. Lemonia Rufus ita de re publica meritus sit
ut eis ornamentis decorari debeat, senatum censere atque
e re publica existimare aedilis curulis edictum quod de funeribus habeant Ser. Sulpici Q. f. Lemonia Rufi funeri
remittere; utique locum sepulcro in campo Esquilino C.
Pansa consul, seu quo in loco videbitur, pedes triginta quoquo versus adsignet quo Ser. Sulpicius inferatur; quod sepulcrum ipsius, liberorum posterorumque eius esset, uti
quod optimo iure publice sepulcrum datum esset."

Servius Sulpicius Rufus, son of Quintus, of the tribe Lemonia, has deserved of the Republic to be honored by the said distinctions, that the senate resolve and deem it in the public interest that the curule aediles suspend their standing order concerning funerals[7] insofar as concerns the funeral of Servius Sulpicius Rufus, son of Quintus, of the tribe Lemonia; further that the consul Gaius Pansa, assign a space thirty feet square for a tomb in the Campus Esquilinus, or wherever shall be thought fitting, to which Servius Sulpicius shall be conveyed, which tomb shall belong to him and his children and descendants with the full legal title appertaining to a tomb by public grant."

[7] The aediles' edict limiting expenditure and display at funerals.

PHILIPPIC 10

INTRODUCTION

At the meeting of the senate on 28 November 44, when provincial governorships were assigned, Macedonia had fallen to Mark Antony's brother Gaius, probably through some manipulation of the lots by Antony (3.24–26). Even though this distribution of provinces had later been re-scinded by a decree of the senate on 20 December 44 (3.37–39), C. Antonius traveled to Macedonia in late 44 / early 43 (10.10), where he was forestalled from taking con-trol of the province by M. Iunius Brutus (10.11). Brutus, instead of going to the province of Crete, which had been assigned to him through Antony's influence, proceeded in the late summer of 44 to Greece, where he raised a sizeable military force (11.27). With that army, Brutus marched into Macedonia, which was being held by the governor Q. Hortensius (son of the famous orator), who re-fused to recognize C. Antonius as his successor. With the cooperation of Hortensius, and with further troops seized from P. Vatinius (governor of the neighboring province of Illyricum), Brutus succeeded in blockading C. Antonius in the town of Apollonia (10.1, 13; Cass. Dio 47.21.4–7).

In mid-February 43, a dispatch from Brutus arrived in Rome, in which he informed the senate of his achieve-ments: he reported that he had brought Macedonia, Illyri-cum, and all Greece into his power and that these regions

were in the control of the senate and the people of Rome
(cf. *Fam.* 12.5.1). Soon after this report became known,
the consul C. Vibius Pansa convened the senate and delivered an opening speech in which he praised Brutus and
his activities (10.1–2). In the general discussion that followed, Q. Fufius Calenus was, again, the first consular to
be called upon to speak (10.2–3). He moved that Brutus'
letter should be acknowledged as "rightly and properly"
written (10.5) but that Brutus should give up his legions
(10.6). In the *Tenth Philippic*, Cicero made the counter-
proposals that Brutus' activities be approved and legiti-
mized, that Brutus be authorized to defend Macedonia,
Illyricum, and all Greece (with provision of the necessary
resources), that he and his troops remain as close to Italy as
possible, and that the proconsul Q. Hortensius act as the
provincial governor of Macedonia until the senate should
appoint a successor (10.25–26). The senate passed this
motion (11.26; 13.30, 32).

INTRODUCTION TO PHILIPPIC 10

STRUCTURE

Exordium

(1–6) Praise for Pansa's initiative and criticism of Calenus' political stance

Narratio

(7–14) Praise of M. Brutus and description of his activities

Refutatio

(15–19a) Refutation of possible objections, esp. fear of offending veterans

Confirmatio

(19b–22) Romans are committed to recovery of freedom

Peroratio

(23–24) Encomium of M. Brutus

Sententia

(25–26) Powers for M. Brutus; Q. Hortensius to retain Macedonia

M. TULLI CICERONIS
IN M. ANTONIUM
ORATIO PHILIPPICA DECIMA

1   [1] Maximas tibi, Pansa, gratias omnes et habere et
agere debemus qui, cum hodierno die senatum te habitu-
rum non arbitraremur, ut M. Bruti, praestantissimi civis,
litteras accepisti, ne minimam quidem moram interposuis-
ti quin quam primum maximo gaudio et gratulatione frue-
remur. Cum factum tuum gratum omnibus debet esse,
tum vero oratio qua recitatis litteris usus es. Declarasti
enim verum esse id quod ego semper sensi, neminem alte-
2   rius qui suae confideret virtuti invidere. Itaque mihi qui
plurimis officiis sum cum Bruto et maxima familiaritate
coniunctus minus multa de illo dicenda sunt. Quas enim
ipse mihi partis sumpseram, eas praecepit oratio tua. Sed
mihi, patres conscripti, necessitatem attulit paulo plura
dicendi sententia eius qui rogatus est ante me; a quo ita
saepe dissentio ut iam verear ne, id quod fieri minime
debet, minuere amicitiam nostram videatur perpetua dissensio.
3   Quae est enim ista tua ratio, Calene, quae mens, ut
numquam post Kalendas Ianuarias idem senseris quod is

MARCUS TULLIUS CICERO'S
TENTH PHILIPPIC ORATION
AGAINST MARCUS ANTONIUS

[1] All of us, Gaius Pansa, ought to feel and express the 1
greatest gratitude to you; for, although we were not expect-
ing you to hold a meeting of the senate today, nevertheless,
after receiving a letter of Marcus Brutus, a most distinguished citizen, you did not let even the slightest of inter-
vals delay our enjoyment of so great a cause for happiness
and congratulation. All should welcome your action, and
particularly the speech that you delivered after the letter
had been read. You proved true something I have always
observed, that a man who is confident of his own worth is
never jealous of another's. And so there is no need for me 2
to say very much about Brutus, to whom I am attached by a
great many good offices and the closest friendship. For the
role for which I had cast myself has been forestalled by
your speech. But the proposal of the gentleman who was
called before me, Members of the Senate, has placed me
under the necessity of saying a little more; I disagree with
him so often that I am beginning to fear that our continual
disagreement may seem to be detracting from our friendship, which should by no means happen.

What is this reasoning of yours, Calenus, what is this 3
thinking, so that never once since the first of January have

qui te sententiam primum rogat, numquam tam frequens senatus fuerit ut unus aliquis sententiam tuam secutus sit? Cur semper tui dissimilis defendis? Cur cum te et vita et fortuna tua ad otium, ad dignitatem invitet, ea probas, ea decernis, ea sentis quae sint inimica et otio communi et dignitati tuae?

4   [2] Nam ut superiora omittam, hoc certe quod mihi maximam admirationem movet non tacebo: quod est tibi cum Brutis bellum? Cur eos quos omnes paene venerari debemus solus oppugnas? Alterum circumsederi non moleste fers; alterum tua sententia spolias eis copiis quas ipse suo labore et periculo ad rei publicae, non ad suum praesidium per se nullo adiuvante confecit. Qui est iste tuus sensus, quae cogitatio, Brutos ut non probes, Antonios probes; quos omnes carissimos habent, tu oderis, quos acerbissime ceteri oderunt, tu constantissime diligas? Amplissimae tibi fortunae sunt, summus honoris gradus, filius, ut et audio et spero, natus ad laudem, cui cum rei publicae

5 causa faveo, tum etiam tua. Quaero igitur, eum Brutine similem malis an Antoni; ac permitto ut de tribus Antoniis eligas quem velis. "Di meliora!" inquies. Cur igitur non eis faves, eos laudas quorum similem tuum filium esse vis? Simul enim et rei publicae consules et propones illi exempla ad imitandum.

---

1 His son-in-law, the consul Pansa.

2 I.e. D. Brutus, besieged by Antony in Cisalpine Gaul, and M. Brutus, controlling military forces in Greece.

you been of the same mind as the gentleman who calls on you first for your view;[1] and that there have never been so many senators present as to provide your motion with a single supporter? Why are you forever supporting persons unlike yourself? Why, while your career and fortune invite you to tranquillity and dignity, do you approve, propose, and advocate what is contrary both to general tranquillity and your individual dignity?

[2] Leaving previous matters aside, this at least I will not pass over in silence, which surprises me most of all: what war do you have with the Bruti?[2] Why do you alone attack men whom all of us ought, I might almost say, to worship? You feel no displeasure that one of them is under siege; the other by your proposal you rob of the forces that he has raised by his own efforts at his own risk, on his own without assistance from any quarter, not for his own protection but for that of the Republic. By what sentiment, what process of thought do you disapprove of the Bruti and approve of the Antonii, hating those whom everyone else holds dearest, whereas those whom other people most bitterly hate, you steadfastly esteem? You are a man of the amplest fortune and the highest official rank; you have a son, as I hear and hope, born for distinction; I wish him well both for the sake of the Republic and particularly for yours. I ask you then: would you prefer him to be like a Brutus or like an Antonius (and I allow you to take your pick among the three Antonii)? "May the gods forbid it!" you will say. Then why do you not support and applaud those whom you wish your son to resemble? For thus you will be looking after the best interests of the Republic and at the same time setting before him models for his imitation.

4

5

Hoc vero, Q. Fufi, cupio sine offensione nostrae ami-
citiae sic tecum ut a te dissentiens senator queri: ita enim
dixisti et quidem de scripto—nam te inopia verbi lapsum
putarem—litteras Bruti "recte et ordine" scriptas videri.
Quid est aliud librarium Bruti laudare, non Brutum?
6 Usum in re publica, Calene, magnum iam habere et debes
et potes. Quando ita decerni vidisti aut quo senatus consulto huius generis—sunt enim innumerabilia—bene scriptas litteras decretum a senatu? Quod verbum tibi non exci-
dit, ut saepe fit, fortuito: scriptum, meditatum, cogitatum
attulisti. [3] Hanc tibi consuetudinem plerisque in rebus
bonis obtrectandi si qui detraxerit, quid tibi quod sibi
quisque velit non relinquetur? Quam ob rem collige te
placaque animum istum aliquando et mitiga; audi viros
bonos, quibus multis uteris; loquere cum sapientissimo
homine, genero tuo, saepius quam ipse tecum: tum denique amplissimi honoris nomen obtinebis. An vero hoc
pro nihilo putas, in quo equidem pro amicitia tuam vicem
dolere soleo, efferri hoc foras et ad populi Romani auris
pervenire, ei qui primus sententiam dixerit neminem adsensum? Quod etiam hodie futurum arbitror. Legiones
abducis a Bruto. Quas? Nempe eas quas ille a C. Antoni
scelere avertit et ad rem publicam sua auctoritate traduxit.

---

3 Cicero chooses to take this frequent formula (e.g. 3.38; 5.36;
10.26) literally, as referring to style or even handwriting. Calenus,
of course, meant it to refer to content according to normal usage.

4 Although senators generally spoke without relying upon a
written text, they sometimes committed their motions to writing
in advance so that they could be transcribed into a decree if
adopted.

On the following point, Quintus Fufius, I wish to re-
monstrate with you, without offense to our friendship, as
one senator disagreeing with another: you said, speaking
from a written draft—for otherwise I should suppose you
made a slip because you were at a loss for a word—, that
Brutus' letter appeared "rightly and properly" written.[3]
That, surely, is to praise Brutus' amanuensis, not Brutus.
By this time, Calenus, you should and can have sufficient   6
experience of public affairs. When have you seen a decree in this form, or in what senatorial decree of this nature—and there are countless such—have you seen it determined by the senate that a letter was well written? You
did not let the phrase fall by chance, as often happens: you
brought it with you, written down, prepared, pondered.[4]
[3] If only someone would rid you of this habit of con-
stantly disparaging decent men, will you not be left with all
a man could desire? So, take stock, calm this mood of yours
at some stage and soften it. Listen to decent men, with
many of whom you are on familiar terms. Speak with your
son-in-law, who is a very wise man, more often than with
yourself. Then at last you will fully possess the title of the
highest office. Does it matter nothing to you (for my part,
as a friend of yours, it often distresses me on your account)
that this is being made public knowledge and reaches the
ears of the Roman people, that nobody has supported the
senator who gave his opinion first? And I believe that this
will be the case today. You take legions from Brutus. Which
legions? Presumably those that he diverted from the criminal enterprise of Gaius Antonius and brought over to the
Republic by his own authority. So you wish to see Brutus

Rursus igitur vis nudatum illum atque solum a re publica relegatum videre.

7   Vos autem, patres conscripti, si M. Brutum deserueritis et prodideritis, quem tandem civem umquam ornabitis, cui favebitis? Nisi forte eos qui diadema imposuerint conservandos, eos qui regni nomen[1] sustulerint deserendos putatis. Ac de hac quidem divina atque immortali laude Bruti silebo quae gratissima memoria omnium civium inclusa nondum publica auctoritate testata est: tantamne patientiam, di boni, tantam moderationem, tantam in iniuria tranquillitatem et modestiam! Qui cum praetor urbanus esset, urbe caruit, ius non dixit, cum omne ius rei publicae recuperavisset, cumque concursu cotidiano bonorum omnium qui admirabilis ad eum fieri solebat praesidioque Italiae cunctae saeptus posset esse, absens iudicio bonorum defensus esse maluit quam praesens manu; qui ne Apollinaris quidem ludos pro sua populique Romani dignitate apparatos praesens fecit, ne quam viam patefa-

8   ceret sceleratissimorum hominum audaciae. [4] Quamquam qui umquam aut ludi aut dies laetiores fuerunt quam cum in singulis versibus populus Romanus maximo clamore et plausu Bruti memoriam prosequebatur? Corpus aberat liberatoris, libertatis memoria aderat; in qua

---

[1] V: regnum omnino *SB*: regis nomen *D*

---

[5] Within less than a month after Caesar's assassination, the praetors M. Brutus and C. Cassius had been forced to withdraw from Rome (and later from Italy) for the sake of their personal safety.

[6] Referring to Antony's attempt to crown Caesar with a diadem at the Lupercalia in Feb. 44 (cf. 2.84–87).

once again[5] as a man banished from the Republic, exposed and isolated.

But you, Members of the Senate, if you should desert 7 and betray Marcus Brutus, to what citizen will you ever show appreciation and favor? Or are you perhaps of the opinion that those who laid a diadem upon a head[6] are to be preserved, while those who abolished the idea of monarchy are to be forsaken? However, I shall not speak of this divine and immortal glory of Brutus, enshrined as it is in the most grateful memory of all our countrymen, though as yet unrecognized by public authority.[7] What patience, good gods, what moderation, what quiet self-effacement in the face of injustice! Though he was city praetor, he stayed away from the city; he did not administer the law, though he had recovered for the Republic all law. And while he might have been fenced around by the daily assembly of all decent men (it was remarkable how they used to cluster to his side) and by the protection of all Italy, he preferred to be defended by the approval of decent men in his absence rather than by their strong arms in his presence. And though he had arranged for the production of the Apollinarian Games in a manner befitting his own and the Roman people's dignity, he did not even oversee their celebration in person, so as not to open a path for the recklessness of vicious criminals.[8] [4] And yet, were any games, 8 any days ever more joyous than when the Roman people revived the memory of Brutus with the greatest outcry and applause in reaction to individual verses? The liberator was absent in the flesh, but the memory of liberation

[7] Cf. 5.35; 11.35.
[8] On the Apollinarian games in 44 cf. 1.36 (and n. 58).

CICERO

Bruti imago cerni videbatur. At hunc eis ipsis ludorum diebus videbam in insu[gu]la[2] c‹l›arissimi adulescentis, ‹M.›[3] Luculli, propinqui sui, nihil nisi de pace et concordia civium cogitantem. Eundem vidi postea Veliae, cedentem Italia ne qua oreretur belli civilis causa propter se. O spectaculum illud non modo hominibus sed undis ipsis et litoribus luctuosum! Cedere e patria servatorem eius, manere in patria perditores! Cassi classis paucis post diebus consequebatur, ut me puderet, patres conscripti, in eam urbem redire ex qua ill‹i› abirent. Sed quo consilio redierim initio audistis, po‹s›t estis experti.

9   Exspectatum igitur tempus a Bruto est. Nam quoad vos omnia pati vidit, usus est ipse incredibili patientia; postea quam vos ad libertatem sensit erectos, praesidia vestrae libertati paravit. At cui pesti quantaeque restitit! Si enim C. Antonius quod animo intenderat perficere potuisset, ut potuisset[4] nisi eius sceleri virtus M. Bruti obstitisset, Macedoniam, Illyricum, Graeciam perdidissemus. Esset vel receptaculum pulso Antonio vel agger oppugnandae Italiae Graecia; quae quidem nunc M. Bruti imperio, auc-

[2] *corr.* V[2]: insulula *Garatoni*: Neside domi *Reid*: Neside *SB dub. in app.*   [3] *add. SB*: Cn. Luculli *Clark*

[4] *SB*: aut potuisset V: potuisset aut‹em› *Poggius*

[9] The large estates of M. Licinius Lucullus, Brutus' cousin, included the small island of Nesis (modern Nisida), located in the Bay of Naples.

[10] Cicero had explained his motives in the *First Philippic* on 2 Sept. 44 (1.7–10) and had taken an active role in the fight against Antony since the *Third* and the *Fourth Philippics* delivered on 20 Dec.

106

was there, and in that memory the likeness of Brutus was clearly to be seen. And during those very days of the festival, I saw Brutus on the island owned by his relative, Marcus Lucullus, a very distinguished young man,[9] where he was pondering nothing except peace and civil concord. Later, I saw him at Velia as he was leaving Italy to prevent some occasion of civil war from arising on his account. Oh, what a mournful sight not only for men, but even for the very waves and beaches! That from our native land its savior was leaving, while in that native land the betrayers remained! Cassius' flotilla followed a few days later; hence I felt ashamed, Members of the Senate, to be returning to the city from which they were departing. But at the outset you heard my purpose in returning, and later you witnessed it in execution.[10]

So, Brutus bided his time. For as long as he saw you 9
putting up with everything, he himself exercised unbelievable patience; but when he perceived that you were ready to fight for freedom,[11] he prepared means to protect your freedom. And what a dreadful vermin he opposed! For if Gaius Antonius had been able to accomplish what he had in mind—as he would have been able, if the valor of Marcus Brutus had not blocked his criminal attempt— we would have lost Macedonia, Illyricum, and Greece. Greece would have become a refuge for Antonius[12] if beaten, or a rampart from which to launch an attack on Italy; the same Greece which now, not merely equipped but even embellished with Marcus Brutus' military com-

[11] When the senate on 20 Dec. 44 rescinded the assignment of provinces under Antony and acknowledged private initiatives against him (cf. 3.37–39).   [12] I.e. Mark Antony.

toritate, copiis non instructa solum sed etiam ornata tendit
dexteram Italiae suumque ei praesidium pollicetur. Quod
qui ab illo abducit exercitum, et respectum pulcherrimum
10 et praesidium firmissimum adimit rei publicae. Equidem
cupio haec quam primum Antonium audire, ut intellegat
non D. Brutum, quem vallo circumsedeat, sed se ipsum
obsideri. [5] Tria tenet oppida to⟨to⟩ in orbe terrarum; habet inimicissimam Galliam; eos etiam quibus confidebat
alienissimos, Transpadanos; Italia omnis infesta est; ex-
terae nationes a prima ora Graeciae usque ad Aegyptum
optimorum et fortissimorum civium imperiis et praesidiis
tenentur. Erat ei spes una in C. Antonio, qui duorum fra-
trum aetatibus medius interiectus viti⟨i⟩s cum utroque
certabat. Is tamquam extruderetur a senatu in Macedoniam et non contra prohiberetur proficisci, ita cucurrit.
11 Quae tempestas, di immortales, quae flamma, quae vasti-
tas, quae pestis Graeciae, nisi incredibilis ac divina virtus
furentis hominis conatum atque audaciam compressisset!
Quae celeritas illa Bruti, quae cura, quae virtus! Etsi ne C.
quidem Antoni celeritas contemnenda est, quam nisi in via
caducae hereditates retardassent, volasse eum, non iter fecisse diceres. Alios ad negotium publicum ire cum cupi-

---

13 Bononia (Bologna), Regium Lepidi (Reggio Emilia), and
Parma (cf. *Fam.* 12.5.2).

14 Since some of the Transpadanes owed their Roman citizenship to legislation passed by Caesar in 49, they might have been
expected to help Antony (cf. 12.10).

15 I.e. west, that closest to Italy.   16 C. Antonius set off,
treating Macedonia as his province on the basis of the distribution
of provinces on 28 Nov. (cf. 3.24–26); yet this had been annulled
by the senate decree of 20 Dec. 44 (cf. 3.37–39).

mand, authority, and forces, holds out her hand to Italy and promises her protection. Whoever withdraws from Brutus his army deprives the Republic of both a most splendid fall-back position and a very powerful bulwark. For my part, I want Antonius to hear of these develop- 10 ments as soon as possible, to make him understand that he himself, and not Decimus Brutus, whom he is surrounding with his palisade, is under siege. [5] He holds three towns[13] in the whole world; Gaul is bitterly hostile to him; even the Transpadanes, on whom he relied,[14] are thoroughly estranged; all Italy is against him; foreign nations, from the nearest coast of Greece[15] as far as Egypt, are held by the military power and forces of excellent and very brave citizens. His only hope was in Gaius Antonius, inserted midway in years between his two brothers and in vices the rival of both. He dashed off to Macedonia as though the senate were thrusting him forth and not, on the contrary, forbidding him to set out.[16] What a storm, by the immortal gods, 11 there would have been, what a conflagration, what devastation, what destruction of Greece, if amazing and divine courage had not quelled the madman's reckless enterprise! How speedily Brutus acted, how circumspectly, how courageously! Not that the speed of Gaius Antonius is to be despised; if his quickness had not been slowed by some unclaimed inheritances along his journey,[17] he might be said to have flown rather than to have made his way. When we want other people to go on a public business, we usually

---

[17] *Caducae hereditates* were inheritances not claimed by the rightful heirs and hence "falling" to the treasury. Cicero suggests that C. Antonius interrupted or delayed his progress out of greed to step in and claim abandoned assets, "falling" his way.

mus, vix solemus extrudere: hunc retinentes extrusimus.[5]
At quid ei cum Apollonia, quid cum Dyrrachio, quid cum
Illyrico, quid cum P. Vatini imperatoris exercitu? Succede-
bat, ut ipse dicebat, Hortensio. Certi fines Macedoniae,
certa condicio, certus, si modo erat ullus, exercitus. Cum
Illyrico vero et cum Vatini legionibus quid erat Antonio?

12 "At ne Bruto quidem": id enim fortasse quispiam impro-
bus dixerit. Omnes legiones, omnes copiae quae ubique
sunt rei publicae sunt: nec enim eae legiones quae M.
Antonium reliquerunt Antoni potius quam rei publicae
fuisse dicentur. Omne enim et exercitus et imperi ius amit-
tit is qui eo imperio et exercitu rem publicam oppugnat.
[6] Quod si ipsa res publica iudicaret aut si omne ius decretis eius statueretur, Antonione an Bruto legiones populi
Romani adiudicaret? Alter advolarat subito ad direptio-
nem pestemque sociorum ut, quacumque iret, omnia vas-
taret, diriperet, auferret, exercitu populi Romani contra
ipsum populum Romanum uteretur; alter eam legem sibi
statuerat, ut, quocumque venisset, lux venisse quaedam et
spes salutis videretur. Denique alter ad evertendam rem
publicam praesidia quaerebat, alter ad conservandam.
Nec vero nos hoc magis videbamus quam ipsi milites a quibus tanta in iudicando prudentia non erat postulanda.

[5] *Muretus*: elusi sumus *SB*: exclusimus *D*: extruinus *V*

---

[18] P. Vatinius was governor of Illyricum in 45–42; the two
towns of Apollonia and Dyrrachium are situated on the Adriatic
coast in the southern part of this province, close to Macedonia.

[19] Four of the six legions stationed there by Caesar had been
transported to Italy in the autumn of 44 for service in Cisalpine
Gaul under Antony, and another one had been given to Dolabella.

have difficulty in thrusting them out; him we thrust out as we tried to hold him back. But what had he to do with Apollonia, with Dyrrachium, with Illyricum, or with the army of the imperator Publius Vatinius?[18] He was succeeding Hortensius, as he said himself. Macedonia has fixed boundaries, fixed terms of tenure, and a fixed army, if there was any.[19] What business did Antonius have with Illyricum and the legions of Vatinius? "But not even Brutus had any," as some ill-disposed person might perhaps say. Yet all legions, all forces, wherever they are, belong to the Republic: and the legions that abandoned Marcus Antonius will not be said to have belonged to Antonius rather than to the Republic. For all right to an army and authority is forfeited by a man who uses his military authority and his army to attack the Republic. [6] If the Republic itself were judge, or if all rights were determined by its decisions, would it adjudge the legions of the Roman people to Antonius[20] or to Brutus? The former had rushed up all of a sudden to plunder and plague our allies in order to ravage, pillage, and carry off everything wherever he went, and to use an army of the Roman people against the Roman people itself; the latter had made it his rule that wherever he had come, some light and a hope of deliverance would seem to have come. In a word, the former was seeking military forces in order to overthrow the Republic, the latter to preserve it. And we did not see this more clearly than the soldiers themselves saw it, from whom we could not expect such wise discrimination. 12

[20] I.e. Gaius Antonius.

13   Cum septem cohortibus esse Apolloniae scribit Antonium, qui iam aut captus est—quod di duint!—aut certe homo verecundus in Macedoniam non accedit ne contra senatus consultum fecisse videatur. Dilectus habitus in Macedonia est summo Q. Hortensi studio et industria; cuius animum egregium dignumque ipso et maioribus eius ex Bruti litteris perspicere potuistis. Legio quam L. Piso ducebat, legatus Antoni, Ciceroni se filio meo tradidit. Equitatus qui in Syriam ducebatur bipertito alter eum quaestorem a quo ducebatur reliquit in Thessalia seseque ad Brutum contulit, alterum in Macedonia Cn. Domitius, adulescens summa virtute, gravitate, constantia, a legato Syriaco abduxit. P. autem Vatinius, qui et antea iure laudatus a vobis et hoc tempore merito laudandus est, aperuit

14   Dyrrachi portas Bruto et exercitum tradidit. Tenet igitur res publica Macedoniam, tenet Illyricum, tuetur Graeciam: nostrae sunt legiones, nostra levis armatura, noster equitatus, maximeque noster est Brutus semperque noster, cum sua excellentissima virtute rei publicae natus tum fato quodam paterni maternique generis et nominis.

[7] Ab hoc igitur viro quisquam bellum timet qui, ante quam nos id coacti suscepimus, in pace iacere quam in bello vigere maluit? Quamquam ille quidem numquam iacuit, neque hoc cadere verbum in tantam virtutis praestantiam potest. Erat enim in desiderio civitatis, in ore, in sermone omnium. Tantum autem aberat a bello ut, cum cupidi-

---

21 Cicero's son Marcus had left his studies in Athens (probably in late 44) to serve under M. Iunius Brutus.
22 Cf. 2.26, n. 24; 3.8, n. 6.

Brutus writes that Gaius Antonius is in Apollonia with   13
seven cohorts; by now either he has been taken prisoner—
may the gods grant this!—or at least the modest fellow
is keeping away from Macedonia so as not to seem to act
contrary to the senate's decree. A levy has been held in
Macedonia, most zealously and energetically directed by
Quintus Hortensius, whose fine spirit, worthy of himself
and his ancestors, you could perceive from Brutus' letter.
The legion that used to be commanded by Antonius' legate, Lucius Piso, surrendered to my son Cicero.[21] Of a
force of cavalry that was being marched to Syria in two sections, one section left the quaestor who was leading it in
Thessaly and joined Brutus; the other division was withdrawn in Macedonia from the legate of the governor of
Syria by Gnaeus Domitius, a young man of the highest
courage, responsibility, and resolution. Moreover, Publius
Vatinius, whom you have rightly commended in the past
and who fully deserves your commendation now, opened
the gates of Dyrrachium to Brutus and handed over his
army. Thus the Republic holds Macedonia, it holds Illyri-   14
cum, and it watches over Greece: the legions are ours, the
light-armed units are ours, the cavalry is ours, and most of
all Brutus is ours, always ours, born for the benefit of the
Republic not only owing to his own outstanding courage
but also to a certain fate attached to the family and name of
both his father and mother.[22]

[7] Does anyone fear war from this man, who, before
we took up arms under compulsion, preferred obscurity in
peace to celebrity in war? Not that he was ever *obscure*;
that word cannot apply to such superiority of worth. He
was what the community longed for, his name was on every
tongue, the theme of everyone's conversation. But war was

tate libertatis Italia arderet, defuerit civium studiis potius
quam eos in armorum discrimen adduceret. Itaque illi ipsi
si qui sunt qui tarditatem Bruti reprehendant tamen idem
moderationem patientiamque mirantur.

15   Sed iam video quae loquantur; neque enim id occulte
faciunt: timere se dicunt quo modo ferant veterani exercitum Brutum habere. Quasi vero quicquam intersit inter A.
Hirti, C. Pansae, D. Bruti, C. Caesaris et hunc exercitum
M. Bruti! Nam si quattuor exercitus ei de quibus dixi prop-
terea laudantur quod pro populi Romani libertate arma ceperunt, quid est cur hic M. Bruti exercitus non in eadem
causa reponatur? At enim veteranis suspectum nomen est
M. Bruti. Magisne quam Decimi? Equidem non arbitror.
Etsi est enim Brutorum commune factum et laudis societas aequa, Decimo tamen iratiores erant ei qui id factum
dolebant quo minus ab eo rem illam dicebant fieri de-
buisse. Quid ergo agunt nunc tot exercitus nisi ut obsidione Brutus liberetur? Qui autem hos exercitus ducunt?
Ei, credo, qui C. Caesaris [res] acta[s]⁶ everti, qui causam
16 veteranorum prodi volunt. [8] Si ipse viveret C. Caesar,
acrius, credo, acta sua defenderet quam vir fortissimus
defendit Hirtius, aut amicior causae quisquam inveniri
potest quam filius! At horum alter nondum ex longinqui-
tate gravissimi morbi recreatus quicquid habuit virium, id
in eorum libertatem defendendam contulit quorum votis
iudicavit se a morte revocatum; alter virtutis robore fir-

⁶ corr. Pluygers

23 Because of Decimus' particularly close ties to Caesar.
24 On A. Hirtius' illness and the prayers of the Roman people
for his recovery cf. 1.37; 7.12; 8.5; 14.4.

so far from his mind that when Italy was aflame with desire for freedom, he disappointed his countrymen's eagerness rather than lead them into armed conflict. Hence, even those who censure Brutus' tardiness, if any such there be, admire his moderation and patience.

But I already see what some are saying; they make no 15 secret of it: they profess to be afraid of how the veterans will take it that Brutus has an army. As though there were a difference between the armies of Aulus Hirtius, Gaius Pansa, Decimus Brutus, and Gaius Caesar and this army of Marcus Brutus! For if those four armies I have just mentioned are commended for taking up arms in defense of the freedom of the Roman people, why should this army of Marcus Brutus not be placed in the same category? But Marcus Brutus' name is suspect to the veterans. More than Decimus'? I do not think so. For though the Bruti share the deed and are equal partners in glory, nevertheless, those who lamented the doing of the deed were angrier with Decimus because they said it was particularly unfitting for him to be involved.[23] Well, what are all these armies trying to achieve at the present time except Brutus' liberation from siege? And who are commanding these armies? Persons, I suppose, who want Gaius Caesar's acts to be overthrown and the cause of the veterans to be betrayed! [8] If Gaius Caesar himself were alive, he would, 16 I suppose, defend his own acts more vigorously than the very brave Hirtius is defending them! Or can any better friend to Caesar's cause be found than his son? And yet the former of these, who had not yet recovered from a lengthy and very serious illness,[24] devoted all the strength he had to defending the freedom of those whose prayers, as he believed, had called him back from death. As for the latter,

mior quam aetatis cum istis ipsis veteranis ad D. Brutum liberandum est profectus. Ergo illi certissimi idemque acer-
rimi Caesaris actorum patroni pro D. Bruti salute bellum
gerunt, quos veterani sequuntur; de libertate enim populi
Romani, non de suis commodis armis decernendum vi-
17   dent. Quid est igitur cur eis qui D. Brutum omnibus opi-
bus conservatum velint M. Bruti sit suspectus exercitus?

   An vero, si quid esset quod a M. Bruto timendum videretur, Pansa id non videret, aut, si videret, non laboraret?
Quis aut sapientior ad coniecturam rerum futurarum aut
ad propulsandum metum diligentior? Atqui huius animum
erga M. Brutum studiumque vidistis: praecepit oratione
sua quid decernere nos de M. Bruto, quid sentire oporteret, tantumque afuit ut periculosum rei publicae M. Bruti
putaret exercitum ut in eo firmissimum rei publicae praesidium et gravissimum poneret. Scilicet hoc Pansa aut non
videt—hebeti enim ingenio est—aut neglegit! Quae enim
Caesar egit, ea rata esse non curat: de quibus confirmandis
et sanciendis legem comitiis centuriatis ex auctoritate nostra laturus est.

   [9] Desinant igitur aut ei qui non timent simulare se timere et prospicere rei publicae, aut ei qui omnia veren-
tur nimium esse timidi, ne illorum simulatio, horum obsit
18   ignavia. Quae, malum, est ista ratio semper optimis causis
veteranorum nomen opponere? Quorum etiam si amplec-
terer virtutem, ut facio, tamen, si essent adrogantes, non

---

   25 In early to mid-Feb. 43 the senate had declared Antony's
laws invalid, and later Pansa re-enacted a select few of those laws
that were regarded as worth preserving, including this *Lex de actis
Caesaris confirmandis*.

stronger in courage than in years, he set out to liberate
Decimus Brutus with those very veterans. And so those
most committed and vigorous champions of Caesar's acts
are waging war to save Decimus Brutus, and the veterans
are following them; for they see that it is the freedom of
the Roman people, not their own benefits, that has to be
decided by arms. Why should those who want Decimus   17
Brutus saved by every means be suspicious of Marcus Brutus' army?

If there were anything that might seem to give us cause
to fear Marcus Brutus, would not Pansa see it; or, seeing it,
would he not be concerned? Is there a man wiser in fore-
casting the future or more conscientious in warding off a
threat? And yet you have seen his attitude toward Marcus
Brutus and his support: in his speech he told us what
we should decree concerning Marcus Brutus and what we
should feel; and he was so far from thinking Marcus Brutus' army a danger to the Republic that he placed in it the
Republic's strongest and weightiest support. Well, I suppose Pansa either does not see it—for he is such a dull
fellow!—or disregards it! After all, he cares nothing for the
validity of Caesar's acts, for the confirmation and ratifica-
tion of which he is about to bring a law before the centuriate assembly on our authority.[25]

[9] Well then, either let those who are not really afraid
cease pretending to be afraid and to be looking out for the
Republic, or let those who fear shadows cease to be overly
timid so that the hypocrisy of the former and the cowardice of the latter may not cause harm. Where, the devil, is   18
the sense in perpetually thrusting the name of the veterans
in the way of every excellent cause? Even if I esteemed
their courage, which I do, I would not be able to put up

possem ferre fastidium. At nos conantis servitutis vincla
rumpere impediet si quis veteranos nolle dixerit? Non
sunt enim, credo, innumerabiles qui pro communi libertate arma capiant! Nemo est praeter veteranos milites vir
qui ad servitutem propulsandam ingenuo dolore excitetur!
Potest igitur[7] stare res publica freta veteranis sine magno
subsidio iuventutis! Quos quidem vos libertatis adiutores
complecti debetis: servitutis auctores sequi non debetis.
19 Postremo—erumpat enim aliquando vera et me digna
vox—si veteranorum nutu mentes huius ordinis gubernan-
tur omniaque ad eorum voluntatem nostra dicta facta refe-
runtur, optanda mors est, quae civibus Romanis semper
fuit servitute potior. Omnis est misera servitus; sed fuerit
quaedam necessaria: ecquodnam principium ponetis[8] libertatis capessendae? An, cum illum necessarium et fatalem paene casum non tulerimus, hunc feremus volunta-
rium?

Tota Italia desiderio libertatis exarsit; servire diutius
non potest civitas; serius populo Romano hunc vestitum
20 atque arma dedimus quam ab eo flagitati sumus. [10] Magna quidem nos spe et prope explorata libertatis causam
suscepimus; sed ut concedam incertos exitus esse belli
Martemque communem, tamen pro libertate vitae periculo decertandum est. Non enim in spiritu vita est, sed ea

[7] *codd*.: *del. SB*   [8] *SB*: et quenam *V* (et quodnam *D*) . . .
putatis (putastis *b*) *codd*.: †et quenam principium putatis† *Fedeli*

---

[26] Under the recent dictatorship of Caesar.
[27] By assassinating the dictator Caesar.   [28] The military
cloak (*sagum*) donned by the populace on 4 Feb. 43, by decree of
the senate (cf. 8.6, 32), as an outward sign of the grave emergency.

with their haughtiness if they were arrogant. But are we going to be hindered in our effort to break the bonds of slavery if somebody tells us that the veterans do not like it? There are not, I suppose, countless numbers to take up arms for the common freedom! There is no man apart from the veteran soldiers to be spurred by noble indignation to ward off slavery! Therefore, the Republic can survive by relying on the veterans, without a large measure of help from the young men! You ought to welcome the veterans as aiders of freedom, but you ought not to follow them as promoters of slavery. Lastly—let the word break out at last, a true word worthy myself—, if the views of this body are governed by a nod from the veterans and all we say and do is subject to their wishes, then death is to be desired, which Roman citizens have always preferred to slavery. Every kind of slavery is miserable, but let us grant that a certain instance of it was unavoidable:[26] will you not lay the foundation for some start at recovering liberty? Or, while we did not put up with that inevitable and almost fate-given plight,[27] shall we endure this voluntary one? 19

All Italy has flared up with desire for freedom; the community can be slaves no longer. We have given the Roman people this garb[28] and these arms but not as promptly as they had called upon us to do. [10] We have taken up the cause of freedom in high and almost assured hopes; but though I admit that the outcome of war is uncertain and that Mars takes both sides,[29] even so, we must fight for freedom at the peril of our lives. For life is not just a 20

[29] The phrase *Mars communis* is proverbial (cf. Hom. *Il.* 18.309; Arist. *Rh.* 2.21: 1395a8–18; Cic. *Fam.* 6.4.1).

nulla est omnino servienti. Omnes nationes servitutem
ferre possunt, nostra civitas non potest, nec ullam aliam ob
causam nisi quod illae laborem doloremque fugiunt, quibus ut careant omnia perpeti possunt, nos ita a maioribus
instituti atque imbuti sumus ut omnia consilia atque facta
ad dignitatem et ad virtutem referremus. Ita praeclara est
recuperatio libertatis ut ne mors quidem sit in repetenda
libertate fugienda. Quod si immortalitas consequeretur
praesentis periculi fugam, tamen eo magis [ea][9] fugienda
videretur quo diuturnior servitus esset. Cum vero dies et
noctes omnia nos undique fata circumstent, non est viri
minimeque Romani dubitare eum spiritum quem naturae
debeat patriae reddere.

21   Concurritur undique ad commune incendium restin-
guendum; veterani qui‹dem›[10] primi Caesaris auctoritatem secuti conatum Antoni reppulerunt; post eiusdem
furorem Martia legio fregit, quarta adflixit. Sic a suis legionibus condemnatus irrupit in Galliam, quam sibi armis
animisque infestam inimicamque cognovit. Hunc A. Hirti,
C. Caesaris exercitus insecuti sunt; post Pansae dilectus
urbem totamque Italiam erexit; unus omnium est hostis.
Quamquam habet secum Lucium fratrem, carissimum populo Romano civem, cuius desiderium ferre diutius civitas
22 non potest. Quid illa taetrius belua, quid immanius? Qui
ob eam causam natus videtur ne omnium mortalium tur-
pissimus esset M. Antonius. Est una Trebellius, qui iam

[9] *del. SB*
[10] *Faërnus*: qui *V*: que *D*: *del. Cobet, praeeunte Orelli*

---

[30] A sarcastic allusion to L. Antonius as the alleged patron of
the Roman people (cf. 6.12–15; 7.16–17).

matter of breathing; a slave has no life at all. All nations can endure slavery, while our community cannot, and for no other reason than because those others shun toil and pain and are ready to put up with anything in order to avoid those hardships, whereas we have been thoroughly schooled by our ancestors to make dignity and valor our touchstones in every decision and act. So splendid is the recovery of freedom that even death is not to be shunned in the struggle to regain it. And if immortality were the consequence of shunning present danger, it would seem all the more something to be avoided since slavery would last longer. But since death in all its forms is all around us day and night, it is not the part of a man, least of all of a Roman, to hesitate to yield up to his native land the breath he owes to nature.

There is a rushing from all quarters to stamp out the 21 general conflagration. The veterans, following Caesar's authority, were the first to beat back Antonius' attempt; afterwards, the Martian Legion broke his fury, and the Fourth dashed it to the ground. Thus condemned by his own legions, he burst into Gaul, which he has found to be his mortal foe in arms and spirit. He was pursued by the armies of Aulus Hirtius and Gaius Caesar; then Pansa's levy roused the city and all Italy; all have a single enemy. True, he has his brother Lucius with him, the favorite citizen of the Roman people; the community cannot bear to be without him much longer.[30] What is more hideous than this 22 beast, what more monstrous? He seems to have been created solely in order that Marcus Antonius should not be the foulest of humankind! He has with him Trebellius, who

cum tabulis novis rediit in gratiam; ‹est›[11] T. Plancus et ceteri pares, qui id pugnant, id agunt ut contra rem publicam restituti esse videantur. Et sollicitant homines imperitos Saxa et Cafo, ipsi rustici atque agrestes, qui hanc rem publicam nec viderunt umquam nec videre constitutam volunt, qui non Caesaris, sed Antoni acta defendunt, quos avertit agri Campani infinita possessio; cuius eos non pudere demiror, cum videant se mimos et mimas habere vicinos.

23   [11] Ad has pestis opprimendas cur moleste feramus quod M. Bruti accessit exercitus? Immoderati, credo, hominis et turbulenti! Videte ne nimium paene patientis. Etsi in illius viri consiliis atque factis nihil nec nimium nec parum umquam fuit. Omnis voluntas M. Bruti, patres conscripti, omnis cogitatio, tota mens auctoritatem senatus, libertatem populi Romani intuetur: haec habet proposita, haec tueri vult. Temptavit quid patientia perficere posset; nihil cum proficeret, vi contra vim experiendum putavit. Cui quidem, patres conscripti, vos idem hoc tempore tribuere debetis quod a.d. XIII Kalendas Ianuarias D. Bruto C. Caesari me auctore tribuistis, quorum privatum de re publica consilium et factum auctoritate vestra est comprobatum atque laudatum. Quod idem in M.

24 Bruto facere debetis, a quo insperatum et repentinum rei publicae praesidium legionum, equitatus, auxiliorum magnae et firmae copiae comparatae sunt. Adiungendus est Q. Hortensius qui, cum Macedoniam obtineret, adiu-

---

[11] *add. SB*

---

[31] Cf. 8.25–26.

has now been reconciled to the proposal for clean slates; Titus Plancus is there and others of his kind, whose one aim and endeavor is to cause their restoration to be seen as an act against the Republic. And Saxa and Cafo stir up naive men, being themselves uncouth, boorish fellows, who never saw nor wish to see this Republic properly established, who defend not Caesar's, but Antonius' acts, who are seduced by the occupation of unlimited areas of Campanian land: I wonder they are not ashamed of it when they see they have mime actors and actresses for neighbors.[31]

[11] Why should we be displeased that Marcus Brutus' army has come to join in crushing these vermin? An intemperate fellow, no doubt, a troublemaker! Rather consider whether he is not almost too patient. And yet, in that great man's decisions and acts nothing was ever too much or too little. Marcus Brutus' every wish, Members of the Senate, his every thought, his whole mind is focused upon the authority of the senate and the freedom of the Roman people: these are his goals, these he wishes to protect. He made trial of what patience could accomplish; when it achieved no success, he thought it time to try force against force. To him, Members of the Senate, you ought to accord at this time the same you accorded to Decimus Brutus and Gaius Caesar on my proposal on the twentieth of December, when their private initiative and action with regard to the Republic were approved and commended by your authority. You ought to do the same in the case of Marcus Brutus, who has raised vast and strong forces comprising legions, cavalry, and auxiliaries as a sudden and unexpected defense of the Republic. With him should be associated Quintus Hortensius, who, while governor of

torem se Bruto ad comparandum exercitum fidissimum et
constantissimum praebuit. Nam de M. Apuleio separatim
censeo referendum, cui testis est per litteras M. Brutus,
eum principem fuisse ad conatum exercitus comparandi.

25   Quae cum ita sint, quod C. Pansa consul verba fecit de
litteris quae a Q. Caepione Bruto pro consule adlatae et in
hoc ordine recitatae sunt, de ea re ita censeo: "Cum Q.
Caepionis Bruti pro consule opera, consilio, industria, virtute difficillimo rei publicae tempore provincia Macedonia et Illyricum et cuncta Graecia et legiones, exercitus,[12]
equitatus, in consulum, senatus populique Romani potestate sint, id Q. Caepionem Brutum pro consule bene et e
re publica pro sua maiorumque suorum dignitate consue-
tudineque rei publicae bene gerendae fecisse; eam rem se-
26   natui populoque Romano gratam esse et fore; utique Q.
Caepio Brutus pro consule provinciam Macedoniam, Illyricum cunctamque Graeciam tueatur, defendat, custodiat
incolumemque conservet, eique exercitui quem ipse constituit, comparavit praesit, pecuniamque ad rem militarem, si qua opus sit, quae publica sit et exigi possit, exigat,
utatur, pecuniasque a quibus videatur ad rem militarem
mutuas sumat, frumentumque imperet, operamque det ut
cum suis copiis quam proxime Italiam sit; cumque ex litteris Q. Caepionis Bruti pro consule intellectum sit, Q. Hortensi pro consule opera et virtute vehementer rem pu-

12 *codd.*: auxilia *SB*

Macedonia, proved Brutus' most loyal and steadfast helper in raising an army. And concerning Marcus Apuleius, I advise that there should be a separate discussion; Marcus Brutus bears witness in his letter that Apuleius took the lead in the endeavor to raise an army.

In view of these facts, and given what the consul Gaius 25 Pansa has said about the letter that has been brought from the proconsul Quintus Caepio Brutus and read out in this body, concerning that matter I move as follows: "Whereas through the agency, strategy, diligence, and courage of the proconsul Quintus Caepio Brutus at a time of great crisis for the Republic, the province of Macedonia and Illyricum, and all Greece, together with legions, troops, and cavalry, are in the control of the consuls, senate, and people of Rome: that the proconsul Quintus Caepio Brutus has acted well and in the public interest, in accordance with his own and his ancestors' dignity and their habit of good service to the Republic; and that this action of his is and will be pleasing to the senate and people of Rome; fur- 26 ther that the proconsul Quintus Caepio Brutus shall protect, defend, guard, and keep safe the province of Macedonia, Illyricum, and all Greece; that he command the army which he himself has established and raised; that if money be required for military purposes, he levy and use such public money as is available and can be levied, and that he borrow monies for military purposes from whom he may see fit; that he requisition grain; and that he see to it that he, with his forces, be as close to Italy as possible. And whereas it has been perceived from the letter of the proconsul Quintus Caepio Brutus that through the agency and courage of the proconsul Quintus Hortensius the Republic has been powerfully assisted and that all his counsels have

125

blicam adiutam omniaque eius consilia cum consiliis Q. Caepionis Bruti pro consule coniuncta fuisse, eamque rem magno usui rei publicae fuisse, Q. Hortensium pro consule recte et ordine exque re publica fecisse, senatuique placere Q. Hortensium pro consule cum quaestore prove quaestore et legatis suis provinciam Macedoniam obtinere quoad ei ex senatus consulto successum sit."

been conjoined with the counsels of the proconsul Quintus Caepio Brutus and as a consequence of this the Republic has derived great benefit: that the proconsul Quintus Hortensius has acted rightly and properly and in the public interest; and that it please the senate that Quintus Hortensius, proconsul, with his quaestor or proquaestor and legates, hold the province of Macedonia until a successor is appointed by decree of the senate."

PHILIPPIC 11

INTRODUCTION

In 44, the consul P. Cornelius Dolabella had been assigned Syria as his proconsular province, and towards the close of the year, in anticipation of the expiration of his consulship, he left Rome to take up this governorship. On his way to Syria, Dolabella passed through the province of Asia, then being administered by the proconsul C. Trebonius, formerly one of Caesar's chief followers and later one of his assassins.

In the second half of February 43, news arrived in Rome that Dolabella had treacherously seized the city of Smyrna, where he had captured Trebonius and put him to death after savagely torturing him (11.1–10). For that act, the senate promptly voted, on the motion of Q. Fufius Calenus, to declare Dolabella a public enemy and to confiscate his property (11.15). The next day, the senate met to decide how best to wage war against Dolabella (11.16): L. Iulius Caesar proposed that an extraordinary command be given to P. Servilius Isauricus, Trebonius' predecessor as governor of Asia in 46–44 (11.19, 25); and another senator, probably Q. Fufius Calenus, moved that the incumbent consuls, A. Hirtius and C. Vibius Pansa, should draw lots for Asia and Syria and go to war against Dolabella in the East, after relieving D. Iunius Brutus of Mark Antony's siege at Mutina (11.21, 24–25).

130

In the *Eleventh Philippic*, delivered during the course of this debate in late February, Cicero argued against the two proposals, characterizing the one as dangerous and the other as inappropriate in the present situation (11.16). He recommended, instead, that C. Cassius Longinus, who was already in Syria and taking action (cf. *Fam.* 12.4; 12.5; 12.7), be given command over the forces and resources in this area, that he be appointed proconsul of Syria with the commission to hunt down Dolabella, and that he be vested with an extraordinary command extending over the provinces of Asia, Bithynia, and Pontus for the purpose of conducting the war against Dolabella. Cicero further proposed that the support of kings and dynasts in the region be officially sanctioned and that the senate discuss the distribution of the consular and praetorian provinces as soon as possible; but until the senate had appointed successors, the provinces were to remain under their present governors (11.29–31).

Yet, influenced by the opposition of the consul Pansa (*Fam.* 12.7.1; *Ad Brut.* 2.4.2), the senate rejected Cicero's recommendation and voted instead to commission the consuls to draw lots for the provinces of Syria and Asia and prosecute the war against Dolabella (*Fam.* 12.14.4; Cass. Dio 47.29). Despite this disposition of the matter, Cassius proceeded to attack Dolabella without any official authorization from the senate and in the end brought him to justice (*Fam.* 12.7.2; 12.11.1; 12.14.4; *Ad Brut.* 2.3.3; 2.4.2).

INTRODUCTION TO PHILIPPIC 11

STRUCTURE

Exordium

(1–3a) Murder of Trebonius as paradigmatic event and wake-up call

Narratio

(3b–15) Murder of Trebonius and its consequences
    (3b–10a) Dramatic account of Trebonius' murder
    (10b–14) Forewarning of similar actions by Antony and
        his followers
    (15) Endorsement of decree (proposed by Calenus) de-
        claring Dolabella a public enemy

Refutatio

(16–25) Arguments against two motions already put for-
        ward:
    (17–20) Extraordinary command for P. Servilius
    (21–25) Distribution of provinces and dispatch of one of
        the consuls

Propositio

(26–28) Cicero's own proposal: Cassius to fight Dolabella
in Syria

Sententia

(29–31) Empower Cassius fully

Confirmatio

Peroratio

M. TULLI CICERONIS
IN M. ANTONIUM
ORATIO PHILIPPICA UNDECIMA

1   [1] Magno in dolore, patres conscripti, vel maerore
potius, quem ex crudeli et miserabili morte C. Treboni,
optimi civis moderatissimique hominis, accepimus, inest
tamen aliquid quod rei publicae profuturum putem. Perspeximus enim quanta in eis qui contra patriam scelerata
arma ceperunt inesset immanitas. Nam duo haec capita
nata sunt post homines natos taeterrima et spurcissima,
Dolabella et Antonius: quorum alter effecit quod optarat;
de altero patefactum est quid cogitaret. L. Cinna crudelis,
C. Marius in iracundia perseverans, L. Sulla vehemens;
neque ullius horum in ulciscendo acerbitas progressa ultra
mortem est; quae tamen poena in civis nimis crudelis puta-
2 batur. Ecce tibi geminum in scelere par, invisitatum, in-
auditum, ferum, barbarum! Itaque quorum summum
quondam inter ipsos odium bellumque meministis, eosdem postea singulari inter se consensu et amore devinxit
improbissimae naturae et turpissimae vitae similitudo.
Ergo id quod fecit Dolabella in quo potuit multis idem mi-

MARCUS TULLIUS CICERO'S
ELEVENTH PHILIPPIC ORATION
AGAINST MARCUS ANTONIUS

[1] In our great sorrow, Members of the Senate, our 1
lamentation rather, at the cruel and pitiable death of Gaius
Trebonius, an excellent citizen and the gentlest of men,
there is nonetheless an element which I believe will prove
beneficial to the Republic. We have now seen what depths
of savagery lie in the hearts of those who have criminally
taken up arms against their native land. For in Dolabella
and Antonius we have the two foulest and filthiest beings
ever born since the birth of mankind: the former of these
has done what he had longed to do; as to the latter, his intentions have been revealed. Lucius Cinna was a cruel
man, Gaius Marius was stubborn in anger, Lucius Sulla
was violent; but in exacting vengeance none of these carried his cruelty further than death; and even that punishment was thought too cruel to be inflicted on fellow
countrymen. And now, behold! A pair of twins in crime, 2
unprecedented, unheard of, bestial, barbarous! You remember the bitter hatred and the war which once existed
between them; later the likeness of their most wicked na-
tures and vile lives knit them together in a remarkable relationship of harmonious affection. And so what Dolabella
has done to the victim in his power, Antonius threatens to

natur Antonius. Sed ille cum procul esset a consulibus exercitibusque nostris neque dum senatum cum populo Romano conspirasse sensisset, fretus Antoni copiis ea scelera suscepit quae Romae iam suscepta arbitrabatur a socio 3 furoris sui. Quid ergo hunc aliud moliri, quid optare censetis aut quam omnino causam esse belli? Omnis, qui libere de re publica sensimus, qui dignas nobis sententias diximus, qui populum Romanum liberum esse voluimus, statuit ille quidem non inimicos, sed hostis; maiora tamen in nos quam in hostem supplicia meditatur: mortem naturae poenam putat esse, iracundiae tormenta atque cruciatum. Qualis igitur hostis habendus est is a quo victore, si cruciatus absit, mors in benefici parte numeretur?

[2] Quam ob rem, patres conscripti, quamquam hortatore non egetis—ipsi enim vestra sponte exarsistis ad libertatis recuperandae cupiditatem—tamen eo maiore animo studioque libertatem defendite quo maiora proposita vic- 4 tis supplicia servitutis videtis. In Galliam invasit Antonius, in Asiam Dolabella, in alienam uterque provinciam. Alteri se Brutus obiecit impetumque furentis atque omnia divexare ac diripere cupientis vitae suae periculo colligavit, progressu arcuit, a reditu refrenavit, obsideri se passus ex utraque parte constrinxit Antonium. Alter in Asiam irrupit. Cur? Si ut in Syriam, ‹cur terra? Sin ut Zmyrnam,›[1] patebat via et certa neque longa: quid opus fuit cum legione?

[1] *add.* SB

---

[1] This judgment reflects Cicero's view since he regards Antony's arrangements for the assignment of provinces as invalid.

[2] D. Brutus was besieged by Antony in Mutina and thereby tied Antony to that place.

do to many. Yet the former was far from our consuls and armies, nor had he yet realized that the senate had become one with the Roman people; relying on Antonius' forces, he perpetrated those crimes which he supposed had already been committed in Rome by his partner in madness. What else then do you suppose the latter is working for and dreaming of? Or what in fact do you think is the cause of the war? All of us who entertained free thoughts about the Republic, who spoke worthily of ourselves, who wished the Roman people to be free, all these Antonius set down as enemies, not merely private but public; though he plans worse fates for us than are inflicted upon a public enemy: he considers that death is the penalty ordained by nature, whereas anger demands the pains of torture. What sort of enemy, then, must we think a man from whom, if he wins, death without torture will be reckoned a favor?

[2] Accordingly, Members of the Senate, although you need no one to urge you—for you yourselves have spontaneously felt a burning desire for regaining liberty—still, defend liberty with all the greater spirit and enthusiasm as you see worse penalties of slavery in store for the defeated. Antonius broke into Gaul, Dolabella into Asia, each of them into a province that did not belong to him.[1] Brutus blocked the former,[2] tying down at the risk of his own life the onslaught of a madman eager for universal plunder and pillage; barring his advance, curbing his retreat, allowing himself to be put under siege, he has bound Antonius fast either way he turns. The other broke into Asia. Why? If he was making for Syria, why by land? But if for Smyrna, a safe road of no great length lay open before him: what need

137

Praemisso Marso nescio quo Octavio, scelerato latrone
atque egenti, qui popularetur agros, vexaret urbis, non ad
spem constituendae rei familiaris, quam tenere eum posse
negant qui norunt—mihi enim hic senator ignotus est—
sed ad praesentem pastum mendicitatis suae, consecutus
5   est Dolabella. Nulla suspicione belli—quis enim id putaret?—secutae collocutiones familiarissimae cum Trebonio
complexusque summae benevolentiae falsi indices exstite-
runt in amore simulato; dexterae, quae fidei testes esse
sole[ba]nt,[2] sunt perfidia et scelere violatae: nocturnus
introitus Zmyrnam quasi in hostium urbem, quae est fidis-
simorum antiquissimorumque sociorum; oppressus Trebonius, si ut ab eo qui aperte hostis esset, incautus; si ut ab
eo qui civis etiam tum speciem haberet, miser. Ex quo nimirum documentum nos capere Fortuna voluit quid esset
victis extimescendum. Consularem hominem consulari
imperio provinciam Asiam obtinentem Samiario exsuli tradidit interficere captum statim noluit, ne nimis, credo, in
victoria liberalis videretur. Cum verborum contumeliis
optimum virum incesto ore lacerasset, tum verberibus ac
tormentis quaestionem habuit pecuniae publicae, idque
per biduum. Post cervicibus fractis caput abscidit, idque
adfixum gestari iussit in pilo; reliquum corpus tractum
6   atque laniatum abiecit in mare. Cum hoc hoste bellandum
est [a][3] cuius taeterrima crudelitate omnis barbaria su-

[2] *corr. C. F. W. Müller*
[3] *del. Poggius*

to take a legion? He sent in advance a wicked and needy bandit, a fellow called Octavius Marsus, to ravage the countryside and harass the towns, not in the hope of making his fortune, which those who know him say he would be incapable of keeping anyway—I myself have no acquaintance with this senator—, but to feed his beggar's appetite for the time being. Dolabella followed. There being 5 no suspicion of war—who would have thought of such a thing?—very friendly conversations with Trebonius ensued; and there were embraces in feigned affection, lying evidence of the heartiest goodwill; right hands, the accustomed pledges of good faith, were violated in treachery and crime. There was an entry into Smyrna by night, as though it were a city of enemies, not of very loyal and ancient allies; Trebonius was overwhelmed: if we think of his assailant as an open enemy, there was a lack of caution on Trebonius' part; if we think of him as still bearing the semblance of a fellow countryman, it is pitiable. It looks indeed as if Fortune wished us to take Trebonius' fate as an example of what the defeated have to fear. Dolabella handed him over, a man of consular rank holding the province of Asia by consular authority, to one Samiarius, an exile. He did not choose to kill his prisoner out of hand; that would have looked too much like generosity in victory. First he lacerated this excellent man with verbal insults from his unclean mouth, then he interrogated him concerning public money under lashes and torments, and he did so for two days together. After which he broke his neck, cut off his head, and ordered it to be stuck on a pike and carried about; the rest of the body, dragged and torn, was flung into the sea. This is the enemy, surpassing all barbarian 6 races in abominable cruelty, whom we have to fight. What

perata est. Quid loquar de caede civium Romanorum, de direptione fanorum? Quis est qui pro rerum atrocitate deplorare tantas calamitates queat? Et nunc tota Asia vagatur, volitat ut rex. Nos alio bello distineri putat: quasi vero non idem unumque bellum sit contra hoc iugum impiorum nefarium. [3] Imaginem M. Antoni crudelitatis in Dolabella cernitis: ex hoc[4] illa efficta est; ab hoc Dolabellae scelerum praecepta sunt tradita. Num leniorem quam in Asia Dolabella fuit in Italia, si liceat, fore putatis Antonium? Mihi quidem et ille pervenisse videtur quoad progredi potuerit feri hominis amentia, neque Antonius ullius supplici adhibendi, si potestatem habeat, ullam esse partem relicturus. Ponite igitur ante oculos, patres conscripti, miseram illam quidem et flebilem speciem, sed ad incitandos nostros animos necessariam: nocturnum impetum in urbem Asiae clarissimam, irruptionem armatorum in Treboni domum, cum miser ille prius latronum gladios videret quam quae res esset audisset; furentis introitum Dolabellae, vocem impuram atque os illud infame, vincla, verbera, eculeum, tortorem carnificemque Samiarium: quae tulisse illum fortiter et patienter ferunt. Magna laus meoque iudicio omnium maxima. Est enim sapientis, quicquid homini accidere possit, id praemeditari ferendum modice esse [si evenerit].[5] Maioris omnino est consili providere ne quid tale accidat, animi non minoris fortiter ferre si evenerit. Ac Dolabella quidem tam fuit immemor humanitatis— quamquam eius numquam particeps fu[er]it[6]—ut suam insatiabilem crudelitatem exercuerit non solum in vivo, sed etiam in mortuo, atque in eius corpore lacerando atque

7

8

---

[4] *V*: ex hac *SB*: ab hoc *D*   [5] *del. Ernesti*: si evenerit[2] *del.* Clark, SB   [6] *cod. Barbadorii*

am I to say of the slaughter of Roman citizens, of the plundering of temples? Who could find words to deplore such calamities as befits their atrocious character? And now he is roaming over all of Asia, moving around like a king. He thinks our attention is held by another war, as though it were not one and the same war against this nefarious pair of villains. [3] In Dolabella you see an image of the cruelty of Marcus Antonius: on him it has been modeled; it is from him that Dolabella's lessons in crimes were received. Do you suppose that Antonius will be more lenient in Italy, given the chance, than Dolabella was in Asia? To me even Dolabella seems to have gone as far as the madness of a savage could go, while Antonius, if he should have the power, seems sure to exploit every variety of physical cruelty to the full. Picture the scene, Members of the Senate, grievous and lamentable indeed, but needful to stir our spirits: the onslaught by night upon a very famous city in Asia; armed men bursting into Trebonius' house, while he, poor wretch, saw the swords of the brigands before he had heard what was going on; the entry of the raging Dolabella, his foul voice and this infamous mouth, the chains, the lashes, the rack, the torturer and executioner Samiarius: they say Trebonius bore it all bravely and patiently. That does him much honor, the highest a man can win in my opinion. For a wise man ought to resolve in advance that all that can happen to a human being must be borne calmly. To make sure that nothing of this kind happens does indeed indicate a greater measure of counsel, but to bear it with fortitude if it happens is a mark of no less courage. So completely did Dolabella forget all human feeling—not that he ever had any—that he exercised his insatiable cruelty not only on the living but on the dead, and fed his eyes,

7

8

vexando, cum animum satiare non posset, oculos pav‹e-
r›it[7] suos.

[4] O multo miserior Dolabella quam ille quem tu miserrimum esse voluisti! "Dolores Trebonius pertulit mag-
nos." Multi ex morbi gravitate maiores, quos tamen non
miseros, sed laboriosos solemus dicere. "Longus fuit dolor." Bidui, at compluribus annorum saepe multorum. Nec
vero graviora sunt carnificum cruciamenta quam interdum
tormenta morborum. Alia sunt, alia, inquam, o perditissi-
mi homines et amentissimi, multo miseriora. Nam quo
maior vis est animi quam corporis, hoc sunt graviora ea
quae concipiuntur animo quam illa quae corpore. Miserior
igitur qui suscipit in se scelus quam is qui alterius facinus
subire cogitur. Cruciatus est a Dolabella Trebonius; et quidem a Carthaginiensibus Regulus. Qua re cum crudelissimi Poeni iudicati sint in hoste, quid in cive de Dolabella
iudicandum est? An vero hoc conferendum est aut dubi-
tandum uter miserior sit, isne cuius mortem senatus populusque Romanus ulcisci cupit, an is qui cunctis senatus
sententiis hostis est iudicatus? Nam ceteris quidem vitae
partibus quis est qui possit sine Treboni maxima contumelia conferre vitam Treboni cum Dolabellae? Alterius consilium, ingenium, humanitatem, innocentiam, magnitudi-

9

[7] corr. Ferrarius

[3] Regulus was sent to Rome by Carthage to negotiate about a
peace treaty or an exchange of prisoners during the First Punic
War. In case the Romans rejected these offers, Regulus was to return to Carthage, to which he committed himself by oath. In
Rome he argued against the Carthaginian proposals in the senate,

since he could not satisfy his soul, by mangling and savaging his victim's body.

[4] Ah, Dolabella, how vastly greater is your misery than that of him whom you wished to be most miserable! "Trebonius suffered terribly." Many endure worse sufferings from severe illness; and yet we do not customarily call them miserable, but sorely tried. "His pain was long drawn out." For two days; but for some, such pain often lasts for many years. The tortures inflicted by executioners are no worse than are sometimes the torments of disease. There 9 are other miseries, others, I repeat, you ruthless criminals, you madmen, far worse than these. In proportion as the mind's power is greater than the body's, so mental pain is worse than physical pain. Therefore, he who takes a crime upon his conscience is more miserable than he who is forced to undergo the misdeed of another. Trebonius was tortured by Dolabella; and so was Regulus by the Carthaginians.[3] Therefore, since the Punic men are held to have treated an enemy with great cruelty, what is to be thought of the way Dolabella treated a fellow countryman? Is there indeed any comparison, or is there any doubt which of the two is the more miserable, the man whose death the senate and people of Rome are eager to avenge, or the man who has been declared a public enemy by a unanimous vote of the senate? As for the rest of their lives, who could compare Trebonius' life to Dolabella's without grossly insulting Trebonius? Who does not know his wisdom, intellect, humanity, integrity, and the greatness of spirit he showed in

which resulted in a negative decree. Thereupon Regulus, true to his oath, returned to Carthage and was savagely tortured to death.

nem animi in patria liberanda quis ignorat? Alteri a puero
pro deliciis crudelitas fuit; deinde ea libidinum turpitudo
ut in hoc sit semper ipse laetatus, quod ea faceret quae sibi
10   obici ne ab inimico quidem possent verecundo. Et hic, di
immortales, aliquando fuit meus! Occulta enim erant vitia
non inquirenti. Neque nunc fortasse alienus ab eo essem,
nisi ille bonis, nisi moenibus patriae, nisi huic urbi, nisi dis
penatibus, nisi aris et focis omnium nostrum, nisi denique
naturae et humanitati inventus esset inimicus.

A quo admoniti diligentius et vigilantius caveamus Antonium. [5] Etenim Dolabella non ita multos secum habuit
notos atque insignis latrones; at videtis quos et quam multos habeat Antonius. Primum Lucium fratrem: quam fa-
cem, di immortales, quod facinus, quod scelus, quem gur-
gitem, quam voraginem! Quid eum non sorbere animo,
quid non haurire cogitatione, cuius sanguinem non bibere
censetis, in cuius possessiones atque fortunas non impu-
11   dentissimos oculos spe et mente defigere? Quid Censorinum? Qui se verbo praetorem esse urbanum cupere dicebat, re certe noluit. Quid Bestiam? Qui consulatum in
Bruti locum se petere profitetur. Atque hoc quidem detes-
tabile omen avertat Iuppiter! Quam absurdum autem, qui
praetor fieri non potuerit, petere eum consulatum! Nisi
forte damnationem pro praetura putat. Alter Caesar Vopis-

---

4 Trebonius joined the plot against Caesar although he owed
his advancement to him.   5 Dolabella was married to Cicero's
only daughter Tullia in 50–46.   6 A sarcastic allusion to the
fact that in 43 L. Marcius Censorinus abandoned the duties of his
praetorship in the city (*urbs*) to join Antony in Gaul; he never actually held the official post of "city praetor" (*praetor urbanus*).

liberating his native land?[4] Dolabella took pleasure in cruelty from boyhood; later he was so depraved in his lusts that he has always found delight in committing acts that even an enemy could not in decency bring up against him. And this man, o immortal gods, was once a member of my family![5] For his vices were concealed, if one did not inquire. Even now perhaps I would not be estranged from him if he had not been found an enemy to decent men, to the walls of his native land, to this city, to the household gods, to the altars and hearths of us all, in fact to nature and humanity.

Warned by him, let us guard ourselves against Antonius with greater care and vigilance. [5] After all, Dolabella did not have very many notorious and eminent cutthroats with him; but you see whom Antonius has and how many they are. First, his brother Lucius: what a firebrand, o immortal gods, what an outrage, what villainy, what a cesspool, what a chasm! What, do you suppose, is he not mentally sucking dry, engulfing in imagination, whose blood is he not drinking, on whose property and fortunes is he not fixing his shameless eyes in hopeful fantasy? What of Censorinus, who used to claim in speeches that he wanted to be city praetor but in fact certainly had no such desire.[6] What of Bestia, who announces his candidacy for the consulship in place of Brutus.[7] May Jupiter avert so abominable an omen! And how absurd that a man who failed to become praetor should stand for consul!—or perhaps he counts a conviction as a praetorship. Well, let him be granted legal

10

11

[7] Cicero suggests that Bestia confidently stepped forward to take over the consulship, if Antony was victorious over D. Brutus, designated as consul for 42 by Caesar.

cus ille summo ingenio, summa potentia, qui ex aedilitate
consulatum petit, solvatur legibus: quamquam leges eum
non tenent propter eximiam, credo, dignitatem! At hic me
defendente quinquiens absolutus est: sexta palma urbana
etiam in gladiatore difficilis. Sed haec iudicum culpa, non
mea est. Ego defendi fide optima; illi debuerunt clarissimum et praestantissimum senatorem in civitate retinere.
Qui tamen nunc nihil aliud agere videtur nisi ut intellega-
mus illos quorum res iudicatas irritas fecimus bene et e re
12 publica iudicavisse. Neque hoc in hoc uno est: sunt alii in
isdem castris honeste condemnati, turpiter restituti. Quod
horum consilium qui omnibus bonis hostes sunt nisi crudelissimum putatis fore? Accedit Saxa nescio quis, quem
nobis Caesar ex ultima Celtiberia tribunum plebis dedit,
castrorum antea metator, nunc, ut sperat, urbis: a qua cum
sit alienus, suo capiti salvis nobis ominetur. Cum hoc vete-
ranus Cafo, quo neminem veterani peius oderunt. His
quasi praeter dotem quam in civilibus malis acceperant
agrum Campanum est largitus Antonius, ut haberent reliquorum nutriculas praediorum. Quibus utinam contenti
essent! Ferremus, etsi tolerabile non erat, sed quidvis pa-

---

8 I.e., Bestia's conduct after his recall from exile by Caesar,
whose acts had been ratified by the senate, proved that Bestia's
original condemnation was justified.

9 I.e., the convictions were honorable to the juries, while the
conduct of these people after restoration was disgraceful to themselves and to those who brought them back.

10 I.e., may the expectation of property being confiscated in
Rome and turned over to Antony's followers (cf. e.g. 8.9) be ful-
filled by the loss of property elsewhere on the part of Saxa (and his
associates).

dispensation, this second Caesar Vopiscus, this marvel of intellect and influence, who stands for the consulship on the basis of an aedileship—even though, I believe, the laws do not apply to so extraordinarily eminent a personage! But I defended him five times and each time he was acquitted: even a gladiator finds it hard to win a sixth palm in the city. However, this is the jury's fault, not mine. I defended him in all good faith; they ought to have kept so illustrious and outstanding a senator in the community. However, he now seems to be solely out to prove to us that the jurors whose verdict we have annulled judged properly and to the public benefit.[8] And this is no isolated case: there are others in the same camp honorably convicted and disgracefully rehabilitated.[9] Do you suppose these enemies of all decent men have any but the cruelest intentions? To these add one Saxa, whom Caesar brought from the farthest parts of Celtiberia and gave us for a tribune of the plebs, formerly a marker-out of military camps, now, as he hopes, of the city. He is a stranger to Rome, so may the omen be on his own head, and we unharmed.[10] Associated with him is the veteran Cafo, than whom no man is more cordially hated by the veterans. On this pair, over and above the dowry, as it were, that they had received in the civil troubles, Antonius bestowed Campanian land,[11] so that they might have wet nurses for the rest of their estates.[12] If only they had been content with them! We would have put up with that, even though it was intolerable; but anything was worth bearing for the sake of avoiding

12

[11] On these allocations of land cf. 2.43, 101; 8.25–26.
[12] I.e., the fertile land in Campania would serve to offset any losses from recently acquired estates elsewhere.

tiendum fuit ut hoc taeterrimum bellum non haberemus.
13 [6] Quid? Illa castrorum M. Antoni lumina, nonne ante
oculos proponitis? Primum duos collegas Antoniorum et
Dolabellae, Nuculam et Lentonem, Italiae divisores lege
ea quam senatus per vim latam iudicavit; quorum alter
commentatus est mimos, alter egit tragoediam. Quid dicam de Apulo Domitio? Cuius modo bona proscripta vidi.
Tanta procuratorum est neglegentia. At hic nuper sororis
filio infudit venenum, non dedit. Sed non possunt non pro-
dige vivere qui nostra bona sperant, cum effundant sua.
Vidi etiam P. Deci auctionem, clarissimi viri, qui maiorum
exempla persequens pro alieno se aere devovit. Emptor tamen in ea auctione inventus est nemo. Hominem ridicu-
lum qui se †exercere†8 aere alieno putet posse, cum vendat
14 aliena! Nam quid ego de Trebellio dicam? Quem ultae videntur Furiae debitorum; vindicis9 enim novarum tabula-
rum novam tabulam vidimus. Quid de T. Planco? Quem
praestantissimus civis, Aquila, Pollentia expulit et quidem
crure fracto: quod utinam illi ante accidisset, ne huc redire

---

8 exercere V: exire D: exserere *Halm*: emergere ⟨ex⟩ C. F. W.
Müller: expedire *Cobet*: exsercire *Schöll*: *alii alia*
9 *Ferrarius*: vindices D: vindicem is V: vindicem *Poggius*

---

13 They were colleagues on the Board of Seven established to
implement the *Lex Antonia agraria* (cf. 5.7 and n. 4), which was
abolished by the senate in early Jan. 43 (cf. 6.14).
14 Or possibly Apulus is a cognomen. Nothing is known of this
person.
15 Cicero facetiously compares the "financial sacrifice" of this
Decius (cf. 13.27) with the heroic self-sacrifice of P. Decius Mus
(cos. 340) and his homonymous son (cos. 295), who were credited

this most dreadful war. [6] Well then, are you not pictur- 13
ing to yourselves the other luminaries of Marcus Antonius' camp? First, those two colleagues of the Antonii and
Dolabella, Nucula and Lento, the parcelers-out of Italy
under a law which the senate has declared to have been
passed by violence.[13] One of them has composed mimes,
the other acted in a tragedy. What am I to say of Domitius
the Apulian?[14] I noticed that his goods were put on the
auction block the other day. His business agents must be
very careless. Recently he gave his sister's son poison, or
rather poured it down his throat. After all, they cannot
help living extravagantly, hoping as they do for our property while they squander their own. I also saw Publius
Decius' auction, that illustrious gentleman who, following
in the footsteps of his ancestors,[15] has offered himself up
for debt. No buyer, however, was found at that auction. A
ridiculous fellow, who thinks he can get himself out of debt
by selling other people's belongings! What am I to say of 14
Trebellius? The Furies of debtors seem to have exacted
their vengeance; for we have seen the new tablet listing the
property of this defender against new tablets.[16] What of Titus Plancus? Aquila, a distinguished citizen, drove him out
of Pollentia, and with a broken leg; if only that had happened to him sooner, to prevent him from coming back

with having offered up their lives for the victory of their armies
and their country in war.   16 Cicero apparently suggests
that Trebellius, who as tribune of the plebs in 47 had opposed a
bill to cancel debts (i.e. to create "clean slates," *tabulae novae*) and
consequently had earned the hatred of debtors, later was forced to
post a "*tabula nova*" (i.e. "an auctioneer's notice board") of his
own, because he himself had fallen into debt (cf. 6.11).

potuisset! Lumen et decus illius exercitus paene praeterii,
T. Annium Cimbrum, Lysidici filium, Lysidicum ipsum
Graeco verbo, quoniam omnia iura dissolvit, nisi forte iure
Germanum Cimber occidit. Cum hanc et huius generis co-
piam tantam habeat Antonius, quod scelus omittet, cum
Dolabella tantis se obstrinxerit parricidiis nequaquam pari
latronum manu et copia?

15   Quapropter, ut invitus saepe dissensi a Q. Fufio, ita
sum eius sententiae libenter adsensus: ex quo iudicare debetis me non cum homine solere, sed cum causa dissidere.
Itaque non adsentior solum sed etiam gratias ago Fufio;
dixit enim severam, gravem, re publica dignam sententiam: iudicavit hostem Dolabellam; bona censuit publice
possidenda. Quo cum addi nihil potuisset—quid enim
atrocius potuit, quid severius decernere?—dixit tamen, si
quis eorum qui post se rogati essent graviorem sententiam
dixisset, in eam se iturum. Quam severitatem quis potest
non laudare?

16   [7] Nunc, quoniam hostis est iudicatus Dolabella, bello
est persequendus. Neque enim quiescit: habet legionem,
habet fugitivos, habet sceleratam impiorum manum. Est

---

17 A broken leg would have hindered Plancus from returning
to Rome when recalled from exile. Or, judging from 13.27, Cicero
sarcastically alludes to the custom of hastening the death of cru-
cified slaves by breaking their legs (cf. Gospel of John 19:31–33), a
fate that would have removed Plancus from Rome forever.

18 The father Lysidicus was probably a freedman. His Greek
name literally means "dissolver (*lys-*) of the principles of law / equity / right (*dike*)"; the added phrase *Graeco verbo* ("according to
the Greek word") points the audience to the literal (Greek) meaning of the word in its application to the son.

19 *Germanus*, meaning both "German" and "a full brother",

here![17] I almost left out the pride and glory of that army, Titus Annius Cimber, Lysidicus' son, and a Lysidicus himself according to the Greek word,[18] since he dissolved all principles of law, unless, perhaps, a Cimbrian lawfully killed a German.[19] With this crew and so many more of the same breed, what crime will Antonius not commit, when Dolabella with so much inferior and smaller a band of ruffians to call upon has made himself guilty of such heinous murders?

Therefore, having often reluctantly disagreed with Quintus Fufius,[20] I gladly assented to his proposal, from which you are to conclude that the differences I am apt to have with him are not related to personality but to substance. So I not only assent to Fufius but thank him; for he put forward a stern, impressive proposal, worthy of the Republic: he has declared Dolabella a public enemy and proposed the confiscation of his property by the authorities. And though this motion admitted of nothing further— what harsher, sterner proposal could he have made?—he added that if any of those who were to be called upon after him made a sterner proposal he would support it. Who is able not to applaud such severity?

[7] Now, since Dolabella has been declared a public enemy, he must be pursued with war. He is not lying low: he has a legion, he has runaways, he has a criminal band of

makes a punning allusion to the charge that Cimber (also the name of a German tribe) allegedly killed his own brother. At 13.26, 28, Cicero adds a further word play with reference to this alleged murder by dubbing Cimber with the nickname "Philadelphus" ("brother-loving").

[20] Cf. 5.1; 7.5; 8.11–19; 10.2–6.

ipse confidens, impotens, gladiatorio generi mortis addic-
tus. Quam ob rem, quoniam Dolabella hesterno die hoste
decreto bellum gerendum est, imperator est deligendus.
Duae dictae sunt sententiae, quarum neutram probo: alteram, quia semper, nisi cum est necesse, periculosam arbitror; alteram, quia alienam his temporibus existimo.

17   Nam extraordinarium imperium populare atque vento-
sum est, minime nostrae gravitatis, minime huius ordinis.
Bello Antiochino magno et gravi, cum L. Scipioni provincia Asia obvenisset, parumque in eo putaretur esse animi,
parum roboris, senatusque ad collegam eius, C. Laelium,
illius Sapientis patrem, negotium deferret, surrexit P. Africanus, frater maior L. Scipionis, et illam ignominiam a
familia deprecatus est, dixitque et in fratre suo summam
virtutem esse summumque consilium neque se ei legatum,
id aetatis eisque rebus gestis, defuturum. Quod cum ab eo
esset dictum, nihil est de Scipionis provincia commuta-
tum. Nec plus extraordinarium imperium ad id bellum
quaesitum quam duobus antea maximis Punicis bellis quae
a consulibus aut a dictatoribus gesta et confecta sunt,
quam Pyrrhi, quam Philippi, quam post Achaico bello,
quam Punico tertio; ad quod populus Romanus ita sibi ipse
delegit idoneum ducem, P. Scipionem, ut eum tamen bel-

---

[21] While the war against Antiochous III the Great was entrusted de facto to the veteran commander Scipio Africanus, his
brother, the consul L. Cornelius Scipio Asiagenus, held the formal
command; with Scipio Africanus serving as his legate, the creation
of a special commission for Africanus was avoided.

[22] All these are wars that Rome fought during the third and
second centuries.

traitors. He himself is confident, unbridled, marked out
for a gladiator's death. Accordingly, since after yesterday's
declaration of Dolabella as a public enemy war must be
waged, we have to choose a commander. Two proposals
have been brought forward, neither of which has my approval: I disapprove of one because I think it is always dangerous except when it is necessary; of the other because I
consider it inappropriate to the present situation.

An extraordinary command smacks of "popular" poli-   17
tics and inconsistency; it does not at all suit our gravity, not
at all suit this body. In the war against Antiochus, a serious
war on a large scale, when the province of Asia had fallen
to Lucius Scipio, who was considered to lack spirit and
strength for the job, and the senate therefore was about
to transfer the task to his colleague, Gaius Laelius, the father of the famous Laelius the Wise, Lucius Scipio's elder
brother, Publius Africanus, rose and asked for such a slight
not to be put upon the family; and he said that his brother
was a man of first-rate courage and judgment and that he
himself, for all his seniority and past record, would not refuse to accompany him as a legate. After he had made this
speech, Scipio's province was left unchanged.[21] No extraordinary command was required for that war any more
than in the two great Punic Wars earlier on, which were
waged and brought to their conclusions by consuls or dic-
tators, or in the war against Pyrrhus, in the war against
Philip, and later in the Achaian War, or in the Third Punic
War.[22] As to the last, the Roman people chose the appropriate general for itself, Publius Scipio, in such a way that it

18   lum gerere consulem vellet. [8] Cum Aristonico bellum
gerendum fuit P. Licinio L. Valerio consulibus. Rogatus est
populus quem id bellum gerere placeret. Crassus consul,
pontifex maximus, Flacco collegae, flamini Martiali, multam dixit, si a sacris discessisset: quam multam populus[10]
remisit; pontifici tamen flaminem parere iussit. Sed ne tum
quidem populus Romanus ad privatum detulit bellum,
quamquam erat Africanus qui anno ante de Numantinis
triumpharat; qui, cum longe omnis belli gloria et virtute
superaret, duas tamen tribus solas tulit. Ita populus Romanus consuli potius Crasso quam privato Africano bellum gerendum dedit. De Cn. Pompei imperiis, summi viri
atque omnium principis, tribuni plebis turbulenti tulerunt. Nam Sertorianum bellum a senatu privato datum est
quia consules recusabant, cum L. Philippus pro consulibus
eum se mittere dixit, non pro consule.

19   Quae igitur haec comitia, aut quam ambitionem constantissimus et gravissimus civis, L. Caesar, in senatum in-

---

10 *D*: populi romani *V*1: populus romanus *V*2

---

23 P. Cornelius Scipio Aemilianus Africanus, the conqueror of
Carthage, was elected consul in 147, although he had not yet
attained the legally required minimum age (cf. 5.47–48).

24 In 131, Aristonicus, a pretender to the throne of Pergamum
in Asia Minor, tried unsuccessfully to block the Romans from taking control of that kingdom under the terms of the will of the last
king, Attalus III, who had died in 133.

25 A. Gabinius in 67 (*Lex Gabinia*) and C. Manilius in 66 (*Lex
Manilia*). The latter's bill to transfer to Pompey the supreme command in the Mithridatic War (74–63) was supported by Cicero in
his extant speech *De imperio Cn. Pompei*.

26 In 77 Pompey was given an extraordinary command to

had him nevertheless conduct the war as consul.[23] [8] In   18
the consulship of Publius Licinius and Lucius Valerius
there was a war to wage with Aristonicus.[24] The people
were asked whom they wished to conduct it. The consul Crassus, who was pontifex maximus, threatened a fine
against his colleague Flaccus, who was the priest of Mars,
if he should abandon his religious duties: the people remit-
ted the fine, but ordered the priest to obey the pontifex.
But not even on that occasion did the Roman people entrust the war to a private individual, though Africanus was
available, who had celebrated his triumph over Numantia
the previous year. Despite standing far above everybody in
military renown and ability, he carried only two tribes. So
the Roman people gave the conduct of the war to the consul Crassus in preference to the private citizen Africanus.
As for the commands of Gnaeus Pompeius, a great man,
indeed the first of men, the legislation was put through by
troublemaking tribunes of the plebs,[25] except that the war
against Sertorius was assigned to him as a private citizen
by the senate because the consuls declined,[26] whereupon
Lucius Philippus said he was sending him, not as proconsul, but in place of the consuls.[27]

    And now what electioneering, what competition for   19
office has a citizen of unimpeachable consistency and responsibility, Lucius Caesar, brought into the senate? He

crush Q. Sertorius (a follower of Marius), who had fled from Italy
after Sulla's victory in 83 and caused unrest in Spain.

    [27] *Pro consulibus*, instead of *pro consule*, but this bitter re-
mark (cf. also Cic. *Leg. Man.* 62; Plut. *Pomp.* 17.4) does not alter
the fact that the senate appointed a private citizen to a command
that should have been given to a consul or ex-consul.

troduxit? Clarissimo viro atque innocentissimo decrevit imperium, privato tamen: in quo maximum nobis onus imposuit. Adsensus ero, ambitionem induxero in curiam; negaro, videbor suffragio meo, tamquam comitiis, honorem homini amicissimo denegavisse. Quod si comitia placet in senatu haberi, petamus, ambiamus, tabella modo detur nobis, sicut populo data est. Cur committis, Caesar, ut aut praestantissimus vir, si tibi non sit adsensum, repulsam tulisse videatur aut unus quisque nostrum praeteritus, si, cum pari dignitate simus, eodem honore digni non pute-

20 mur? At enim—nam id exaudio—C. Caesari adulescentulo imperium extraordinarium mea sententia dedi. Ille enim mihi praesidium extraordinarium dederat: cum dico "mihi," senatui dico populoque Romano. A quo praesidium res publica, ne cogitatum quidem, tantum haberet ut sine eo salva esse non posset, huic extraordinarium imperium non darem? Aut exercitus adimendus aut imperium dandum fuit. Quae est enim ratio aut qui potest fieri ut sine imperio teneatur exercitus? Non igitur, quod ereptum non est, id existimandum est datum. Eripuissetis C. Caesari, patres conscripti, imperium nisi dedissetis. Milites veterani qui illius auctoritatem, imperium, nomen secuti pro re publica arma ceperant volebant sibi ab illo imperari; legio Martia et legio quarta ita se contulerant ad auctoritatem senatus et rei publicae dignitatem ut deposcerent impera-

---

28 In the *Fifth Philippic*, where, however, Cicero talks of *imperium* and not of *imperium extraordinarium* (esp. 5.45).

has proposed to give the command to a person of the highest distinction and integrity, who is, however, a private citizen, thereby putting us in a very awkward position. Suppose I support the motion: I shall be bringing electioneering into the senate-house; suppose I say no: it will look as though I have refused an honor to a close friend by my vote, as in an election. Well, if elections are to be held in the senate, let us present ourselves as candidates, let us canvass, but let us be given a ballot as are the people. Why put us in such a dilemma, Caesar, that it will appear that a most eminent personage has been rejected if your motion fails, or each one of us will seem to have been passed over if we are not deemed worthy of the same honor though equals in rank? But I think I hear a murmur that I proposed a motion giving an extraordinary command to young Gaius Caesar.[28] Well, he had given me extraordinary protection—when I say "me," I mean the senate and people of Rome. Was I not to give an extraordinary command to one from whom the Republic had received extraordinary, undreamed-of protection, failing which it could not have survived? The choice lay between taking his army away or granting him military authority. For by what rationale or how can an army be held without such authority? So we must not regard as granted that which was not snatched away. Members of the Senate, you would have snatched military authority away from Gaius Caesar if you had not granted it. The veteran soldiers who, following his authority, command, and name, had taken up arms on behalf of the Republic wished to be commanded by him; the Martian Legion and the Fourth Legion had given their support to the authority of the senate and the dignity of the Republic, but at the same time they demanded Gaius Caesar as

20

torem et ducem C. Caesarem. Imperium C. Caesari belli
necessitas, fascis senatus dedit. Otioso vero et nihil agenti
privato, obsecro te, L. Caesar—cum peritissimo homine
mihi res est—quando imperium senatus dedit? [9] Sed de
hoc quidem hactenus, ne refragari homini amicissimo ac
de me optime merito videar. Etsi quis potest refragari non
modo non petenti verum etiam recusanti?

21   Illa vero, patres conscripti, aliena consulum dignitate,
aliena temporum gravitate sententia est, ut consules Dolabellae persequendi causa Asiam et Syriam sortiantur. Dicam cur inutile rei publicae, sed prius quam turpe consulibus sit videte. Cum consul designatus obsideatur, cum in
eo liberando salus sit posita rei publicae, cum a populo Romano pestiferi cives parricidaeque desciverint, cumque id
bellum geramus quo bello de dignitate, de libertate, de
vita decernamus, si in potestatem quis Antoni venerit, proposita sint tormenta atque cruciatus, cumque harum rerum omnium decertatio consulibus optimis et fortissimis
commissa et commendata sit, Asiae et Syriae mentio fiet,
ut aut suspicioni crimen aut invidiae materiam dedisse vi-
22 deamur? At vero ita decernunt ut "liberato Bruto": id enim
restabat ut "relicto, deserto, prodito." Ego vero mentionem omnino provinciarum factam dico alienissimo tempore. Quamvis enim intentus animus tuus sit, C. Pansa,
sicut est, ad virum fortissimum et omnium clarissimum
liberandum, tamen rerum natura coget te necessario re-

---

[29] D. Brutus in Mutina.

their general and leader. The necessity of war gave Gaius Caesar the command, the senate only gave him the fasces. But when, I beg you, Lucius Caesar—I am dealing with a man very well versed in these matters—did the senate give a command to a private individual living at his ease and leisure? [9] But enough on this subject. I would not wish to seem to be opposing the appointment of a close friend to whom I owe a great deal. Yet, who can oppose a man who is not seeking the assignment, indeed is actually refusing it?

That other proposal, Members of the Senate, ill accords with the dignity of the consuls or the gravity of the situation, namely that the consuls draw lots for Asia and Syria with a view to pursuing Dolabella. I shall explain why this is disadvantageous to the Republic, but first just see how discreditable it would be to the consuls. When a consul-elect is under siege,[29] when the survival of the Republic depends on his release, when pernicious citizens and traitors have defected from the Roman people, when we are fighting a war for dignity, liberty, and life, and whoever falls into Antonius' power faces the agonies of torture, when the conflict to determine all these matters has been committed and commended to our excellent and very brave consuls, will there be talk of Asia and Syria, letting us seem to have given a reason for suspicion or a cause for jealousy? But the motion includes the condition "when Brutus has been relieved"; it just falls short of saying "abandoned, forsaken, betrayed." But I maintain that the very mention of provinces comes at a most inappropriate moment. Although your mind, Gaius Pansa, may be intent, as indeed it is, on relieving that most courageous and illustrious gentleman of all, yet in the nature of things you would necessarily be forced at times to put your thoughts

ferre animum aliquando ad Dolabellam persequendum et
partem aliquam in Asiam et Syriam derivare curae et cogi-
tationis tuae. Si autem fieri posset, vel pluris te animos habere vellem quos omnis ad Mutinam intenderes. Quod
quoniam fieri non potest, isto t⟨e⟩ animo quem habes
praestantissimum atque optimum nihil volumus nisi de
23 Bruto cogitare. Facis tu id quidem et eo maxime incumbis,
intellego; duas tamen res, magnas praesertim, non modo
agere uno tempore sed ne cogitando quidem explicare
quisquam potest. Incitare et inflammare tuum istuc praestantissimum studium, non ad aliam ulla ex parte curam
transferre debemus.

[10] Adde istuc sermones hominum, adde suspiciones,
adde invidiam. Imitare me, quem tu semper laudasti: qui
instructam ornatamque a senatu provinciam deposui ut incendium patriae omissa omni[11] cogitatione restinguerem.
Nemo erit praeter unum me, quicum profecto, si quid interesse tua putasses, pro summa familiaritate nostra com-
municasses, qui credat te invito provinciam tibi esse decretam. Hanc, quaeso, pro tua singulari sapientia reprime
famam atque effice ne id quod non curas cupere videare.
24 Quod quidem eo vehementius tibi laborandum est quia in
eandem cadere suspicionem collega, vir clarissimus, non
potest. Nihil horum scit, nihil suspicatur; bellum gerit, in
acie stat, de sanguine et de spiritu decertat; ante provin-

[11] *codd.*: omissa ⟨alia⟩ omni *add. Halm in app.*, *SB*

[30] When consul in 63, Cicero resigned in advance his proconsular command for the following year (cf. *Pis.* 5; *Mur.* 42; *Cat.*
4.23; *Fam.* 5.2.3; *Att.* 2.1.3), so as to be able to concentrate exclusively on fighting the Catilinarian conspiracy.

on pursuing Dolabella and divert some part of your attention and consideration to Asia and Syria. But if it were possible, I should wish you had more than one mind so that you could fix them all on Mutina. Since that is not possible, we want you to use that excellent and outstanding mind you have for thinking of nothing except Brutus. That is   23
what you are doing, that is the object of your strenuous effort, I realize. All the same, no one can do two things, especially two important things, at once or even work them out in his mind. We should be spurring and firing your admirable zeal to that purpose, not transferring any part of it to another preoccupation.

[10] And besides, consider the talk of the people, the suspicions, the jealousy. Follow my example; you have always commended me: I resigned a province already furnished and equipped by the senate in order to put aside every concern but that of extinguishing our native land's conflagration.[30] Except for me alone, with whom you would surely have communicated in keeping with our very close friendship if you had thought your interests were in any way involved, nobody will believe that you have been assigned a province against your wish. Like the wise man you are, check such talk, I beg you, and do not let yourself appear to be coveting an appointment for which you care nothing. You should be the more anxious not to let that   24
happen because your colleague, an illustrious gentleman, cannot fall under the same suspicion.[31] He knows nothing; he suspects nothing of all this. He is fighting a war, standing in the battle line, risking his blood and breath. He will

[31] Because Pansa's colleague A. Hirtius was absent from Rome, engaged in military action against Antony.

ciam sibi decretam audiet quam potuerit tempus ei rei datum suspicari. Vereor ne exercitus quoque nostri, qui non dilectus necessitate, sed voluntariis studiis se ad rem publicam contulerunt, tardentur animis, si quicquam aliud a nobis nisi de instanti bello cogitatum putabunt. Quod si provinciae consulibus expetendae videntur, sicut saepe ⟨a⟩[12] multis clarissimis viris expetitae sunt, reddite prius nobis Brutum, lumen et decus civitatis; qui ita conservandus est ut id signum quod de caelo delapsum Vestae custodiis continetur; quo salvo salvi sumus futuri. Tunc vel in caelum vos, si fieri potuerit, umeris nostris tollemus; provincias certe dignissimas vobis deligemus. Nunc quod agitur agamus; agitur autem liberine vivamus an mortem obeamus, quae certe servituti anteponenda est.

25   Quid si etiam tarditatem adfert ista sententia ad Dolabellam persequendum? Quando enim veniet consul? An id exspectamus quoad ne vestigium quidem Asiae civitatum atque urbium relinquatur? At mittent aliquem de suo numero. Valde mihi probari potest, qui paulo ante clarissimo viro privato imperium extra ordinem non dedi! At hominem dignum mittent. Num P. Servilio digniorem? At eum quidem civitas non habet. Quod ergo ipse nemini putavi dandum, ne a senatu quidem, id ego unius iudicio delatum comprobem?

[12] add. Halm

[32] The Palladium was an old-fashioned idol of an armed goddess that supposedly fell from the sky and was kept in Troy as a safeguard of that city. According to Roman tradition, it later came to Rome, where it was kept in the innermost room of the Temple of Vesta and served the same talismanic function.

[33] A legate sent by the absent consular commander (Hirtius or

hear that a province has been assigned to him before he could suspect that any time has been given to this issue. I fear that our armies too, who have come to the aid of the Republic in voluntary enthusiasm, not under the compulsion of a levy, may lose something of their ardor if they think we have anything under consideration except the present war. But if you consuls think it right to seek provinces, as they have often been sought by many illustrious men, first give us back Brutus, the pride and glory of the community, who must be treasured like the image that fell from the sky and is kept by the guardians of Vesta; if this is safe, we will be safe.[32] Then we shall even carry you to heaven on our shoulders if we can; at least, we shall choose for you provinces entirely worthy of yourselves. But now, let us attend to the business in hand; and that business is whether we are to live free or die, which latter is certainly preferable to slavery.

Moreover, does not this proposal actually hold up the 25 pursuit of Dolabella? When will the consul arrive? Are we waiting until the communities and cities of Asia are wiped out completely? But perhaps the consuls will send one of their staff.[33] Am I expected to approve of that, when just now I opposed an extraordinary command for a most illustrious person who is a private citizen! But they will send a worthy man. Worthier than Publius Servilius? But our community contains nobody of that description. I was against the command being given to anybody even by the senate: am I to approve of an appointment made by a single individual?

Pansa) to act on his behalf would not be a private individual, but as a mere subordinate would lack the standing required for such a major military operation.

26   Expedito nobis homine et parato, patres conscripti, opus est et eo qui imperium legitimum habeat, qui praeterea auctoritatem, nomen, exercitum, perspectum animum in re publica liberanda. [11] Quis igitur is est? Aut M. Brutus aut C. Cassius aut uterque. Decernerem plane, sicut multa, "consules, alter ambove," ni Brutum colligassemus in Graecia et eius auxilium ad Italiam vergere quam ad Asiam maluissemus; non ut ex [ea]¹³ acie respectum haberemus, sed ut ipsa acies subsidium haberet etiam transmarinum. Praeterea, patres conscripti, M. Brutum retinet etiam nunc C. Antonius, qui tenet Apolloniam, magnam urbem et gravem; tenet, opinor, Byllidem, tenet Amantiam, instat Epiro, urget Oricum, habet aliquot cohortis, habet equitatum. Hinc si Brutus erit traductus ad aliud bellum, Graeciam certe amiserimus. Est autem etiam de Brundisio atque illa ora Italiae providendum. Quamquam miror tam diu morari Antonium; solet enim ipse accipere manicas nec diutius obsidionis metum sustinere. Quod si confecerit Brutus et intellexerit plus se rei publicae profuturum si Dolabellam persequatur quam si in Graecia maneat, aget ipse per sese, ut adhuc quoque fecit, neque in tot incendiis quibus confestim succurrendum est exspec-
27 tabit senatum. Nam et Brutus et Cassius multis iam in rebus ipse sibi senatus fuit. Necesse est enim in tanta conver-

---

¹³ *del. Rau*: ex ea acie *D*: eo ex acie *Ferrarius*

---

³⁴ Byllis and Amantia were cities situated southeast of Apollonia; Oricum was on the coast. All these places are in the region of Epirus and Illyricum.

³⁵ I.e., C. Antonius normally takes to his heels at the first sign of a siege. The metaphor of donning "gloves" (which were typi-

What we need, Members of the Senate, is a man who is 26
unoccupied and at the ready, who possesses lawful military
power, and besides that, authority, a name, an army, and
a spirit proved in the liberation of the Republic. [11] Who
is that man? Either Marcus Brutus or Gaius Cassius or
both. In fact I should propose, as in many things, "the consuls, one or both," if we had not tied Brutus down in
Greece and preferred that the aid he offers be turned towards Italy rather than Asia, not for us to have a place of
refuge from the battle line but so that the battle line itself
should have some support from overseas. Furthermore,
Members of the Senate, Marcus Brutus is still detained by
Gaius Antonius, who holds the large and important city
of Apollonia; he holds as well, I imagine, Byllis, holds
Amantia, threatens Epirus, presses upon Oricum,[34] has
some cohorts and has cavalry. If Brutus is drawn away from
this theater of action to another war, we shall certainly
have lost Greece. We also have to look after Brundisium
and the adjacent coast of Italy. Yet I am surprised that
Antonius is hanging about for so long: he usually puts on
long gloves himself and does not endure the fear of siege
for very long.[35] However, if Brutus finishes his business
and reaches the conclusion that he will better serve the Republic if he pursues Dolabella instead of remaining in
Greece, he will act on his own initiative, as he has done
hitherto, and not wait for the senate when there are so
many trouble spots calling for immediate attention. For 27
both Brutus and Cassius have already been their own senate on a number of occasions. In such great and complete

cally worn by women and hindered proper use of one's hands) sarcastically adds an aspect of effeminacy to his cowardice.

sione ‹et› perturbation‹e omni›um rerum[14] temporibus
potius parere quam moribus. Nec enim nunc primum aut
Brutus aut Cassius salutem libertatemque patriae legem
sanctissimam et morem optimum iudicabit.[15] Itaque si ad
nos nihil referretur de Dolabella persequendo, tamen ego
pro decreto putarem cum essent tali[16] virtute, auctoritate,
nobilitate summi viri,[17] quorum alterius iam nobis notus
esset exercitus, alterius auditus. [12] Num igitur Brutus
exspectavit decreta nostra, cum studia nosset? Neque
enim est in provinciam suam Cretam profectus: in Macedoniam alienam advolavit; omnia sua putavit quae vos vestra esse velitis; legiones conscripsit novas, excepit veteres;
equitatum ad se abduxit Dolabellae atque eum nondum
tanto parricidio oblitum hostem sua sententia iudicavit.
Nam ni ita esset, quo iure equitatum a consule abduceret?
28 Quid? C. Cassius, pari magnitudine animi et consili prae-
ditus, nonne eo ex Italia consilio profectus est ut prohiberet Syria Dolabellam? Qua lege, quo iure? Eo quod Iuppiter ipse sanxit, ut omnia quae rei publicae salutaria essent
legitima et iusta haberentur. Est enim lex nihil aliud nisi
recta et[iam][18] a numine deorum tracta ratio, imperans honesta, prohibens contraria. Huic igitur legi paruit Cassius,
cum est in Syriam profectus, alienam provinciam, si homi-

---

[14] *Ferrarius*: conversione et concursatione perturbatarum rerum *SB*: concursatione (concursione *t*: conversione *v*) perturba-
tionum rerum *D*   [15] *SB*: iudicavit *D*
[16] *Faërnus*: tales *D*   [17] *D*: ‹ei› summi viri *Clark*: summa
viri *Faërnus*   [18] *del. Poggius*

---

[36] A reference to Caesar's assassination, led by the two men.
[37] M. Brutus had officially been allotted the province of Crete

upheaval and confusion one must be guided by the circumstances, not by standard procedures. This will not be the first time for either Brutus or Cassius to regard the safety and freedom of their native land as the most sacred law and the best possible procedure.[36] So if nothing were referred to us concerning the pursuit of Dolabella, I should still take it as the equivalent of a decree since there are eminent men, men of such valor, high standing, and nobility, whose armies in the one case are already known to us and in the other heard tell of. [12] So did Brutus wait for our decrees when he knew our aims? For instead of going to Crete, his own province, he hastened to somebody else's, Macedonia.[37] He considered as his everything which you would like to be yours. He raised new legions, took over old ones. He drew away Dolabella's cavalry to himself and by his personal decision judged him a public enemy, though not yet stained with so foul a murder. For were it otherwise, what right had he to draw cavalry away from a consul? And did not Gaius Cassius, his equal in greatness of spirit and judgment, set out from Italy with the design of keeping Dolabella out of Syria? Under what law, by what right? By the right which Jupiter himself established, that all things beneficial to the Republic be held lawful and proper. Law is nothing but a code of right conduct derived from the will of the gods, ordaining what is good and forbidding its opposite. This law, then, Cassius obeyed when he went to Syria; another man's province, if

28

in summer 44 while Mark Antony secured Macedonia for himself and later had it allotted to his brother C. Antonius; this arrangement was in force till the distribution of provinces under Antony was annulled by the senate on 20 Dec. 44 (cf. 3.37–39).

nes legibus scriptis uterentur, eis vero oppressis suam lege
naturae.

29   Sed ut ea vestra quoque auctoritate firmetur, ⟨ita⟩[19]
censeo: "Cum P. Dolabella quique eius crudelissimi et tae-
terrimi facinoris ministri, socii, adiutores fuerunt hostes
populi Romani a senatu iudicati sint, cumque senatus P.
Dolabellam bello persequendum censuerit, ut is qui omnia deorum hominumque iura novo, inaudito, inexpiabili
scelere polluerit nefarioque se patriae parricidio obstrinxerit poenas dis hominibusque meritas debitasque persol-
30 vat, senatui placere C. Cassium pro consule provinciam
Syriam obtinere, ut qui optimo iure eam provinciam ob-
tinuerit, eum a Q. Marcio Crispo pro consule, L. Staio
Murco pro consule, A. Al⟨l⟩ieno legato exercitus accipere,
eosque ei tradere, cumque eis copiis et si quas praeterea
paraverit bello P. Dolabellam terra marique persequi. Eius
belli gerendi causa quibus ei videatur navis, nautas, pecuniam ceteraque quae ad id bellum gerendum pertineant,
ut imperandi in Syria, Asia, Bithynia, Ponto ius potesta-
temque habeat, utique, quamcumque in provinciam eius
belli gerendi causa advenerit, ibi maius imperium C. Cassi
pro consule sit quam eius erit qui eam provinciam tum ob-
tinebit cum C. Cassius pro consule in eam provinciam ve-
31 nerit; regem Deiotarum patrem et regem Deiotarum
filium, si, ut multis bellis saepe numero imperium populi
Romani iuverint, item C. Cassium pro consule copiis suis
opibusque iuvissent, senatui populoque Romano gratum

[19] *add.* SB

people were following written laws, but such laws having
been overthrown, his by the law of nature.

But in order that this may be strengthened by your au-   29
thority, I move as follows: "Whereas Publius Dolabella and
those who were the instruments, partners, and aides of his
most cruel and abominable act have been declared enemies of the Roman people by the senate, and whereas the
senate has determined that Publius Dolabella shall be pursued with war, to the end that he who has defiled all the
laws of gods and men by a novel, unheard-of, inexpiable
crime and made himself guilty of a criminal assault upon
his native land may pay a due and proper penalty to gods
and men: that it please the senate that Gaius Cassius, pro-   30
consul, shall hold the province of Syria as governor in
full status; and that he take over from Quintus Marcius
Crispus, proconsul, Lucius Staius Murcus, proconsul, and
Aulus Allienus, legate, their armies and that they hand the
said armies over to him, and that with these forces, and
any which he may raise in addition, he pursue Publius
Dolabella with war by land and sea; that for the purpose of
waging this war he have the right and power in Syria, Asia,
Bithynia, and Pontus to requisition ships, crews, money,
and all else pertaining to the prosecution of this war from
whomsoever he may see fit; and that whatever province he
enter in order to prosecute this war, the authority of Gaius
Cassius, proconsul, shall supersede that of the governor of
that province at the time when Gaius Cassius, proconsul,
shall enter that province; that if king Deiotarus the father   31
and king Deiotarus the son, as in many wars they have often aided the empire of the Roman people, shall likewise
aid Gaius Cassius, proconsul, with their forces and resources, their action shall be pleasing to the senate and

CICERO

esse facturos. Itemque si ceteri reges, tetrarchae dynas-
taeque fecissent, senatum populumque Romanum eorum
offici non immemorem futurum. Utique C. Pansa A. Hirtius consules, alter ambove, si eis videretur, re publica recuperata de provinciis consularibus, praetoriis, ad hunc
ordinem primo quoque tempore ⟨re⟩ferant. Interea provinciae ab eis a quibus obtinentur obtineantur quoad
cuique ex senatus consulto successum sit."

32   [13] Hoc senatus consulto ardentem inflammabitis et
armatum armabitis Cassium; nec enim animum eius potes-
tis ignorare nec copias. Animus is est quem videtis; copiae
quas audistis: ⟨primum legiones quas ducunt Q. Marcius
et L. Staius⟩,[20] fortes et constantes viri, qui ne vivo quidem
Trebonio Dolabellae latrocinium in Syriam penetrare si-
vissent. Al⟨l⟩ienus, familiaris et necessarius meus, post
interitum Treboni profecto ne dici quidem se legatum Dolabellae volet. Est Q. Caecili Bassi, privati illius quidem,
sed fortis et praeclari viri, robustus et victor exercitus,
33   Deiotari regis et patris et fili et magnus et nostro more
institutus exercitus. Summa in filio spes, summa ingeni in-
doles, summa virtus. Quid de patre dicam? cuius benevo-
lentia in populum Romanum est ipsius aequalis aetati; qui
non solum socius imperatorum nostrorum fuit in bellis verum etiam dux copiarum suarum. Quae de illo viro Sulla,
quae Murena, quae Servilius, quae Lucullus, quam ornate,
quam honorifice, quam graviter saepe in senatu praedica-

20 *add. SB, praeeunte Madvig* (primum legiones Q. Marci,
deinde L. Stati)

people of Rome; and that if other kings, tetrarchs, and dynasts do likewise, the senate and people of Rome will not be unmindful of their service; and that Gaius Pansa and Aulus Hirtius, consuls, one or both, if they see fit, shall open a discussion in this body concerning the consular and praetorian provinces as soon as possible after the Republic has been recovered; and that in the meantime the provinces shall remain under their present governors until such time as a successor to each be appointed by decree of the senate."

[13] By this decree you will put fire into Cassius' heart,   32 which is already aflame, and arms into his hands, which already grasp them; for neither his spirit nor his forces can be unknown to you. His spirit is as you see, his forces as you have heard: first, the legions commanded by Quintus Marcius and Lucius Staius, men of courage and resolution, who would not have allowed Dolabella's bandits to gain entrance into Syria even while Trebonius was alive. Allienus, my good friend and connection, will surely not wish even to be called Dolabella's legate after Trebonius' death. There is the stout and victorious army of Quintus Caecilius Bassus; he holds no office, but he is a fine, gallant man. There is the army of the two kings, Deiotarus father   33 and son, large and trained in our fashion. The son is a man of the highest promise, highest mental capacity, and highest courage. What shall I say of his father? His goodwill to the Roman people is as long as his life; he was not only the ally of our generals in their wars but led his troops in person. Think of all the eloquent, flattering, impressive tributes often paid to that monarch in the senate by Sulla,

34 verunt! Quid de Cn. Pompeio loquar? Qui unum Deiotarum in toto orbe terrarum ex animo amicum vereque
benevolum, unum fidelem populo Romano iudicavit. Fuimus imperatores ego et M. Bibulus in propinquis finiti-
misque provinciis: ab eodem rege adiuti sumus et equitatu
et pedestribus copiis. Secutum est hoc acerbissimum et
calamitosissimum civile bellum in quo quid faciendum
Deiotaro, quid omnino rectius fuerit dicere non est necesse, praesertim cum contra ac Deiotarus sensit victoria
belli iudicarit. Quo in bello si fuit error, communis ei fuit
cum senatu; sin recta sententia, ne victa quidem causa
vituperanda est. Ad has copias accedent alii reges, etiam
35 dilectus accedent. Neque vero classes deerunt: tanti Tyrii
Cassium faciunt, tantum eius in Syria nomen atque Phoenice est. [14] Paratum habet imperatorem C. Cassium, patres conscripti, res publica contra Dolabellam nec paratum
solum sed peritum atque fortem. Magnas ille res gessit
ante Bibuli, summi viri, adventum, cum Parthorum nobilissimos duces maximas copias fudit Syriamque immani
Parthorum impetu liberavit. Maximam eius et singularem
laudem praetermitto; cuius enim praedicatio nondum omnibus grata est, hanc memoriae potius quam vocis testimo-
nio conservemus.

---

38 King Deiotarus, who shared with his homonymous son the
rule of his kingdom of Galatia in Asia Minor, assisted the Roman
generals mentioned in a succession of wars in Asia Minor (87–63).

39 In 63/62 Pompey recognized Deiotarus as royal ruler and
assigned a large area to his royal power.

40 In 51–50, Deiotarus gave support to M. Calpurnius Bibulus, who governed Syria, and to Cicero, who was proconsul in
Cilicia (cf., e.g., *Fam.* 15.1.6; 15.2.2; 15.4.5).

Murena, Servilius, Lucullus.[38] What am I to say of Gnaeus 34
Pompeius? He declared that the Roman people had one
sincere friend, one true and faithful well-wisher in the
whole world: Deiotarus.[39] Marcus Bibulus and I commanded armies in provinces near to, in fact adjoining one
another: we were aided by this same king with both cavalry
and infantry units.[40] Then came this most cruel and disastrous civil war. What Deiotarus should have done, what
was on the whole the more proper course, does not have to
be said, especially as victory in the war went contrary to
Deiotarus' sentiments. If in that war he made a mistake,
the senate shared it; but if his was the right decision, it
should not be blamed, even though the cause was defeated.[41] To these forces will accrue other kings and also
levies. Nor will navies be lacking. Cassius is a hero to the 35
Tyrians, a mighty name in Syria and Phoenicia. [14] In Gaius Cassius, Members of the Senate, the Republic has a
general ready to fight Dolabella, and not only ready but experienced and brave. He won great victories before the arrival of the eminent Bibulus, routing celebrated Parthian
commanders and a mighty force, delivering Syria from a
massive Parthian invasion.[42] His greatest, unique glory I
pass by;[43] since its celebration is not yet agreeable to everyone, let us preserve it by the testimony of memory rather
than of words.

[41] In 49–48, King Deiotarus the father supported Pompey in
the Civil War (cf. 2.93–94).   [42] After the major defeat of
Roman forces under M. Licinius Crassus at Carrhae in 53, the
Parthians posed a serious threat to Roman territory in Syria and
Asia Minor until they were beaten back in 51 by C. Cassius Lon-
ginus, who had served as quaestor under Crassus.

[43] I.e. Caesar's assassination (cf. 5.35; 10.7).

36   Animadverti, patres conscripti, exaudivi etiam nimium
a me Brutum, nimium Cassium[21] ornari, Cassio vero sententia mea dominatum et principatum dari. Quos ego
orno? Nempe eos qui ipsi sunt ornamenta rei publicae.
Quid? D. Brutum nonne omnibus sententiis semper orna-
vi? Num igitur reprehenditis? An Antonios potius orna-
rem, non modo suarum familiarum sed [p.] Romani[22] nominis probra atque dedecora? An Censorinum ornem in
bello hostem, in pace sectorem? An cetera ex eodem latrocinio naufragia colligam? Ego vero istos oti, concordiae, legum, iudiciorum, libertatis inimicos tantum abest ut ornem ut effici non possit quin eos tam oderim quam rem
publicam diligo.

37   "Vide," inquit, "ne veteranos offendas"; hoc enim vel
maxime exaudio. Ego autem veteranos tueri debeo, sed
eos quibus sanitas est; certe timere non debeo. Eos vero
veteranos qui pro re publica arma ceperunt secutique sunt
C. Caesaris[23] auctoritatem[24] beneficiorum ⟨memores⟩[25]
paternorum, hodieque rem publicam defendunt vitae
suae periculo, non tueri solum sed etiam commodis augere
debeo. Qui autem quiescunt, ut septima, ut octava legio, in
magna gloria et laude ponendos puto. Comites vero Anto-

---

21 nimium cassium *bns*: brutum cassium *t*: *del. Halm*
22 *corr. Ferrarius*   23 *SB*: Caesarem *D*
24 *n*: auctoritate *sv*: auctore *b*[1]: auctorem *b*[2]
25 *suppl. SB*

---

44 The Antonii (on the paternal side) and the Iulii (on the maternal side).   45 Cicero introduces an unspecified critic who
cautions against a decree conferring power on Cassius, one of
Caesar's assassins.

I have noticed, Members of the Senate, I have even 36
heard it murmured, that I honor Brutus overmuch and
Cassius overmuch; moreover that my motion gives Cassius
a position of dominance and primacy. Whom do I honor?
Why, men who are themselves an honor to the Republic.
What? Have I not always honored Decimus Brutus in all
my speeches and proposals? Do you censure me for that?
Or should I rather have honored the Antonii, a reproach
and disgrace not only to their families[44] but to the Roman
name? Or should I honor Censorinus, an enemy in war,
a liquidator of confiscated properties in peace? Or am I to
assemble the rest of the wreckage from the same robber
band? No, far from honoring these foes of peace, concord,
laws, law courts, and liberty, there is no way that I shall not
hate them as much as I love the Republic.

"Mind you don't offend the veterans," he says;[45] for this 37
in particular I hear murmured. Now I have a duty to look
after the veterans, but only those of sound sentiments; I
certainly have no duty to be afraid of them. Those veterans
who took up arms for the Republic and followed Gaius
Caesar's authority, mindful of his father's benefits, and are
today risking their lives in defense of the Republic, those I
am bound not only to defend but to honor by increas-
ing their benefits. The ones who remain quiet, like the Seventh and like the Eighth Legions,[46] I consider deserving of
great praise and glory. But the men with Antonius, who af-

[46] The veterans recruited by Octavian from these two legions
in Campania in Oct. 44 later returned to their colonies and took no
part in the fighting when they discovered that they would be opposing the Caesarian Mark Antony.

ni, qui, postquam beneficia Caesaris comederunt, consulem designatum obsident, huic urbi ferro ignique minitantur, Saxae se et Cafoni tradiderunt ad facinus praedamque natis, num quis est qui tuendos putet? Ergo aut boni sunt, quos etiam ornare, aut quieti, quos conservare debemus, aut impii, quorum contra furorem bellum et iusta arma 38 cepimus. [15] Quorum igitur veteranorum animos ne offendamus veremur? Eorumne qui D. Brutum obsidione cupiunt liberare? Quibus cum Bruti salus cara sit, qui possunt Cassi nomen odisse? An eorum qui utrisque armis vacant? Non vereor ne acerbus c‹u›ivis[26] quisquam istorum sit qui otio delectantur. Tertio vero generi, non militum veteranorum sed importunissimorum hostium, cupio quam acerbissimum dolorem inurere. Quamquam, patres conscripti, quousque sententias dicemus veteranorum arbitratu? Quod eorum tantum fastidium est, quae tanta adrogantia ut ad arbitrium illorum imperatores etiam 39 deligamus? Ego autem—dicendum est enim, patres conscripti, quod sentio—non tam veteranos metuendos nobis arbitror quam quid tirones milites, flos Italiae, quid novae legiones ad liberandam patriam paratissimae, quid cuncta Italia de vestra gravitate sentiat. Nihil enim semper floret; aetas succedit aetati. Diu legiones Caesaris viguerunt; nunc vigent Pansae, vigent Hirti, vigent Caesaris fili, vigent Planci. Vincunt numero, vincunt aetatibus; nimirum etiam auctoritate vincunt; id enim bellum gerunt quod ab omnibus gentibus comprobatur. Itaque his praemia pro

[26] *corr. Sternkopf*

ter squandering Caesar's benefits are besieging a consul-
elect and threatening this city with sword and fire, who
have handed themselves over to Saxa and Cafo, those
born malefactors and plunderers: does anyone think they
should be looked after? So there are either decent men,
whom we ought even to honor, or quiet ones, whom we
should preserve, or villainous ones, against whose madness
we have taken up arms in a just war. [15] To which veter-   38
ans, then, do we fear to give offence? Those who are anxious to free Decimus Brutus from siege? How can they
hate the name of Cassius when they hold Brutus' life dear?
Or those who stand neutral? I am not afraid that any of
these peace-loving folk will be bitter against anybody. As
for the third category, not veteran soldiers but most savage
enemies, I wish to sear them with the bitterest possible
pain. After all, Members of the Senate, how much longer
shall we voice our opinions at the discretion of the veterans? What presumption, what arrogance on their part, to
expect us even to choose commanders at their pleasure!
For my part—I have to speak as I feel, Members of the   39
Senate—I do not think we should be apprehensive of the
veterans so much as of how the recruits, the flower of Italy,
how the new legions, who stand fully ready to liberate our
native land, and how the whole of Italy are going to judge
of your steadfastness. Nothing blooms forever; generation
succeeds generation. Caesar's legions flourished for a long
while; now it is the turn of Pansa's legions, and Hirtius',
and young Caesar's, and Plancus'. They have the advantage in number, in youth, and also, one might add, in respect; for they are fighting a war that is approved by all nations. And so these soldiers have been promised rewards,
whereas the others have already received them. Let the

missa sunt, illis persoluta. Fruantur illi suis, persolvantur his quae spopondimus. Id enim deos immortalis spero aequissimum iudicare.

40   Quae cum ita sint, eam quam dixi sententiam vobis, patres conscripti, censeo comprobandam.

latter enjoy their own, and let the former be paid in full what we have pledged. That I trust is fairest in the judgment of the immortal gods.

In view of which, Members of the Senate, I conceive 40 that the proposal I have made deserves your approval.

PHILIPPIC 12

INTRODUCTION

About the beginning of March 43, the consulars Q. Fufius
Calenus and L. Calpurnius Piso, who were supporters of
Antony, spread reports that Antony was now ready to come
to terms (12.1). The mood in Rome at that time seems to
have shifted briefly in favor of Cicero's political opponents.
They pressed their advantage after Cicero's setback in failing to win senatorial approval for his motion in the *Eleventh Philippic* to assign a military command to the tyran-
nicide C. Cassius in Syria (11.26–31). In that climate, the
consul Pansa wavered for a time in his support for pursuing military action against Antony (12.6, 18), and the senate authorized another peace embassy to Mutina. Possibly
they did so partly out of fear for the safety of Decimus
Brutus, in case he should fall into Antony's hands and suffer torture and execution after the fashion of Trebonius,
who had been treacherously put to death by Dolabella
(12.3). The new embassy was to consist of five consulars (13.36), viz. Calenus, Piso, L. Caesar, P. Servilius
Isauricus, and amazingly, Cicero (12.18); it was given no
special charge or powers to negotiate with Antony (12.28),
apart from exploring Antony's willingness to cease hostilities (12.16). Then, at a slightly later meeting, Servilius indicated a desire to withdraw from serving on the embassy

(12.5), and Pansa delivered a lengthy retraction of his recent enthusiasm for peace (12.6).[1]

At that same meeting, Cicero took advantage of the change in mood to deliver the *Twelfth Philippic*, in which he denounced the senate's decision to send a second embassy (12.7–16a) and argued against his own participation in that mission (12.16b-30a). He stopped short, however, of refusing outright to serve as an envoy (12.30b) because evidently he still did not have sufficient support for his demand that the mission be cancelled. Even later, when Cicero delivered the *Thirteenth Philippic* on 20 March, he stops short of claiming that the embassy will never leave Rome, although he continues to express his own unwillingness to participate (13.47). In the end, the outbreak of fighting in April and Antony's withdrawal from Mutina made a peace embassy a moot point.

Cicero's part in the affair of this second embassy is a curious one because he claims in the *Fourteenth Philippic* of 21 April that from 1 January onwards he had *never* voted in favor of sending envoys to Antony (14.20). However, the opening of the *Twelfth Philippic* certainly conveys the opposite impression. At the very least, Cicero had not op-

[1] The date of the senate's meeting can have been no later than *c.* 10 March since Mark Antony in his letter received in Rome on 20 March (see Introduction to *Phil.* 13) appears to signal his awareness of the second thoughts that were voiced in opposition to sending a second embassy (13.47). Since 5 to 6 days is roughly the time it takes a speedy messenger to cover the approximately 200 miles between Rome and Mutina (*Fam.* 11.6.1), we must allow at least that much time for news of the meeting to travel to Antony in Mutina and the same length of time for Antony's letter to be carried back by 20 March.

posed the sending of the second peace mission when it was authorized at the earlier meeting (12.6), and he even allowed himself to be included among the five ambassadors. By Cicero's own admission, he had briefly shared the delusion that Antony had become amenable (12.2–3).

INTRODUCTION TO PHILIPPIC 12

STRUCTURE

Exordium

(1–4a) General deception by a false hope for peace

Propositio

(4b–5a) Plans for a second peace embassy should be scrapped

Confirmatio

(5b–30a) Arguments against a second embassy
  (5b–6) P. Servilius and Pansa are no longer in favor of the embassy
  (7–10) News of embassy will dampen ardor
  (11–16a) No terms are possible; bridges have been burned
  (16b–30a) Cicero can play no useful role in this embassy because
    (16b–19a) his participation is an inappropriate choice
    (19b–20) his personal feelings will get in the way
    (21–30a) it will be too dangerous for him to go

Peroratio

(30b) Time is needed for Cicero to reflect further on the best course of action

M. TULLI CICERONIS
IN M. ANTONIUM
ORATIO PHILIPPICA DUODECIMA

1   [1] Etsi minime decere videtur, patres conscripti, falli,
decipi, errare eum cui vos maximis saepe de rebus ad-
sentiamini, consolor me tamen quoniam vobiscum pariter
et una cum sapientissimo consule erravi. Nam cum duo
consulares spem honestae pacis nobis attulissent, quod
erant familiares M. Antoni, quod domestici, nosse aliquod
eius vulnus quod nobis ignotum esset videbantur. Apud alterum uxor, liberi; alter cotidie litteras mittere, accipere,
2   aperte favere Antonio. Hi subito hortari ad pacem, quod
iam diu non fecissent, non sine causa videbantur. Accessit
consul hortator. At qui consul? Si prudentiam quaerimus,
qui minime falli posset; si virtutem, qui nullam pacem pro-
baret nisi cum cedente atque victo; si magnitudinem animi, qui praeferret mortem servituti. Vos autem, patres
conscripti, non tam immemores vestrorum gravissimorum

---

¹ L. Calpurnius Piso and Q. Fufius Calenus, as revealed in §3.

² The plural noun *liberi* can stand for any number of children:
here it refers to Antony's son Antyllus, by his wife Fulvia.

³ Cf. 7.5. At 12.18 Calenus is called Antony's "agent" (*procura-
tor*).

MARCUS TULLIUS CICERO'S TWELFTH PHILIPPIC ORATION AGAINST MARCUS ANTONIUS

[1] Members of the Senate, although it seems by no means fitting that one to whose views on matters of the highest importance you frequently give your assent, should be deceived, be misled, be in error, nevertheless, I console myself inasmuch as I erred in common with you and in the company of our very astute consul. For when two consulars[1] brought us hope of peace with honor, we supposed that they, because they were close friends of Marcus Antonius and part of his domestic circle, knew of some reverse that had befallen him of which we were ignorant. His wife and children[2] are staying with one of these individuals, while the other sends and receives letters daily from Antonius and openly supports him.[3] Their suddenly urging us to make peace, something they had not been doing previously, could not be without any reason, we thought. The consul added his encouragement. And what sort of a consul is he? If we seek prudence, the sort of man who was least capable of being tricked; if courage, the sort of man to approve no peace except with a yielding and defeated adversary; if a lofty spirit, the sort of man to prefer death to slavery. As for you, Members of the Senate, it was not as though you had forgotten your weighty decrees but

187

decretorum videbamini quam spe adlata deditionis, quam
amici pacem appellare mallent, de imponendis, non acci-
piendis legibus cogitare. Auxerat autem meam quidem
spem, credo item vestram, quod domum Antoni adflictam
maestitia audiebam, lamentari uxorem. Hic etiam fautores
Antoni, quorum in vultu habitant oculi mei, tristiores vide-
3 bam. Quod si non ita est, cur a Pisone et Caleno potissimum, cur hoc tempore, cur tam improviso, cur tam repente pacis est facta mentio? Negat Piso scire se, negat
audisse quicquam; negat Calenus rem ullam novam adla-
tam esse. Atque id nunc negant, postea quam nos pacifica-
toria legatione implicatos putant. Quid ergo opus est novo
consilio, si in re nihil omnino novi est?

[2] Decepti, decepti, inquam, sumus, patres conscripti.
Antoni est acta causa ab amicis eius, non publica. Quod videbam equidem, sed quasi per caliginem; praestrinxerat
aciem animi D. Bruti salus. Quod si in bello dari vicarii so-
lerent, libenter me ut D. Brutus emitteretur pro illo inclu-
4 di paterer. Atque hac voce Q. Fufi capti sumus: "Ne si a
Mutina quidem recesserit, audiemus Antonium, ne si a
senatus quidem potestate futurum se dixerit?" Durum videbatur; itaque fracti sumus, cessimus. Recedit igitur a
Mutina? "Nescio." Paret senatui? "Credo," inquit Calenus,
"sed ita ut teneat dignitatem." Valde hercules vobis laborandum est, patres conscripti, ut vestram dignitatem amittatis, quae maxima est, Antoni, quae neque est ulla neque

rather were thinking of laying down terms, not accepting them, since you had been given reason to hope for a surrender which Antonius' friends preferred to call a peace. My hopes rose, as I expect yours did as well, from the report that gloom reigned in Antonius' house and that his wife was in tears. Here too I saw his backers, whose faces my eyes keep under constant observation, looking glum. If this is not the case, why the mention of peace by Piso and Calenus of all people, why at this time, why so unexpectedly and suddenly? Piso says he knows nothing, has heard nothing. Calenus says that nothing new has come his way. They make these denials now, after they think we have entangled ourselves in a peacemaking embassy. Well, where is the need for a new policy, if there is nothing whatever new in the circumstances? 3

[2] We have been misled, Members of the Senate, misled, I say. Antonius' friends have pleaded *his* cause, not that of our country. I saw it indeed, but I saw it through a fog as it were; my vision was blurred by my anxiety for Decimus Brutus. If the giving of substitutes were customary in war, I would gladly let myself be shut in instead of him so as to secure Decimus Brutus' release. Moreover, we 4 were taken in by these words of Quintus Fufius: "Shall we not listen to Antonius even if he withdraws from Mutina, even if he promises to be under the senate's control?" It seemed obstinate of us; consequently we softened, we gave in. Well, does he withdraw from Mutina? "I don't know," is the reply. Is he obedient to the senate? "I believe so," (Fufius) Calenus says, "but with the proviso that he maintain his dignity." Of course, by god, Members of the Senate, you must make every effort to throw away your own dignity, which is very great, and keep intact Antonius'

189

esse potest, retineatis, ut eam per vos reciperet quam per se perdidit!

Si iacens vobiscum aliquid ageret, audirem fortasse; quamquam—sed hoc malo dicere, audirem: stanti resis-
5 tendum est aut concedenda una cum dignitate libertas. At non est integrum: constituta legatio est. Quid autem non integrum est sapienti quod restitui potest? Cuiusvis hominis est errare; nullius nisi insipientis perseverare in errore. Posteriores enim cogitationes, ut aiunt, sapientiores solent esse. Discussa est illa caligo quam paulo ante dixi; diluxit, patet, videmus omnia, neque per nos solum, sed admonemur a nostris.

Attendistis paulo ante praestantissimi viri quae esset oratio. "Maestam," inquit, "domum offendi, coniugem, liberos. Admirabantur boni viri, accusabant amici quod spe pacis legationem suscepissem." Nec mirum, P. Servili: tuis enim ⟨se⟩verissimis[1] gravissimisque sententiis omni est non dico dignitate sed etiam spe salutis spoliatus Antonius.
6 Ad eum ire te legatum quis non miraretur? De me experior: cuius idem consilium quod tuum sentio quam reprehendatur. Nos reprehendimur soli? Quid? Vir fortissimus Pansa sine causa paulo ante tam accurate locutus est tam diu? Quid egit nisi uti falsam proditionis a se suspicionem depelleret? Unde autem ista suspicio est? Ex pacis patrocinio repentino quod subito suscepit eodem captus errore quo nos.

[1] *corr. Gulielmius*

[4] A proverbial expression, e.g., Eur. *Hipp.* 436.

dignity, which does not and cannot exist, so that he may recover through you the dignity that he destroyed by his own
doing!

If he were prepared to negotiate with you on his knees,
perhaps I would listen, even though—but I prefer to say, I
would listen. Given, however, that he stands upright, we
must resist him or surrender freedom along with dignity.
But, it may be objected, the matter is closed; the delega- 5
tion has been appointed. Yet, to a man of sense everything
is open that can be corrected. Anyone can make a mistake,
but only a fool persists in error. Second thoughts, as they
say, are usually wiser.[4] That fog of which I spoke a little earlier is dispersed. Light has broken through, all is plain, we
see everything, and not only with our own eyes, but our
families and friends warn us.

You heard a little while ago the speech of a very distinguished gentleman: "I found in mourning," he said, "my
household, my wife, my children. Decent men were aston-
ished, and my friends criticized me for accepting the mission in the hope of peace." No wonder, Publius Servilius! It
was your most stern and weighty proposals that deprived
Antonius of all hope of survival, let alone dignity. Who 6
would not be surprised to see you go to him as envoy? I
speak from my own experience. I took the same view as
you, and I see how strongly it is censured. Nor are the two
of us the only targets for criticism. Was it without good
cause that our gallant Pansa spoke just now in such detail
and at such length? What was his purpose except to free
himself from a false suspicion of treachery? And whence
arose that suspicion? From his sudden advocacy of peace,
which he launched on the spur of the moment, having
been deceived by the same error as ourselves.

7   Quod si est erratum, patres conscripti, spe falsa atque fallaci, redeamus in viam. Optimus est portus paenitenti mutatio consili. [3] Quid enim potest, per deos immortalis, rei publicae prodesse nostra legatio? Prodesse dico? Quid si etiam obfutura est? Obfutura? Quid si iam nocuit atque obfuit? An vos acerrimam illam et fortissimam populi Romani libertatis recuperandae cupiditatem non imminutam ac debilitatam putatis legatione pacis audita? Quid municipia censetis? Quid colonias? Quid cunctam Italiam? Futuram eodem studio quo contra commune incendium exarserat? An non putamus fore ut eos paeniteat professos esse et prae se tulisse odium in Antonium qui pecunias polliciti sunt, qui arma, qui se totos et animis et corporibus in salutem rei publicae contulerunt? Quem ad modum nostrum hoc consilium Capua probabit, quae temporibus his Roma altera est? Illa impios civis iudicavit, eiecit, exclusit. Illi, inquam, urbi fortissime ‹constringere›[2] conanti e manibus

8 est ereptus Antonius. Quid? Legionum nostrarum nervos nonne his consiliis incidimus? Quis est enim qui ad bellum inflammato animo futurus sit spe pacis oblata? Ipsa illa Martia caelestis et divina legio hoc nuntio languescet et mollietur atque illud pulcherrimum nomen [Martium][3] amittet: excident gladii, fluent arma de manibus. Senatum enim secuta non arbitrabitur se graviore odio debere esse in Antonium quam senatum. Pudet huius legionis, pudet quartae, quae pari virtute nostram auctoritatem probans non ut consulem et imperatorem suum, sed ut hostem et

---

[2] *SB: suppl. Koch (post* conanti)   [3] *del. Manutius*

---

[5] The new colonists brought in by Antony in the spring of 44; cf. 2.100.

Well, Members of the Senate, if we have been led   7
astray by a false, delusive hope, let us get back to our path.
The best recourse when experiencing regret is a change of
policy. [3] For, in name of the immortal gods, what good
can our mission do the Republic? "What good," do I say?
But supposing it is even going to do harm? *Going* to do
harm? Supposing it already *has* done harm and been detri-
mental? Or do you imagine that the Roman people's ardent, courageous desire to recover its freedom has not
been diminished and enfeebled by the news of a peace
mission? How do you think the municipalities have been
affected, and the colonies, and the whole of Italy? Will the
enthusiasm that previously flamed up to fight the common
peril be the same? Must we not expect that those who have
promised money and arms, who have committed themselves unreservedly body and soul to the survival of the Republic, will regret having professed and declared their hatred of Antonius? How will Capua, which is a second Rome
these days, approve this initiative of ours? She judged the
traitors, threw them out, kept them out.[5] Yes, Antonius was
barely snatched from that city's grasp as she bravely tried
to lay hold of him. What of our legions? Have we not ham-   8
strung them by this peace initiative? What heart will burn
for war once the hope of peace has been held out? Even
that godlike, superhuman Martian legion will droop at the
news and soften and lose its splendid name; the swords will
fall, the shields will drop from their hands. They followed
the senate, and will not feel it right to show more hatred towards Antonius than the senate does. One feels shame in
the sight of this legion and of the Fourth too, which with
equal courage approved our authority and abandoned Antonius, not as their consul and imperator but as an enemy

193

oppugnatorem patriae reliquit Antonium; pudet optimi
exercitus qui coniunctus est ex duobus, qui iam lustratus,
qui profectus ad Mutinam est; qui si pacis, id est timo-
ris nostri, nomen audierit, ut non referat pedem, insistet
certe. Quid enim revocante et receptui canente senatu

9   properet dimicare? [4] Quid autem hoc iniustius quam nos
inscientibus eis qui bellum gerunt de pace decernere, nec
solum inscientibus sed etiam invitis? An vos A. Hirtium,
praeclarissimum consulem, C. Caesarem, deorum beneficio natum ad haec tempora, quorum epistulas spem victoriae declarantis in manu teneo, pacem velle censetis?
Vincere illi expetunt pacisque dulcissimum et pulcherrimum nomen non pactione, sed victoria concupiverunt.
Quid? Galliam quo tandem animo hanc rem audituram
putatis? Illa enim huius belli propulsandi, administrandi,
sustinendi principatum tenet. Gallia D. Bruti nutum ipsum, ne dicam imperium, secuta armis, viris, pecunia belli
principia firmavit; eadem crudelitati M. Antoni suum totum corpus obiecit; exhauritur, vastatur, uritur: omnis aequo animo belli patitur iniurias, dum modo repellat peri-

10   culum servitutis. Et ut omittam reliquas partis Galliae—
nam sunt omnes pares—Patavini alios excluserunt, alios
eiecerunt missos ab Antonio, pecunia, militibus, et, quod
maxime deerat, armis nostros duces adiuverunt. Fecerunt
idem reliqui, qui quondam in eadem causa erant et prop-

---

6 Octavian's and Hirtius'.

7 Lit. "purified," i.e., ritually sanctified prior to setting out on
campaign.

and assailant of their native land. One feels shame in the
sight of that excellent army, made up of two armies,[6] which
has already been reviewed[7] and has set out for Mutina. If
they hear the name of peace, that is, of our fear, they will
undoubtedly halt, if not turn around. Why should they has-
ten to do battle, when the senate calls them back, sounding
the signal for retreat? [4] And what can be more improper   9
than for us to decide upon peace without the knowledge of
those who are fighting the war—and not only without their
knowledge but against their will? Or do you imagine that
Aulus Hirtius, our splendid consul, or Gaius Caesar, born
by the grace of the gods to match these times, whose letters declaring their hope for victory I hold in my hand—do
you imagine they want peace? They aim at being victorious, and they have set their hearts on peace, that sweetest
and most beautiful of words, through victory, not bargain-
ing. Again, how do you think Gaul will feel about this
news? She plays the leading role in repelling, conducting,
and sustaining this war. Gaul, following Decimus Brutus'
simple nod—I won't say his order—strengthened the war's
beginnings with arms, men, and money. That same province put her whole body in the way of Marcus Antonius'
cruelty; she is being drained, ravaged, burned. She calmly
endures all the injuries of war, if only she can thrust back
the danger of slavery. And to say nothing of the other   10
parts of Gaul—for they are all equal—the people of Patavium kept out some of the men sent by Antonius and threw
out others, while helping our commanders with money,
troops, and what they needed most, weapons. The rest did
likewise, though formerly they were in the same cause as
Antonius and were believed to be alienated from the sen-

ter multorum annorum iniurias alienati a senatu putaban-
tur: quos minime mirum est communicata cum eis re publica fidelis ‹esse›,[4] qui etiam expertes eius fidem suam
semper praestiterunt. [5] His igitur omnibus victoriam
sperantibus pacis nomen adferemus, id est desperationem
victoriae?

11   Quid si ne potest quidem ulla esse pax? Quae enim est
condicio pacis in qua ei cum quo pacem facias nihil concedi potest? Multis rebus ‹nefariis ante commissis›[5] a nobis
est invitatus ad pacem Antonius: bellum tamen maluit.
Missi legati repugnante me, sed tamen missi; delata mandata: non paruit. Denuntiatum est ne Brutum obsideret, a
Mutina discederet: oppugnavit etiam vehementius. Et ad
eum legatos de pace mittemus qui pacis nuntios repudiavit? Verecundioremne coram putamus in postulando fore
quam fuerit tum cum misit mandata ad senatum? Atqui
tum ea petebat quae videbantur improba omnino sed tamen aliquo modo posse concedi; nondum erat vestris tam
gravibus tamque multis iudiciis ignominiisque concisus:
nunc ea petit quae dare nullo modo possumus, nisi prius
12 volumus bello nos victos confiteri. Senatus consulta falsa
delata ab eo iudicavimus: num ea vera possumus iudicare?
Leges statuimus per vim et contra auspicia latas eisque
nec populum nec plebem teneri: num eas restitui posse

[4] *add. Poggius*   [5] *add. SB, cf. 6.2*

---

[8] Cicero refers to the inhabitants of Cisalpine Gaul north of
the Po River, where Patavium was situated. The senate had opposed for decades the aspirations of the people in that region to
gain Roman citizenship, a goal that was finally realized by legislation passed in March 49, after Caesar seized control of Italy and
Rome (*MRR* 2.258).

ate because of the wrongs of many years.[8] But it is not at all surprising that, having always shown their loyalty even when they had no share in the Republic, they should be faithful now that they have been given a stake in it. [5] Since, therefore, all of them hope for victory, shall we offer them the name of peace, which means despair of victory?

What if it is not even possible for there to be any peace? 11 For what can be the terms of a peace in which no concession can be made to the party with whom you are making peace? After committing many acts of wickedness, Antonius was invited by us to make peace, but still he preferred war. Envoys were dispatched, despite my opposition, but they were dispatched nonetheless. Instructions were delivered: he disobeyed. He was warned not to besiege Brutus, to withdraw from Mutina: he attacked with even greater vigor. Shall we send envoys concerning peace to a man who rebuffed messengers of peace? Do we suppose he will be more modest in his demands face to face than he was when he sent directives to the senate? All the same, his requests at that time appeared wicked to be sure, but in some way within the limits of possible concession. He had not yet been mauled by so many condemnatory judgments and black marks at your hands. Now he is asking what we cannot possibly grant, unless we first choose to acknowledge ourselves defeated in the war. We have declared that 12 he entered false decrees of the senate: surely we cannot declare them genuine, can we? We have determined that laws were passed by violence and contrary to auspices and that neither people nor plebs[9] are bound by them: surely

[9] *Populus* = the whole citizen body, *plebs* = the same with patricians excluded. The latter could legislate for the whole people.

censetis? Sestertium septiens miliens avertisse Antonium pecuniae publicae iudicavistis: num fraude poterit carere peculatus? Immunitates ab eo, civitates, sacerdotia, regna venierunt: num figentur rursus eae tabulae quas vos decretis vestris refixistis?

[6] Quod si ea quae decrevimus obruere, num etiam memoriam rerum delere possumus? Quando enim obliviscetur ulla posteritas cuius scelere in hac vestitus foeditate fuerimus? Ut centurionum legionis Martiae Brundisi profusus sanguis eluatur, num elui praedicatio crudelitatis potest? Ut media praeteream, quae vetustas tollet operum circum Mutinam taetra monumenta, sceleris indicia latrocinique vestigia?

13   Huic igitur importuno atque impuro parricidae quid habemus, per deos immortalis, quod remittamus? An Galliam ultimam et exercitum? Quid est aliud non pacem facere, sed differre bellum, nec solum propagare bellum sed concedere etiam victoriam? An ille non vicerit, si quacumque condicione in hanc urbem cum suis venerit? Armis nunc omnia tenemus; auctoritate valemus plurimum; absunt tot perditi cives, nefarium secuti ducem; tamen eorum ora sermonesque qui in urbe ex eo numero relicti sunt ferre non possumus. Quid censetis, cum tot uno tempore irruperint, nos arma posuerimus, illi non depo-

---

10 The military cloak (*sagum*), donned by decree of the senate as a sign of a state of emergency (8.6).

11 Demanded by Antony in previous negotiations as a concession for his giving up claim to Cisalpine Gaul (8.27).

you do not think they can be restored, do you? You have declared that Antonius embezzled seven hundred million sesterces of public money: surely embezzlement cannot escape penalty, can it? He sold exemptions from levies, Roman citizenship, priesthoods, kingdoms: surely those tablets, which you took down by your decrees, will not be replaced, will they?

[6] Suppose, however, we can bury our decrees, surely we cannot wipe out the memory of events as well, can we? For when will any future generation forget whose crime it was that made us put on this repellent dress?[10] Even supposing that the blood of the centurions of the Martian Legion shed at Brundisium may be washed away, surely the recital of that atrocity cannot be washed away, can it? To pass over all that happened in between, what lapse of years will remove the sinister memorials of the siege works surrounding Mutina, the evidence of crime, the traces of banditry?

So, what do we have, by the immortal gods, that we can 13 make as a concession to this savage, foul traitor? Outer Gaul and an army?[11] That would not be making peace but simply deferring the war, and not only prolonging the war but even conceding victory. For will he not have won if he comes back to this city with his followers on whatever terms? At present, we are in control of everything by means of our arms; our authority has enormous weight; so many reckless citizens are absent from Rome as a result of having followed their wicked leader: and yet we cannot tolerate the countenances and talk of those of their number who are left in Rome. How do you think it will be when so many of them have burst in at the same time, when we have laid aside our arms, and they have not laid down

suerint, nonne nos nostris consiliis victos in perpetuum
14 fore? Ponite ante oculos M. Antonium consularem; spe-
rantem consulatum Lucium adiungite; supplete ceteros
neque nostri ordinis solum honores et imperia meditan-
tis: nolite ne Tirones quidem Numisios et Mustelas Seios
contemnere. Cum eis facta pax non erit pax, sed pactio servitutis. L. Pisonis, amplissimi viri, praeclara vox a te non
solum in hoc ordine, Pansa, sed etiam in contione iure laudata est. Excessurum se ex Italia dixit, deos penatis et sedes patrias relicturum, si—quod di omen avertant!—rem
15 publicam oppressisset Antonius. [7] Quaero igitur a te, L.
Piso, nonne oppressam rem publicam putes, si tot tam impii, tam audaces, tam facinerosi recepti sint? Quos nondum tantis parricidiis contaminatos vix ferebamus, hos
nunc omni scelere coopertos tolerabilis censes civitati
fore? Aut isto tuo, mihi crede, consilio erit utendum, ut cedamus, abeamus, vitam inopem et vagam persequamur,
aut cervices latronibus dandae atque in patria cadendum
est. Ubi sunt, C. Pansa, illae cohortationes pulcherrimae
tuae quibus a te excitatus senatus, inflammatus populus
Romanus non solum audivit sed etiam didicit nihil esse ho-
16 mini Romano foedius servitute? Idcircone saga sumpsi-
mus, arma cepimus, iuventutem omnem ex tota Italia ex-
cussimus, ut exercitu florentissimo et maximo ‹confecto›[6]
legati ad pacem mitterentur? Si accipiendam, cur non ro-
gamur? Si postulandam, quid timemus?

[6] *add. SB*

---

[12] Sc. by Antonius to send envoys for negotiations.
[13] I.e., if we in the senate are in a position to demand peace on
our own terms, what have we to fear (i.e., why send a mission at
all)?

theirs? Shall we not have been defeated once and for all
through our own decisions? Picture Marcus Antonius, the   14
consular. Add Lucius, aspirant to the consulship. Throw in
the rest, and not only those who are members of this body,
whose minds are on offices and commands. Don't despise
even the likes of Tiro Numisius or Mustela Seius. Peace
made with them will be no peace, but a pact of slavery. Not
only in this body but also in a public meeting, Pansa, you
rightly praised a fine saying of Lucius Piso, a distinguished
gentleman. He declared that he would leave Italy, abandon his household gods and his ancestral home, if—may
the gods avert the omen!—Antonius crushed the Republic. [7] Then I ask you, Lucius Piso, would you not regard   15
the Republic as crushed if so many who are so wicked, so
bold, and so vicious are taken back? We had all we could do
to put up with them before they had polluted themselves
with such atrocities against their country. Do you think the
community will find them tolerable now that they are
steeped in every crime? Believe me, we shall either have to
follow your plan to leave, retire, and lead the life of needy
wanderers, or we shall have to permit our throats to be slit
by the criminals and fall in our native land. Where now,
Gaius Pansa, are those noble exhortations of yours with
which you roused the senate and fired the people, as they
not only heard but also learned that to a Roman no fate is
more horrible than slavery? Did we put on military cloaks,   16
take up arms, rouse up all young men of military age from
all over Italy with a view to sending envoys on a peace mission after we had raised a great and most splendid army?
If to accept a peace, why are we not being asked?[12] If to
demand it, what are we afraid of?[13]

In hac ego legatione sim aut ad id consilium admiscear in quo ne si dissensero quidem a ceteris sciturus populus Romanus sit? Ita fiet ut, si quid remissum aut concessum sit, meo semper periculo peccet Antonius, cum ei peccandi potestas a me concessa videatur. Quod si habenda cum M. Antoni latrocinio pacis ratio fuit, mea tamen persona ad istam pacem conciliandam minime fuit deligenda. Ego numquam legatos mittendos censui; ego ante reditum legatorum ausus sum dicere, pacem ipsam si adferrent, quoniam sub nomine pacis bellum lateret, repudiandam; ego princeps ⟨sumendorum⟩[7] sagorum; ego semper illum appellavi hostem, cum alii adversarium, semper hoc bellum, cum alii tumultum. Nec haec in senatu solum: eadem ad populum semper egi; neque solum in ipsum sed in eius socios facinorum et ministros, et praesentis et eos qui una sunt, in totam denique M. Antoni domum sum semper invectus. Itaque ut alacres et laeti spe pacis oblata inter se impii cives, quasi vicissent, gratulabantur, sic me iniquum eierabant, de me querebantur. Diffidebant etiam Servilio: meminerant eius sententiis confixum Antonium. L. Caesarem fortem quidem illum et constantem senatorem, avunculum tamen; Calenum procuratorem; Pisonem familiarem. Te ipsum, Pansa, vehementissimum et fortissimum

17

18

---

[7] *add. SB, cf. 5.44; 7.23; 14.20, 26*

---

[14] In 7.7–25, esp. §19.
[15] Pansa is singled out because he had earlier supported sending the embassy (§6).

Am *I* to be a member of this delegation, or am I to be added to that council in which even if I dissent from the rest, the Roman people are not going to know it? The consequence will be that if there should be any relaxation or concession, Antonius will commit further wrongdoings with my good name continually at risk, since it will appear that the power to do wrong was conceded to him by me. But even supposing peace with Marcus Antonius' banditry 17 was something to be considered, still, I was the last person who should have been chosen to negotiate such a peace. I was never in favor of sending envoys. Before the envoys returned, I was bold enough to say that even if they brought peace itself, it should be rejected, inasmuch as under the name of peace war would lurk.[14] I took the lead in the putting on of military cloaks. I consistently called Antonius a public enemy, while others called him an adversary; I consistently called this a war, while others called it a public emergency. And this I did not in the senate only; I always used the same language before the people. And I have all along inveighed not only against Antonius but against the partners and ministers of his crimes, both those present and those who are with him, in fact against the whole family circle of Marcus Antonius. And so, traitorous citi- 18 zens, when they were lively and cheerful at the prospect of peace and were congratulating each other as though they had triumphed, were for rejecting me as biased, were protesting about me. Neither did they trust Servilius, remembering how Antony had been impaled by his views expressed in this body. Lucius Caesar, though a brave and resolute senator, they bore in mind was nonetheless Antonius' uncle, Calenus his agent, and Piso his close friend. As for yourself, Pansa,[15] our most energetic and valiant

203

consulem, factum iam putant leniorem; non quo ita sit
aut esse possit, sed mentio a te facta pacis suspicionem
multis attulit immutatae voluntatis. Inter has personas me
interiectum amici Antoni moleste ferunt: quibus geren-
dus mos est, quoniam semel liberales esse coepimus. [8]
19 Proficiscantur legati optimis ominibus, sed ei proficiscantur in quibus non offendatur Antonius.

Quod si de Antonio non laboratis, mihi certe, patres
conscripti, consulere debetis. Parcite oculis saltem meis et
aliquam veniam iusto dolori date. Quo enim aspectu videre potero—omitto hostem patriae, ex quo mihi odium in
illum commune vobiscum est—sed quo modo aspiciam
mihi uni crudelissimum hostem, ut declarant eius de me
acerbissimae contiones? Adeone me ferreum putatis ut
cum eo congredi aut illum aspicere possim qui nuper, cum
in contione donaret eos qui ei de parricidis audacissimi videbantur, mea bona donare se dixit Petusio Urbinati, qui
ex naufragio luculenti patrimoni ad haec Antoniana saxa
20 proiectus est? An L. Antonium aspicere potero, cuius ego
crudelitatem effugere non potuissem, nisi me moenibus et
portis et studio municipi mei defendissem? Atque idem
hic myrmillo Asiaticus, latro Italiae, collega Lentonis et
Nuculae, cum Aquilae primi pili nummos aureos daret,
de meis bonis se dare dixit: si enim de suis dixisset, ne
Aquilam quidem ipsum crediturum putavit. Non ferent,

---

16 Possibly the hints of threats to Cicero's safety while at Tusculum, near Rome, in late May and early June 44 (*Att.* 15.8.2;
15.12.2) may help to account for his decision to withdraw to
Arpinum for a time in July. See also SB on *Fam.* 9.24.1.

17 Cf. 5.20.

consul, they believe you have now been made more amenable; not that this is true or could be, but your introduction of the topic of peace made many suspect a shift of attitude. The friends of Antonius are annoyed that I have been
thrust among these participants, and we ought to humor
them, seeing that we have started to be obliging once already. [8] Let the envoys set out with the best of omens,   19
but only those who will not offend Antonius.

But if you are not worried about Antonius' feelings,
Members of the Senate, you ought at least to have some regard for mine. Spare my eyes at any rate and make some al-
lowance for a legitimate indignation. With what expression
on my face shall I be able to behold—I do not say the enemy of our native land, since you have as much cause as I to
hate him on that account—but how shall I look at an enemy so cruel to me especially, as his very savage harangues
about me declare? Do you think I am so made of iron that I
can meet with him or look at that man who the other day,
when announcing rewards at a public meeting to the bold-
est-seeming among his traitor band, said that he was granting my property to Petusius of Urbinum, a fellow who was
flung from the wreck of a fine patrimony onto these Antonian rocks? Or shall I be able to look at Lucius Antonius,   20
whose cruelty I escaped only under the protection of the
walls and gates and goodwill of my native town?[16] When
this same Asiatic myrmillo,[17] robber of Italy, colleague of
Lento and Nucula,[18] gave some gold pieces to Aquila, a
chief centurion, he said that he was giving them out of my
property; for if he had said they came out of his own resources, he thought that even Aquila would not believe

18 On the Board of Seven for the distribution of land.

205

inquam, oculi Saxam, Cafonem, non duo praetores, non tribunos plebis [non][8] duo designatos [tribunos],[9] non Bestiam, non Trebellium, non T. Plancum. Non possum animo aequo videre tot tam importunos, tam sceleratos hostis; nec id fit fastidio meo, sed caritate rei publicae.

21   Sed vincam animum mihique imperabo: dolorem iustissimum, si non potuero frangere, occultabo. Quid? Vitae censetisne, patres conscripti, habendam mihi aliquam esse rationem? Quae mihi quidem minime cara est, praesertim cum Dolabella fecerit ut optanda mors esset, modo sine cruciatu atque tormentis; vobis tamen et populo Romano vilis meus spiritus esse non debet. Is enim sum, nisi me forte fallo, qui vigiliis, curis, sententiis, periculis etiam, quae plurima adii propter acerbissimum omnium in me odium impiorum, perfecerim ut non obstarem rei pu-
22   blicae, ne quid adrogantius videar dicere. [9] Quod cum ita sit, nihilne mihi de periculo meo cogitandum putatis? Hic cum essem in urbe ac domi, tamen multa saepe temptata sunt, ubi me non solum amicorum fidelitas sed etiam universae civitatis oculi custodiunt: quid censetis, cum iter ingressus ero, longum praesertim, nullasne insidias extimescendas?

Tres viae sunt ad Mutinam—quo festinat animus ut quam primum illud pignus libertatis populi Romani, D. Brutum, aspicere possim; cuius in complexu libenter extremum vitae spiritum ediderim, cum omnes actiones ho-

---

[8] *del. SB*
[9] *del. SB*

---

[19] Censorinus and Ventidius, cf. 13.2, 26.
[20] Hostilius Tullus and Insteius, cf. 13.26.

him. My eyes, I say, will not bear the sight of Saxa and Cafo, of the two praetors,[19] of the two tribunes-elect of the plebs,[20] of Bestia, of Trebellius, of Titus Plancus. I cannot calmly behold such a large number of such savage, such wicked public enemies. That is not because I am squeamish, but because I love the Republic.

But I shall conquer my feelings and force myself along.   21
If I cannot overcome my most legitimate indignation, I shall hide it. What? Do you think, Members of the Senate, that I ought to have some regard for my life? Indeed I set little store by it, especially now that thanks to Dolabella death is a thing to wish for, provided it not be accompanied by the pains of torture. But in your eyes and those of the Roman people, my life should not be of little account. For if I do not perchance deceive myself, I am one who by his vigils, anxieties, views expressed in this body, and even by risks, which I have often encountered on account of the bitter hatred felt for me by all traitors, has managed—let me avoid any appearance of arrogant speech—to be of no disservice to the Republic. [9] That being so, do you think I   22
ought not to take any thought for the risks I should be exposed to? Even here, as I live in Rome, in my home, many attempts have often been made, where I am guarded not only by the loyalty of friends but also by the eyes of the whole community. How do you suppose it will be when I have set out on a journey, particularly a long one? Will there be no need for fear of an ambush?

There are three roads to Mutina, the town to which I am hastening in spirit so that I may behold as soon as possible that pledge of the Roman people's freedom, Decimus Brutus. In his embrace I would gladly breathe my last, when all that I have been doing and recommending these

rum mensum, omnes sententiae meae pervenerint ad eum
qui mihi fuit propositus exitum. Tres ergo, ut dixi, viae: a
supero mari Flaminia, ab infero Aurelia, media Cassia.
23 Nunc, quaeso, attendite num aberret a coniectura suspicio
periculi mei. Etruriam discriminat Cassia. Scimusne igitur, Pansa, quibus in locis nunc sit Lentonis Caesenni septemviralis auctoritas? Nobiscum nec animo certe est nec
corpore. Si autem aut domi est aut non longe a domo, certe
in Etruria est, id est in via. Quis igitur mihi praestat Lentonem uno capite esse contentum? Dic mihi praeterea, Pansa, Ventidius ubi sit, cui fui semper amicus ante quam ille
rei publicae bonisque omnibus tam aperte est factus inimicus. Possum Cassiam vitare, ⟨tenere⟩[10] Flaminiam: quid si
Anconam, ut dicitur, Ventidius venerit? Poterone Ariminum tuto accedere? Restat Aurelia. Hic quidem etiam
praesidia habeo; possessiones enim sunt P. Clodi. Tota
familia occurret; hospitio invitabit propter familiaritatem
notissimam.
24   [10] Hisce ego me viis committam, qui Terminalibus
nuper in suburb⟨an⟩um,[11] ut eodem die reverterer, ire
non sum ausus? Domesticis me parietibus vix tueor sine
amicorum custodiis. Itaque in urbe maneo, si licebit, ma-
nebo. Haec mea sedes est, haec vigilia, haec custodia, hoc
praesidium stativum. Teneant alii castra, gerant res bellicas, oderint hostem; nam hoc caput est: nos, ut dicimus

[10] *suppl. Poggius*
[11] *corr. SB*

[21] While on Caesar's Spanish campaign in 45, Lento had
hunted down and killed Pompey's elder son.
[22] On 23 February.

past months has reached the end I had in view. Well, as
I have said, there are three roads: the Flaminian along
the east coast, the Aurelian along the west coast, and the
Cassian in the middle. Now consider, please, whether my 23
suspicion of personal danger strays from a reasonable in-
ference. The Cassian Way divides Etruria. Do we know,
Pansa, the present whereabouts of that pillar of the Board
of Seven, Lento Caesennius? He certainly is not with us,
either in body or spirit. And if he is either at home or not
far from home, he is certainly in Etruria; that is, on my
route. Who guarantees me that Lento is content with one
life?[21] Tell me, furthermore, Pansa, where Ventidius is, a
man with whom I was always on friendly terms before he
became so open an enemy to the Republic and to all decent men. Well, I can avoid the Cassian Way and follow the
Flaminian. What if Ventidius comes to Ancona, as it is said
he will? Shall I be able to approach Ariminum safely? That
leaves the Aurelian Way. Now here I even have protection.
These are the lands of Publius Clodius. The whole household will turn out to meet me and offer hospitality because
of our notorious friendship.

[10] Shall I then entrust myself to those roads, when re- 24
cently at the Festival of Terminus[22] I did not dare to go to a
house near Rome[23] and return the same day? I can scarcely
protect myself within the walls of my house without my
friends' keeping guard. So I stay in Rome; if I am permitted, I shall continue to do so. This is my dwelling-place,
this my watch and ward, this my standing guard. Let others
occupy camps, wage war, hate the enemy; for this is the

[23] Cicero's Tusculan villa (a favorite spot of his to spend a holi-
day)?

semperque fecimus, urbem et res urbanas vobiscum pariter tuebimur.

Neque vero recuso munus hoc: quamquam populum Romanum video pro me recusare. Nemo me minus timidus, nemo tamen cautior. Res declarat. Vicesimus annus est cum omnes scelerati me unum petunt. Itaque ipsi, ne dicam mihi, rei publicae poenas dederunt: me salvum adhuc res publica conservavit sibi. Timide hoc dicam—scio enim quidvis homini accidere posse—verum tamen: ‹numquam imprudens oppressus sum›.[12] Semel circumsessus ‹col›lectis[13] valentissimorum hominum viribus cecidi sciens ut honestissime possem exsurgere.

25 Possumne igitur satis videri cautus, satis providus, si me huic itineri tam infesto tamque periculoso commisero? Gloriam in morte debent ei qui in re publica versantur, non culpae reprehensionem et stultitiae vituperationem relinquere. Quis bonus non luget mortem Trebonī? Quis non dolet interitum talis et civis et viri? At sunt qui dicant, dure illi quidem, sed tamen dicunt, minus dolendum quod ab homine impuro nefarioque non caverit. Etenim qui multorum custodem se profiteatur, eum sapientes sui primum capitis aiunt custodem esse oportere. Cum saeptus sis legibus et iudiciorum metu, non sunt omnia timenda neque ad omnis insidias praesidia quaerenda. Quis enim audeat luci, quis in militari via, quis bene comitatum, quis illustrem ag-

[12] *suppl. SB*
[13] *corr. Busche*

[24] When driven into exile in March 58 by his enemy, the tribune P. Clodius.

main point: I, as I say and as I have always done, shall attend to Rome and its affairs along with you gentlemen.

But at the same time, I am not refusing this commission, though I perceive that the Roman people are refusing it for me. No man is less timid than I, but no man is more cautious. The facts declare it. For twenty years past, all the villains have attacked me alone. Well, they themselves paid their penalties, I will not say to me personally but to the Republic, while the Republic has up to this time preserved me for its service. I shall say this with hesitation—for I know that anything can happen to mortal man—but anyhow: I was never taken unawares, though on one occasion,[24] surrounded by the massed strength of some very powerful people, I fell, deliberately, so that I could rise again in triumph.

Can I, then, appear adequately cautious, adequately   25
prudent, if I trust myself to this journey so fraught with menace and peril? Those who take part in public affairs should leave a legacy of glory when they die, not a legacy of censure and reproach for shortcoming and folly. What honest man does not mourn the death of Trebonius? Who does not grieve for the destruction of such a man and such a citizen? And yet there are those who say (unsympathetically, indeed, but they say it) that our grief should be diminished by the fact that he was not on his guard against a villainous traitor. Wise men say that a person who sets himself up as the guardian of many should first of all be the guardian of his own life. When one is protected by laws and the fear of the courts, there is no need to be afraid of everything or to seek defenses against all manner of plots. For who would dare to attack a well-known public figure traveling well-attended by daylight on a military highway?

26 gredi? Haec neque hoc tempore neque in me valent. Non
modo enim poenam non extimescet qui mihi vim attulerit
sed etiam gloriam sperabit a latronum gregibus et praemia. [11] Haec ego in urbe provideo: facilis est circum-
spectus unde exeam, quo progrediar, quid ad dexteram,
quid ad sinistram sit. Num idem in Appennini tramitibus
facere potero? In quibus etiam si non erunt insidiae, quae
facillime esse poterunt, animus tamen erit sollicitus, ut nihil possit de officiis legationis attendere. Sed effugi insidias, perrupi Appenninum: nempe in Antoni congressum
colloquiumque veniendum est. Quinam locus capietur? Si
extra castra, ceteri viderint: ego me vix tuto futurum puto.
Novi hominis furorem, novi effrenatam violentiam. Cuius
acerbitas morum immanitasque naturae ne vino quidem
permixta temperari solet, hic ira dementiaque inflammatus adhibito fratre Lucio, taeterrima belua, numquam profecto a me sacrilegas manus atque impias abstinebit.

27   Memini colloquia et cum acerrimis hostibus et cum
gravissime dissidentibus civibus. Cn. Pompeius Sex. f.
consul me praesente, cum essem tiro in eius exercitu, cum
P. Vettio Scatone, duce Marsorum, inter bina castra collo-
cutus est: quo quidem memini Sex. Pompeium, fratrem
consulis, ad colloquium ipsum Roma venire, doctum virum atque sapientem. Quem cum Scato salutasset, "quem
te appellem?" inquit. At ille: "voluntate hospitem, necessitate hostem." Erat in illo colloquio aequitas; nullus timor,
nulla suberat suspicio, mediocre etiam odium. Non enim
ut eriperent nobis socii civitatem, sed ut in eam reciperen-

---

25 An attack on Cicero would be "sacrilegious" because he was
an ambassador.

26 In 89, during the Social War.

Such considerations do not apply at this time or in my case. 26
Anyone who employs violence against me will not only
have no fear of punishment but will even hope for glory
and rewards from the robber bands. [11] In Rome I take
precautions against this. It is easy to look around, to the
rear and to the front, right and left. Shall I be able to do the
same on the paths over the Apennines? Even if there is no
ambush, which can very easily take place, my mind will
nevertheless be distracted so that it will be unable to attend to the duties of the mission. But imagine I have escaped an attack, forced my way through the Apennines: I
must then presumably meet and talk with Antonius. What
venue, I ask you, will be chosen? If outside the camps, I
leave it to others: as for myself, I scarcely think I shall
be safe. I know the man's fury, I know his unbridled violence. His savage ways and natural cruelty are seldom tem-
pered, even when mingled with wine. Ablaze with wrath
and madness, with that horrible beast of a brother Lucius
at his elbow, he will surely never keep his impious, sacrilegious[25] hands off my person.

I remember parleys both with Rome's bitterest for- 27
eign foes and with fellow countrymen in open revolt. The
consul Gnaeus Pompeius, son of Sextus, conferred with
Publius Vettius Scato, the Marsian leader, between their
two camps in my presence, when I was a recruit in
Pompeius' army.[26] I remember that Sextus Pompeius, the
consul's brother, a man of learning and good sense, came
down from Rome to take part in the parley. When Scato
had greeted him, he added: "What am I to call you?" And
the other replied: "'Guest-friend' by my choosing, 'enemy'
by necessity." There was fair play at that parley; no covert
fear, no suspicion; even the hostility was not extreme. Our
allies, after all, were not seeking to take our citizenship

213

tur petebant. Sulla cum Scipione inter Cales et Teanum,
cum alter nobilitatis florem, alter belli socios adhibuisset,
de auctoritate senatus, de suffragiis populi, de iure civitatis
leges inter se ⟨et⟩[14] condiciones contulerunt. Non tenuit
omnino colloquium illud fidem: a vi tamen periculoque
afuit. [12] Possumusne igitur in Antoni latrocinio aeque
esse tuti? Non possumus; aut, si ceteri possunt, me posse
diffido.

28   Quod si non extra castra congrediemur, quae ad colloquium castra sumentur? In nostra ille numquam veniet;
multo minus nos in illius. Reliquum est ut et accipiantur et
remittantur postulata per litteras. Ergo erimus in castris,
meaque ad omnia postulata una sententia; quam cum hic
vobis audientibus dixero, isse [et][15] redisse me putatote:
legationem confecero. Omnia ad senatum mea sententia
reiciam, quaecumque postulabit Antonius. Neque enim
licet aliter neque permissum est nobis ab hoc ordine, ut
bellis confectis decem legatis permitti solet more maiorum, neque ulla omnino a senatu mandata accepimus.
Quae cum agam in consilio non ⟨n⟩ullis,[16] ut arbitror, re-
pugnantibus, nonne metuendum est ne imperita militum
29   multitudo per me pacem distineri putet? Facite hoc meum
consilium legiones novas non improbare; nam Martiam
et quartam nihil cogitantis praeter dignitatem et decus
comprobaturas esse certo scio. Quid veteranos? Non veremur—nam timeri se ne ipsi quidem volunt—quonam

14 add. Garatoni
15 del. Clark, cf. 2.78, 89
16 corr. Poggius

27 In 83, to try to arrive at a peaceful settlement in the civil
war.

away from us but to be admitted to a part in it. Sulla and Scipio met between Cales and Teanum,[27] one with the flower of the nobility at his side, the other with his wartime allies, to discuss terms and conditions relating to the authority of the senate, the votes of the people, and the right of citizenship. Faith was not kept at that conference, it is true, but there was no violence or danger.[28] [12] Can we be equally safe in the midst of Antonius' brigand band? We cannot; or if *others* can, I do not believe I can.

But if we do not meet outside the camps, which camp will be chosen for the parley? He will never come into ours; much less we into his. There remains the possibility of receiving and returning demands by letter. Well then, we shall be in camp, and I shall have only one opinion in reply to all his demands, and when I tell you who are listening to me here what it is, picture in your mind that I have gone and come back: I shall have discharged the mission. I shall be for referring all Antonius' demands to the senate, whatever their nature. That is the only permissible course; we have not received discretion from this body, such as is wont to be given by traditional custom to delegations of ten after the conclusion of a war; nor have we received any mandates whatsoever from the senate. When I take this line in council, probably against some opposition, is there not a danger that the mass of uninstructed soldiery will think I am obstructing a peace? Suppose the new legions do not disapprove of this advice of mine—for I am sure that the Martian and Fourth, who have no thought but of honor and glory, will approve of it—what of the veterans? Have we no apprehensions—they themselves indeed have

28

29

---

[28] Although Sulla took advantage of the truce to win over Scipio's army and make Scipio his prisoner, he spared Scipio's life.

modo accipiant severitatem meam? Multa enim falsa de
me audierunt, multa ad eos improbi detulerunt; quorum
commoda, ut vos optimi testes estis, semper ego sententia,
auctoritate, oratione firmavi: sed credunt improbis, credunt turbulentis, credunt suis. Sunt autem fortes illi quidem, sed propter memoriam rerum quas gesserunt pro
populi Romani libertate et salute rei publicae nimis fero-
30 ces et ad suam vim omnia nostra consilia revocantes. Horum ego cogitationem non vereor; impetum pertimesco.

Haec quoque tanta pericula si effugero, satisne tutum
reditum putatis fore? Cum enim et vestram auctoritatem
meo more defendero et meam fidem rei publicae constan-
tiamque praestitero, tum erunt mihi non ei solum qui me
oderunt sed illi etiam qui invident extimescendi.

Custodiatur igitur vita mea rei publicae eaque, quoad
vel dignitas vel natura patietur, patriae reservetur; mors
aut[em][17] necessitatem habeat fati aut, si ante oppetenda
est, oppetatur cum gloria.

Haec cum ita sint, etsi hanc legationem res publica, ut
levissime dicam, non desiderat, tamen si tuto licebit ire,
proficiscar. Omnino, patres conscripti, totum huiusce rei
consilium non periculo meo, sed utilitate rei publicae me-
tiar. De qua mihi quoniam liberum est spatium, multum
etiam atque etiam considerandum puto idque potissimum
faciendum quod maxime interesse rei publicae iudicaro.

---

[17] *corr. Faërnus*

---

[29] On foreign campaigns, not in helping Caesar to establish his
dictatorship.
[30] Lit. "the necessity of fate"; cf. 1.10 fin.

no wish to be *feared*—as to how they will take my hard line? They have heard many untruths about me; unscrupulous persons have told them many tales, though as you are best able to testify, I have always upheld their benefits by means of my proposals, my influence, and my speeches. But they believe the unscrupulous persons, they believe the troublemakers, they believe the members of their own side. Moreover, they are brave men to be sure, but the memory of what they have done for the freedom of the Roman people and the survival of the Republic[29] makes them overbearing and inclined to regard their force as arbiter in all our decisions. I am not afraid of their considered views, 30 but I dread their impetuosity.

If I escape also these grave dangers, do you think my return will be sufficiently safe? For when I have defended your authority in my usual way and kept my faith resolutely with the Republic, I shall have to fear not only those who hate me but also those who are jealous of me.

Therefore let my life be safeguarded for the benefit of the Republic and reserved for our native land, so long as honor and nature allow. Let my death either come by natural necessity,[30] or, if it must be met sooner, let it be met gloriously.

In these circumstances, although the Republic, to put it very mildly, does not need this embassy, nevertheless I shall go, if I shall be able to do so safely. In weighing this whole question, Members of the Senate, I shall adopt as my sole criterion the advantage of the Republic, not my personal risk. And since I have plenty of time, I am of the opinion that I must give much further consideration to the matter and do most of all whatever I shall judge to be in the best interest of the Republic.

PHILIPPIC 13

INTRODUCTION

We can be certain that the *Thirteenth Philippic* was delivered no later than 20 March 43 because in a letter written on that date (*Fam.* 10.6) Cicero informed L. Munatius Plancus, the then governor of Outer Gaul, that the senate had politely rejected two letters advocating a peaceful settlement with Mark Antony. One of those letters was from Plancus himself. The other was from M. Lepidus, the governor of Narbonese Gaul and Hither Spain, and Cicero's reaction to Lepidus' proposal can be read in the *Thirteenth Philippic* (13.7b–21, 49), as well as in a letter written to Lepidus on or about 20 March (*Fam.* 10.27). Next, we know that the consul C. Pansa left Rome to join his troops in the latter part of March (*Fam.* 10.10.1), some time after 19 March, when his presence in Rome is last explicitly attested, on the occasion of a meeting of the senate over which he presided (*Fam.* 12.25.1). Moreover, the way in which Pansa and his colleague Hirtius are referred to in the *Thirteenth Philippic* reveals that both consuls were most likely already in the field, on campaign against Antony (13.16, 23, 39), and this conclusion is bolstered by the fact that the *Thirteenth Philippic* makes no reference at all to Pansa as presiding magistrate. By contrast, all the preceding senatorial *Philippics* in 43 B.C. invariably address either both Pansa and his colleague (5.52) or Pansa alone,

after Hirtius left Rome to assume command of his army (7.27; 8.1; 9.3; 10.1; 11.22; 12.14). If, then, the *Thirteenth Philippic* was delivered after Pansa's departure, it can fall no earlier than 19 March, when Pansa was still in Rome, and as noted above, it can be no later than 20 March, the date of Cicero's report to Plancus on the debate in the senate. Hence, 20 March must be the date of the speech, and this means that the presiding magistrate was almost certainly the urban praetor M. Caecilius Cornutus, who is known to have discharged the duties of chief executive in the absence of the consuls from late March onwards (*Fam.* 10.12.3–4; 10.16.1; *ad Brut.* 2.5.3).

What calls for some explanation is the complete absence of any reference to Plancus' letter in the *Thirteenth Philippic*. Where Plancus is mentioned at all, he is portrayed as standing ready to lend vigorous support to the fight against Antony (13.16, 44). If the senate was in fact debating a dispatch from Plancus advocating a peaceful settlement with Antony, one would expect it to be difficult, if not impossible, for Cicero to contradict so offhandedly Mark Antony's claim at 13.44 that Plancus was in sympathy with him. It is true that Plancus' legate C. Fannius had conveyed orally to the senate a pledge of loyalty from Plancus that clashed with his written dispatch (*Fam.* 10.6.1). Even so, in the delivered version of the speech, Cicero must have been forced to say *something* at the very least about the contradiction between the oral and written communications, a topic that is conspicuously absent from the published version. What is likely to have influenced Cicero to drop the sections addressing this issue is a letter from Plancus attested by *Fam.* 10.10 (of 30 March) but no longer extant. That letter arrived a few days

after the delivery of the *Thirteenth Philippic* and assured Cicero of Plancus' unwavering loyalty to the campaign against Antony. In the light of the later communication, Cicero doubtless considered it counterproductive to retain in the published version of his speech any reference to peace initiatives from Plancus. On top of which, Cicero's tactful rejection of Lepidus' peace proposal could be read as extending to Plancus' recommendation as well, while the later written pledge of loyalty from Plancus made it a moot point to preserve in the revised version of the speech any shadow of doubt as to where Plancus' true sympathy might lie. To have included a separate discussion of Plancus' peace proposal in the published speech could only have served to cloud the issue.

As we can tell from the *Twelfth Philippic* and from the message that Antony claims to have received from Octavian and Hirtius (13.36), there had indeed been a momentary reawakening in the senate of a willingness to explore the possibility of a peaceful settlement with Antony through negotiation. Word of that mood will help to explain the timing of the two dispatches from Lepidus and Plancus, which must have arrived in Rome nearly simultaneously, just as two later dispatches from those same governors did in May (*Fam.* 10.16.1). By the date of the *Thirteenth Philippic*, however, the senate's resolve to press ahead with the war against Antony had begun to stiffen again, and so Cicero argued that the peace initiatives from Lepidus (and by implication from Plancus) were ill timed. He did so tactfully, not wanting to offend two governors who commanded approximately ten legions between them.

What played nicely into Cicero's hands was the arrival

223

in Rome of a letter written by Antony to Hirtius and Octavian, one that was no doubt intended by its author for open circulation. It was in the nature of a white paper, of the sort that Antony wanted to be copied and circulated so as to make known his policies and his complaints against Cicero and his enemies in the senate (cf. 7.5). A copy of that letter was forwarded to Cicero by Hirtius (13.22), and Cicero devoted more than half of his *Thirteenth Philippic* (§§22–48) to reproducing the text of Antony's communication and replying to its assertions, sometimes quoting and commenting on it phrase by phrase. In all, some sixteen and a half text pages of the *Thirteenth Philippic*, out of thirty pages in the present edition, are given over to a refutation of Antony's claims and assertions. The rhetorical strategy adopted by Cicero was brilliant because (a) it permitted him to divert attention away from the unwelcome peace proposals contained in the letters from Lepidus and Plancus, which he dared not criticize harshly, and (b) he could profess, as he does at 13.22 and 48, to use Antony's own words to show that peace with Antony was impossible.

There is, however, a further motive on the part of Cicero that should not to be overlooked because it may even outweigh the other two aims, and it certainly had a great influence on the ultimate form given to the speech as a whole. That is, the *Thirteenth Philippic* is unique in that no other speech in the corpus of 58 extant Ciceronian orations devotes so much space to the quotation of the words of another: in this instance, nearly 550 words of Antony. Furthermore, careful examination of this speech reveals that it borrows heavily from material contained in the *Second Philippic*, which was composed after the fact to simulate a direct reply in the senate to Antony's invective

against Cicero on 19 Sept. 44.[1] No such reply was ever directly made because Cicero failed to attend the senate on 19 September. Ever since that day, Cicero must have longed for an opportunity to meet his mortal enemy in a verbal duel, which he was confident of winning (as he states in 2.2), but now that Antony was hundreds of miles from Rome and armies separated the two antagonists, a meeting between the two in the senate was impossible. The dilemma was solved, however, when Cicero obtained the text of Antony's letter and proceeded to use it to produce the semblance of a live, face-to-face debate in the senate between himself and his archenemy. What we find in 13.22–48 is an *altercatio*, a lively exchange of words of the sort that is known to have taken place on occasion between colleagues in the senate (e.g. *Att.* 1.16.10). The way in which Antony's letter is refuted in the *Thirteenth Philippic*, point by point, produces the illusion of a genuine confrontation in the senate between two bitter antagonists.

[1] Reversion to topics and even specific language previously used by Cicero in his *Second Philippic* is too frequent to be dismissed as mere coincidence. Furthermore, nothing in Antony's letter directly calls for Cicero to reuse the earlier themes and language found in *Phil.* 2, but rather, he appears to have done so by conscious choice, presumably because he wanted his rejoinders to Antony's letter to recall the previous occasion. E.g., (1.) letter of an opponent read out in senate and used as a weapon (2.7; 13.22–48a); (2.) Antony's shameless purchase and occupation of Pompey's *domus* and *horti* (2.67–68, 72; 13.10, 12, 34); (3.) Antony styled *"sector Pompei"* (2.39, 65 [2x], 75; 13.30); (4.) fatal act of Trebonius in taking Antony aside on Ides (2.34; 13.22; cf. *Fam.* 10.28.1); (5.) Antony failed to have himself installed as *flamen* ("priest") of the deified Caesar (2.110; 13.41, 47); and many more.

This synthetic debate brought closure to the long-delayed face-off between Antony and Cicero, which happens to have been postponed precisely six months, as reckoned by the Roman calendar, from the 13th day before the Kalends (1st) of October (19 Sept. 44) to the 13th day before the Kalends of April (20 Mar. 43).

STRUCTURE

Exordium

(1–2a) Civil war is a great evil

Propositio

(2b–3) Peace is not always possible
  (2b) Major premise: Peace at the price of liberty is to be rejected
  (2c–3) Minor premise: Peace can be made with Antony only at the price of liberty

Confirmatio

(4–7a) Of both premises
  (4–5a) Of minor premise: Antony is bent on annihilating or enslaving his enemies
  (5b–7a) Of major premise: True wisdom puts liberty ahead of mere survival

INTRODUCTION TO PHILIPPIC 13

Refutatio

(7b–48a) Of Lepidus' proposal and views expressed in Antony's letter
- (7b–21) Of Lepidus' peace proposal
  - (7b–13a) Praise of Lepidus for making peace with Sextus Pompeius
  - (13b–14) Lepidus must use his power as directed by the senate and the people
  - (15–21) The state is fighting for its very survival
- (22–48a) Of four themes in Antony's letter to Hirtius and Octavian, viz.
  - (22–33a) that Hirtius and Octavian are fighting on the wrong side
  - (33b–35) that Caesar's veterans are being duped into fighting on the wrong side
  - (36–44) that no compromise is possible with their diehard, mutual enemies in the senate
  - (45–48a) that the only hope for self-preservation is for Hirtius and Octavian to come over to Antony's side

Peroratio

(48b–49) Lepidus would never advocate peace with such a madman

Sententia

(50) Cicero supports Servilius' motion to reject Lepidus' recommendation of peace and proposes a vote of thanks for Sextus Pompeius

M. TULLI CICERONIS
IN M. ANTONIUM ORATIO
PHILIPPICA TERTIA DECIMA

1   [1] A principio huius belli, patres conscripti, quod cum
impiis civibus consceleratisque suscepimus, timui ne condicio insidiosa pacis libertatis recuperandae studia restin-
gueret. Dulce enim etiam nomen est pacis, res vero ipsa
cum iucunda tum salutaris. Nam nec privatos focos nec
publicas leges videtur nec libertatis iura cara habere quem
discordiae, quem caedes civium, quem bellum civile de-
lectat, eumque ex numero hominum eiciendum, ex finibus
humanae naturae exterminandum puto. Itaque sive Sulla
sive Marius sive uterque sive Octavius sive Cinna sive iterum Sulla sive alter Marius et Carbo sive qui alius civile
bellum optavit, eum detestabilem civem rei publicae na-
2 tum iudico. Nam quid ego de proximo dicam cuius acta
defendimus, auctorem ipsum iure caesum fatemur? Nihil
igitur hoc cive, nihil hoc homine taetrius, si aut civis aut
homo habendus est, qui civile bellum concupiscit.

    Sed hoc primum videndum est, patres conscripti, cum

---

    1 Cicero seems to be recalling Nestor's words in the *Iliad*
(9.63–64, trans. A. T. Murray): "a clanless, lawless, heartless man
is he that loveth dread strife among his own folk."

    2 Cf. 8.7; 14.23.   3 Caesar.

MARCUS TULLIUS CICERO'S
THIRTEENTH PHILIPPIC ORATION
AGAINST MARCUS ANTONIUS

[1] From the outset of this war, Members of the Senate,   1
which we have undertaken against traitorous and wicked
citizens, I have been afraid that a seductive proposal of
peace might quell enthusiasm for the recovery of freedom.
Even the name of peace is sweet; the reality is beneficial,
as well as agreeable. For a man who delights in strife and
the slaughter of his countrymen and civil war surely holds
dear neither private hearths nor public laws nor the rights
of liberty.[1] Such a man, I think, ought to be excluded from
membership in the human race, banished beyond the con-
fines of human nature. Whoever has desired civil war, be it
Sulla or Marius or both, be it Octavius or Cinna, be it Sulla
a second time or the other Marius and Carbo,[2] or anyone
else, I hold him a citizen born accursed to the Republic.
Why should I speak of the latest example, a man whose acts   2
we defend while admitting that their author was justly
slain.[3] There is no fouler thing than such a citizen, such a
man, if he is to be deemed a citizen or a man, who desires a
civil war.

But one point has to be considered at the outset, Mem-

omnibusne pax esse possit an sit aliquod bellum inexpiabile, in quo pactio pacis lex sit servitutis. Pacem cum Scipione Sulla sive faciebat sive simulabat, non erat desperandum, si convenisset, fore aliquem tolerabilem statum civitatis. Cinna si concordiam cum Octavio confirmare voluisset, ⟨aliqua⟩[1] [hominum][2] in re publica sanitas remanere potuisset. Proximo bello si aliquid de summa gravitate Pompeius, multum de cupiditate Caesar remisisset, et pacem stabilem et aliquam rem publicam nobis habere licuisset.

[2] Hoc vero quid est? Cum Antoniis pax potest esse? Cum Censorino, Ventidio, Trebellio, Bestia, Nucula, Munatio, Lentone, Saxa? Exempli causa paucos nominavi: genus infinitum immanitatemque ipsi cernitis reliquorum.

3 Addite illa naufragia Caesaris amicorum, Barbas Cassios, Barbatios Polliones; addite Antoni collusores et sodalis, Eutrapelum, Melam Pontium, Caelium, Crassicium, Tironem, Mustelam, Petusium: comitatum relinquo, duces nomino. Huc accedunt Alaudae ceterique veterani, seminarium iudicum decuriae tertiae, qui suis rebus exhaustis, beneficiis Caesaris devoratis, fortunas nostras concupiverunt.

4 O fidam dexteram Antoni qua ille plurimos civis trucidavit, o ratum religiosumque foedus quod cum Antoniis fecerimus! Hoc si Marcus violare conabitur, Luci eum

---

[1] *add. SB*   [2] *del. SB*: hominum . . . potuisset *om.* V[1]

---

[4] In 83; cf. 12.27.   [5] Apparently a reference to actual negotiations in 87 mentioned in Appian (*B Civ.* 1.69–70).

[6] Doubtless L. Pontius P. f. Mela, attested in *ILS* 917 (poss. to be dated to 44 B.C.) and 917a, about whom nothing further is

bers of the Senate: is peace with all men possible, or is there such a thing as an inexpiable war, in which a pact of peace is a prescription for slavery? When Sulla tried, or pretended to try, to make peace with Scipio,[4] it was not unreasonable to hope that if they came to terms a tolerable state of the community would emerge. If Cinna had been willing to come to an agreement with Octavius,[5] the Republic might have retained some degree of health. In the latest war, if Pompeius had been a little less stiffly steadfast and Caesar a great deal less greedy, we could have had a stable peace and some semblance of a Republic.

[2] But what of the present? Can there be peace with the Antonii? Or with Censorinus, Ventidius, Trebellius, Bestia, Nucula, Munatius, Lento, Saxa? I have named a few as examples; you see for yourself the endless number and the savagery of the rest. Add the flotsam of Caesar's 3 friends, a Barba Cassius, a Barbatius Pollio, add Antonius' gambling partners and cronies, Eutrapelus, Mela Pontius,[6] Caelius, Crassicius, Tiro, Mustela, Petusius: I name only the captains; the rank and file I leave out of account. After these come the Larks and the rest of the veterans, the seedbed of jurymen of the third panel,[7] who, after running through their own property and devouring Caesar's bounties, have cast covetous eyes on our possessions.

Trusty indeed is Antonius' right hand, the hand which 4 has slaughtered so many of our countrymen! Binding and sacred indeed will be the treaty we make with the Antonii! Should Marcus try to break it, the virtuous Lucius will call

known. We thank John D. Morgan for pointing out this inscriptional evidence.

[7] See 1.20.

sanctitas a scelere revocabit. Illis locus si in hac urbe fuerit,
ipsi urbi locus non erit. Ora vobis eorum ponite ante oculos
et maxime Antoniorum, incessum, aspectum, vultum, spiritum, latera tegentis alios, alios praegredientis amicos.
Quem vini anhelitum, quas contumelias fore censetis mi-
nasque verborum! Nisi forte eos pax ipsa leniet maximeque, cum in hunc ordinem venerint, salutabunt benigne, comiter appellabunt unum quemque nostrum. [3]
5 Non recordamini, per deos immortalis, quas in eos sententias dixeritis? Acta M. Antoni rescidistis; leges refixistis;
per vim et contra auspicia latas decrevistis; totius Italiae
dilectus excitavistis; collegam et scelerum socium omnium
hostem iudicavistis. Cum hoc quae pax potest esse? Hostis
si esset externus, id ipsum vix talibus factis, sed posset aliquo modo. Maria, montes, regionum magnitudines inter-
essent; odisses eum quem non videres. Hi in oculis haere-
bunt et, cum licebit, in faucibus; quibus enim saeptis tam
immanis beluas continebimus?

At incertus exitus belli. Est omnino fortium virorum,
quales vos esse debetis, virtutem praestare—tantum enim
6 possunt—fortunae culpam non extimescere. Sed quoniam
ab hoc ordine non fortitudo solum verum etiam sapientia
postulatur—quamquam vix videntur haec posse seiungi,
seiungamus tamen—fortitudo dimicare iubet, iustum odium incendit, ad confligendum impellit, vocat ad periculum: quid sapientia? Cautioribus utitur consiliis, in poste-

him back from such a crime. If there is to be a place for those people here in Rome, there will be no place for Rome itself. Picture to yourselves their faces, above all those of the Antonii, their gait, appearance, expression, disposition, and their friends, some covering their flanks, others walking in front. Imagine the reek of wine, the abusive, threatening language. Or will the very fact of peace perhaps mollify them? In particular, when they come into this body, will they have a friendly greeting, a pleasant word for each of us? [3] By the immortal gods, don't you remember the votes you cast against them? You rescinded Marcus Antonius' acts, tore down his laws, decreed that they had been passed by violence and contrary to the auspices; you raised levies all over Italy; you declared his colleague, the partner in all his crimes, a public enemy. What peace can there be with him? If he were a foreign enemy, such a thing would scarcely be possible after such doings, but it could be carried off somehow or other. There would be seas, mountains, wide tracts of land to separate us. One would hate him without seeing him. But these fellows will cling to our sight and, when they get the chance, be at our throats. For with what cages shall we confine such monstrous beasts?

But still, uncertain is the issue of the war . It is entirely the place of brave men, such as you should be, to do their best—they can do no more—and not to fear what is Fortune's fault. But since not only courage but wisdom too is demanded from this body—the two seem hardly separable, but let us separate them all the same—well, courage commands us to fight, kindles just hatred in our hearts, urges us to contend, summons us to danger. And what does wisdom do? She employs more cautious counsels,

rum providet, est omni ratione tectior. Quid igitur censet?
Parendum est enim atque id optimum iudicandum quod
sit sapientissime constitutum. Si hoc praecipit ne quid vita
existimem antiquius, ne decernam capitis periculo, fugiam
omne discrimen, quaeram ex ea: "Etiamne, si erit, cum id
fecero, serviendum?" Si adnuerit, ne ego sapientiam istam, quamvis sit erudita, non audiam. Sin responderit: "Tu
vero ita vitam corpusque servato, ita fortunas, ita rem
familiarem, ut haec libertate posteriora ducas itaque his
uti velis, si libera re publica possis, nec pro his libertatem,
sed pro libertate haec proicias tamquam pignora iniuriae
⟨oblata⟩,"[3] tum sapientiae vocem audire videar eique uti
7 deo paream. Itaque si receptis illis esse possumus liberi,
vincamus odium pacemque patiamur; sin otium incolumi-
bus eis esse nullum potest, laetemur decertandi oblatam
esse fortunam. Aut enim interfectis illis fruemur victrice
re publica aut oppressi—quod omen avertat Iuppiter!—si
non spiritu, at virtutis laude vivemus.

[4] At enim nos M. Lepidus, imperator iterum, pontifex
maximus, optime proximo civili bello de re publica meritus, ad pacem adhortatur. Nullius apud me, patres conscripti, auctoritas maior est quam M. Lepidi vel propter ipsius virtutem vel propter familiae dignitatem. Accedunt
eodem multa privata magna eius in me merita, mea quaedam officia in illum. Maximum vero eius beneficium nu-

---

[3] *add.* SB

---

[8] I.e., to avoid being stripped of his material possessions, a rich
man may be inclined to bend to the will of a tyrant.
[9] By striking peace with Sextus Pompeius (cf. 5.39).

she looks ahead to consequences, she is altogether more guarded. What, then, is her advice? For it must be obeyed; the wisest decision is to be judged the best. If she instructs me to deem nothing more important than life, not to risk my life in perilous battle, to shun all danger, I shall ask her a question: "Even if, having done all this, I am to be a slave?" If she nods assent, then I for one shall refuse to listen to that wisdom, whatever her learning. But if she replies: "No. Preserve your life and body, your fortunes and property, but only as valuing them less than freedom and as desiring to enjoy them only if you can do so in a free Republic, and do not sacrifice liberty in exchange for those things but them for liberty, regarding them as pledges exposed to ill-usage,"[8] then I would think I am hearing the voice of wisdom and would obey as I would obey a god. Therefore, if we can take those people back and still be free, let us conquer our hatred and put up with peace. But if there can be no quiet in the community if they are part of it, let us rejoice that we have been given the opportunity to fight it out. For either they will be killed and we shall enjoy a victorious Republic or, if overwhelmed—may Jupiter avert the omen!— we shall live, if not with breath, yet with the glory of valor.

[4] But we are being urged to make peace by Marcus Lepidus, imperator for the second time, pontifex maximus, who has deserved excellently of the Republic in the most recent civil war.[9] No man's authority, Members of the Senate, stands higher with me than that of Marcus Lepidus whether by reason of his own worth or the dignity of his family. Added to these considerations are his many great private services to me and certain good offices of mine to him. But I count it as his greatest benefaction that he feels

mero quod hoc animo in rem publicam est, quae mihi vita
8 mea semper fuit carior. Nam cum Magnum Pompeium,
clarissimum adulescentem, praestantissimi viri filium,
auctoritate adduxit ad pacem remque publicam sine armis
maximo civilis belli periculo liberavit, tum me eius beneficio plus quam pro virili parte obligatum putavi. Itaque et
honores ei decrevi quos potui amplissimos, in quibus mihi
vos estis adsensi, nec umquam de illo et sperare optime et
loqui destiti. Magnis et multis pignoribus M. Lepidum res
publica illigatum tenet. Summa nobilitas est, omnes honores, amplissimum sacerdotium, plurima urbis ornamenta, ipsius, fratris maiorumque monumenta; probatissima
uxor, optatissimi liberi, res familiaris cum ampla tum casta
a cruore civili. Nemo ab eo civis violatus, multi eius beneficio et misericordia liberati. Talis igitur vir et civis opi-
nione labi potest, voluntate a re publica dissidere nullo
pacto potest.
9   Pacem vult M. Lepidus. Praeclare, si talem potest ef-
ficere qualem nuper effecit, qua pace Cn. Pompei filium
res publica aspiciet suoque sinu complexuque recipiet,
neque solum illum, sed cum illo se ipsam sibi restitutam
putabit. Haec causa fuit cur decerneretis statuam in rostris cum inscriptione praeclara, cur absenti triumphum.
Quamquam enim magnas res bellicas gesserat et triumpho

---

10 Perhaps alluding to the personal ties between Cicero and
the elder Pompey.   11 Cf. 5.40–41.
12 Such as the Basilica Aemilia built by Lepidus' ancestor, the
censor of 179, and restored by his brother, L. Aemilius Paullus,
consul in 50. Lepidus himself had a part in the construction of a
shrine to Felicitas on the site of the old senate-house (Cass. Dio
44.5.2).

as he does toward the Republic, which has always been more dear to me than my own life. For when Lepidus by means of the weight of his prestige induced young Magnus Pompeius, the illustrious son of so eminent a father, to accept peace and so delivered the Republic without a sword drawn from a very grave threat of civil war, I then conceived myself under more than my individual share of obligation for the benefit received from him.[10] Accordingly I proposed for Lepidus the most ample honors I could, in respect to which you gave me your assent;[11] nor have I ever ceased both to hope and to speak of him in the highest terms. The Republic holds Marcus Lepidus bound to it by many great pledges. His birth is of the highest, he has passed through the gamut of offices, he holds the most elevated priesthood, and many adornments of Rome commemorate him, his brother, and their ancestors;[12] his wife is greatly respected, his children are all that could be desired, his wealth is ample and untainted by civil bloodshed. No fellow countryman has been harmed by him; many have been rescued by his kindness and compassion. Such a man and such a citizen can make an error of judgment, but in his sympathies he cannot by any manner of means be at variance with the Republic.

Marcus Lepidus wants peace. Admirable, if he can make peace of the sort he has recently made, whereby the Republic will see and take into her arms the son of Gnaeus Pompeius, and not him alone: she will deem that along with him she has experienced her own restoration. This was the reason why you voted him a statue on the Rostra with a splendid inscription and a triumph in absentia. He had indeed achieved important military successes worthy of a triumph, but that did not warrant our granting

8

9

dignas, non erat tamen ei tribuendum quod nec L. Aemilio
nec Aemiliano Scipioni nec superiori Africano nec Mario
nec Pompeio, qui maiora bella gesserunt; sed quod silentio
bellum civile confecerat, cum primum licuit, honores in
10 eum maximos contulistis. [5] Existimasne igitur, M. Lepide, qualem Pompeium res publica habitura sit civem, talis futuros in re publica Antonios? In altero pudor, gravitas,
moderatio, integritas; in illis—et cum hos compello, prae-
tereo animo ex grege latrocini neminem—libidines, scelera, ad omne facinus immanis audacia.

Deinde vos obsecro, patres conscripti, quis hoc vestrum non videt quod Fortuna ipsa quae dicitur caeca vidit?
Salvis enim actis Caesaris, quae concordiae causa defendimus, Pompeio sua domus patebit, eamque non minoris
quam emit Antonius redimet; redimet, inquam, Cn. Pompei domum filius. O rem acerbam! Sed haec satis diu mul-
tumque defleta sunt. Decrevistis tantam pecuniam Pompeio quantam ex bonis patriis in praedae dissipatione
11 inimicus victor redegisset. Sed hanc mihi dispensationem
pro paterna necessitudine et coniunctione deposco: redimet hortos, aedis, urbana quaedam quae possidet Antonius. Nam argentum, vestem, supellectilem, vinum amittet aequo animo, quae ille helluo dissipavit. Albanum,
Formianum a Dolabella recuperabit; etiam ab Antonio

---

13 Cf. 5.41; actually, Pompey *had* been awarded a gilt equestrian statue on the Rostra (Vell. 2.61.3; cf. *Phil.* 1.36, n. 56).

14 Cf. §12 fin.

15 Caesar. The senate voted this compensation for Sextus
Pompeius in the late summer or autumn of 44, on the motion of
Antony (App. *B Civ.* 3.4; Cass. Dio 45.10.6).

to him what was not granted to Lucius Aemilius or to Aemilianus Scipio or to the elder Africanus or to Marius or to Pompeius, men who conducted greater wars.[13] But because he had brought a civil war to a conclusion without an uproar, you conferred the greatest honors upon him at the first opportunity. [5] Well, Marcus Lepidus, do you expect   10 the Antonii to be such citizens in the Republic as the Republic will have in Sextus Pompeius? In him is modesty, responsibility, moderation, integrity; in them—and when I name them, I mentally include every member of that robber band—are lusts, crimes, monstrous audacity stopping at nothing.

Next, I beg you, Members of the Senate: which of you does not see what Fortune herself has seen,[14] who is said to be blind? With no violation of Caesar's acts, which we defend for the sake of concord, Pompeius' own house will lie open to him, and he will repurchase it for not less than Antonius paid for it. I repeat, Gnaeus Pompeius' son will repurchase his father's house. A bitter thought! But enough tears, and for long enough, have been shed over these things. You voted Sextus Pompeius a sum of money equal to that which his father's property realized for his victorious enemy[15] in the dispersal of the plunder. But I   11 claim for myself the management of this matter in virtue of my friendship and close association with his father. Pompeius will repurchase the suburban estate, the town house, and certain urban properties now occupied by Antonius. As for the silverplate, fabrics, furniture, and wine which that wastrel has squandered, Pompeius will take their loss philosophically. He will recover the villas at Alba and Formiae from Dolabella and the villa at Tusculum, again,

Tusculanum; eique qui nunc Mutinam oppugnant, D. Brutum obsident, de Falerno Anseres depellentur. Sunt alii plures fortasse, sed ‹e›[4] mea memoria dilabuntur. Ego etiam eos dico qui hostium numero non sunt Pompeianas possessiones quanti emerint filio reddituros. Satis inconsiderati fuit, ne dicam audacis, rem ullam ex illis attingere; retinere vero quis poterit clarissimo domino restituto? An is non reddet qui domini patrimonium circumplexus quasi thesaurum draco, Pompei servus, libertus Caesaris, agri Lucani possessiones occupavit? Atque illud bis[5] miliens, quod adulescenti, patres conscripti, spopondistis, ita discribetur ut videatur a vobis Cn. Pompei filius in patrimonio suo collocatus.

Haec senatus: reliqua populus Romanus in ea familia quam vidit amplissimam persequetur, in primis paternum auguratus locum, in quem ego eum, ut quod a patre accepi filio reddam, mea nominatione cooptabo. Utrum igitur augurem Iuppiter Optimus Maximus cuius interpretes internuntiique constituti sumus, utrum populus Romanus libentius sanciet, Pompeiumne an Antonium? Mihi quidem numine deorum immortalium videtur hoc Fortuna

[4] *suppl. Clark*
[5] *nescio quis coni. teste SB*: septiens *D*

16 Presumably brothers. One of them may have been the poet Anser mentioned by Ovid, *Tr.* 2.435; cf. Serv. on Verg. *Ecl.* 9.36.
17 Name unknown.   18 The sum of 200 million—*bis* (*II*) for *septiens* (*VII*) of the MSS—is restored on the basis of App. *B Civ.* 3.4. The corruption may have arisen from Cicero's frequent mention of the sum of 700 million that was allegedly embezzled by Antony from the Temple of Ops (e.g., 2.93).

from Antonius. The Ansers,[16] who are now attacking Mutina and blockading Decimus Brutus, will be ousted from the Falernian property. There are quite a few others, perhaps, but they escape my memory. I also declare that those who are not in the number of our enemies will restore Pompeius' possessions to his son at the price they paid for them. It was inconsiderate enough, not to say audacious, to touch any one of those items; yet who will have the effrontery to hold on to such after the restoration of its illustrious owner? There is a former slave of Gnaeus Pompeius and freedman of Caesar's[17] who has taken possession of lands in Lucania, coiled round his master's property like a dragon around a treasure: will he not give it back? And that two hundred million,[18] which you have promised the young man, Members of the Senate, will be so disposed that Gnaeus Pompeius' son will be seen to have been established by you in his own patrimony.

12

This much the senate will do. The Roman people will attend to the rest in the case of the most illustrious family it has ever seen:[19] first and foremost, his father's place in the College of Augurs, into which I shall co-opt him by my nomination, thus returning to the son what I received from the father.[20] So which of these two will Jupiter Best and Greatest, of whom we augurs have been constituted interpreters and intermediaries, which of them will the Roman people more willingly ratify as augur, Pompeius or Antonius? For my part, I think it is by the will of the immortal

[19] Or "a family which it (once) saw as the epitome of greatness."

[20] Cicero was nominated by Pompey and Hortensius in 53 or 52.

241

voluisse, ut actis Caesaris firmis ac ratis Cn. Pompei filius
posset et dignitatem et fortunas patrias recuperare.

13   [6] Ac ne illud quidem silentio, patres conscripti, prae-
tereundum puto quod clarissimi viri legati, L. Paul<l>us,
Q. Thermus, C. Fannius, quorum habetis cognitam voluntatem in rem publicam eamque perpetuam atque constantem, nuntiant se Pompei conveniendi causa devertisse
Massiliam eumque cognovisse paratissimo animo ut cum
suis copiis iret ad Mutinam, ni vereretur ne veteranorum
animos offenderet. Est vero eius patris filius qui sapienter
faciebat non minus multa quam fortiter. Itaque intellegitis
et animum ei praesto fuisse nec consilium defuisse.

Atque etiam hoc M. Lepido providendum est, ne quid
14   adrogantius quam eius mores ferunt facere videatur. Si
enim nos exercitu terret, non meminit illum exercitum senatus populique Romani atque universae rei publicae esse,
non suum. At uti potest pro suo. Quid tum? Omniane bonis viris quae facere possunt facienda sunt? Etiamne si tur-
pia, si perniciosa erunt, si facere omnino non licebit? Quid
autem turpius aut foedius aut quod minus deceat quam
contra senatum, contra civis, contra patriam exercitum ducere? Quid vero magis vituperandum quam id facere quod
non liceat? Licet autem nemini contra patriam ducere
exercitum, si quidem licere id dicimus quod legibus, quod
more maiorum institutisque conceditur. Neque enim,
quod quisque potest, id ei licet, nec, si non obstatur, prop-

---

21 *Devertisse* (lit. "turned aside") must imply that these envoys
had another destination. Perhaps they were going to Lepidus.

gods that Fortune has chosen to allow the son of Gnaeus Pompeius to recover his father's dignity and possessions while Caesar's acts remain firmly established.

[6] There is another point, Members of the Senate, which I think should not be passed over in silence. Our illustrious envoys, Lucius Paullus, Quintus Thermus, and Gaius Fannius, whose unflagging, steadfast patriotism you know well, report that they stopped along the way at Massilia[21] in order to meet with Pompeius and found him perfectly ready to go to Mutina with his forces, if he were not afraid of offending the veterans. Truly he is the son of his father, whose acts of wisdom were no less numerous than his acts of valor. So you see that his courage was ready and his discretion did not fail him.

Moreover, Marcus Lepidus should guard against the appearance of behaving with an arrogance that is out of character. If he seeks to intimidate us with his army, he forgets that that army belongs to the senate and the people of Rome and the entire Republic, not to him personally. Ah, but he can use it as though it did belong to him personally. What then? Are upright men to do all things that lie in their power, even things dishonorable and destructive, even things quite impermissible? What can be more dishonorable and ugly and unseemly than to lead an army against the senate and one's fellow countrymen and one's native land? And what is more blameworthy than to do the impermissible? Now to no one is it permitted to lead an army against his native land, if indeed by "permitted" we mean what is allowed by laws and by the customs and institutions of our ancestors. It is not permissible for a man to do everything he is able to do; and even if no opposition is put in his way, it does not follow that he is allowed. To you,

13

14

terea etiam permittitur. Tibi enim exercitum, Lepide, tamquam maioribus tuis patria pro se dedit. Hoc tu arcebis hostem, finis imperi propagabis: senatui populoque Romano parebis, si quam ad aliam rem te forte traduxerit.

15   [7] Haec si cogitas, es M. Lepidus, pontifex maximus, M. Lepidi, pontificis maximi, pronepos; sin hominibus tantum licere iudicas quantum possunt, vide ne alienis exemplis eisque recentibus uti quam et antiquis et domesticis malle videare. Quod si auctoritatem interponis sine armis, magis equidem laudo, sed vide ne hoc ipsum non sit necesse. Quamquam enim est tanta in te auctoritas quanta debet in homine nobilissimo, tamen senatus se ipse non contemnit, nec vero fuit umquam gravior, constantior, fortior. Incensi omnes rapimur ad libertatem recuperandam. Non potest ullius auctoritate tantus senatus populique Romani ardor exstingui. Odimus, irati pugnamus; extorqueri ⟨e⟩ manibus arma non possunt; receptui signum aut revocationem a bello audire non possumus; speramus optima,

16 pati vel difficillima malumus quam servire. Caesar confecit invictum exercitum; duo fortissimi consules adsunt cum copiis; L. Planci, consulis designati, varia et magna auxilia non desunt; in D. Bruti salute certatur; unus furiosus gladiator cum taeterrimorum latronum manu contra patriam, contra deos penatis, contra aras et focos, contra quattuor

---

22 Just the opposite was, in fact, the case with reference to his immediate ancestor: Lepidus' father, consul in 78, died leading a rebellion in 78–77.

23 An adaptation of a line of the second-century poet Lucilius quoted in *Tusc.* 4.48: *odi hominem, iratus pugno . . .*

Lepidus, your native land has given an army, just as she did to your ancestors, for her own benefit. With it you will ward off the enemy and extend the boundaries of empire. You will obey the senate and people of Rome, if they happen to transfer you to some other assignment.

[7] If you think along these lines, you are Marcus Lepidus, pontifex maximus, great-grandson of Marcus Lepidus, pontifex maximus. But if you judge that people are permitted to do anything they have the power to do, consider lest you seem to be preferring to follow recent precedents drawn from outside your family rather than ancient and familial ones.[22] If, however, you are bringing into play the respect in which you are held without any implication of armed force, the more credit to you, say I; but consider whether even this very act is unnecessary. Granted you enjoy all the respect that is due to your exalted birth, nevertheless, the senate does not undervalue itself, nor indeed was it ever more dignified, resolute, and courageous. Our fiery enthusiasm for the recovery of liberty sweeps us onward, nor can the passionate ardor of the senate and people of Rome be quelled by respect for any man. We hate, we fight, roused to anger.[23] Our arms cannot be wrenched out of our hands. We cannot hear a signal for retreat, a recall from battle. We hope for the best, but would rather suffer any extremity than be slaves. Caesar has raised an army which has never known defeat. Two very valiant consuls and the forces they command are with him. Large subsidiary forces of various kinds under consul-elect Lucius Plancus are not wanting. The struggle is for the survival of Decimus Brutus. A single frantic gladiator with a band of horrible brigands makes war upon our native land, upon our household gods, upon our altars and hearths, upon

15

16

245

consules gerit bellum. Huic cedamus, huius condiciones audiamus, cum hoc pacem fieri posse credamus?

[8] At periculum est ne opprimamur. Non metuo ne is qui suis amplissimis fortunis nisi bonis salvis frui non potest prodat salutem suam. Bonos civis primum natura efficit, adiuvat deinde Fortuna. Omnibus enim bonis expedit salvam esse rem publicam, sed in eis qui fortunati sunt

17 magis id apparet. Quis fortunatior Lepido, ut ante dixi, quis eodem sanior? Vidit eius maestitiam atque lacrimas populus Romanus Lupercalibus; vidit quam abiectus, quam confectus esset, cum Caesari diadema imponens Antonius servum se illius quam collegam esse malebat. Qui si reliquis flagitiis et sceleribus abstinere potuisset, tamen unum ob hoc factum dignum illum omni poena putarem. Nam si ipse servire poterat, nobis dominum cur imponebat? Et si eius pueritia pertulerat libidines eorum qui erant in eum tyranni, etiamne in nostros liberos dominum et tyrannum compararet?[6] Itaque illo interfecto qualem in nos eum esse voluit, talis ipse in ceteros exstitit.

18 Qua enim ‹in ›[7] barbaria quisquam tam taeter, tam crudelis tyrannus quam in hac urbe armis barbarorum stipatus Antonius? Caesare dominante veniebamus in senatum, si non libere, at tamen tuto. Hoc archipirata—quid enim dicam tyranno?—haec subsellia ab Ituraeis occupaban-

---

[6] *SB*: comparabat *D*   [7] *add.* ς

---

[24] The two consuls-elect, D. Brutus and Plancus, are included.
[25] I.e., by backing Antony. The argument is quite flimsy and shows Cicero's distrust of Lepidus. The latter, in the end, cut a deal with Antony and Octavian to form the Triumvirate and share power over the whole Roman world.

four consuls.[24] Are we to yield to him? Are we to listen to his terms? Are we to believe it possible for peace to be made with him?

[8] Still, it may be urged that there is a danger of our being overwhelmed. I am not afraid that one who cannot enjoy his own ample fortunes if honest men perish will betray his own welfare.[25] Good citizens are made in the first place by nature, then are aided by Fortune. For while the well-being of the Republic is to the advantage of all honest men, that is more obviously the case with the fortunate among them. As I have already observed, who is more fortunate than Lepidus, who of sounder mind than he? The Roman people saw his distress, his tears, at the Lupercalia, saw how cast down, how crushed he was when Antonius tried to put the diadem on Caesar and preferred to be Caesar's slave than his colleague. Even if Antonius had been able to hold back from his other infamies and crimes, I should still count him deserving of every punishment because of this one act. For if he found slavery bearable for himself, why foist a master on *us*? If in his boyhood days he endured the lusts of those who tyrannized over him, was he also to produce a master and tyrant over our children? And so, when Caesar was killed, Antonius became to the rest of the community what he wanted Caesar to be to us.

In what barbarous land was there ever so grim and cruel a tyrant as was Antonius in Rome, surrounded by armed barbarians? Under Caesar's despotism we used to come to the senate in safety, if not in freedom. With this pirate chief ("tyrant" is too good for him) these benches were occupied by Ituraeans. Suddenly he burst forth to Brun-

17

18

tur. Prorupit subito Brundisium ut inde agmine quadrato
ad urbem accederet; lautissimum oppidum nunc munic-
ip[i]um[8] honestissimorum, quondam colonorum, Suessam
fortissimorum militum sanguine implevit; Brundisii in
sinu non modo avarissimae sed etiam crudelissimae uxoris
delectos Martiae legionis centuriones trucidavit. Inde se
quo furore, quo ardore ad urbem, id est ad caedem optimi
cuiusque rapiebat!

Quo tempore di ipsi immortales praesidium improvi-
sum nec opinantibus nobis obtulerunt. [9] Caesaris enim
incredibilis ac divina virtus latronis impetus crudelis ac
furibundos retardavit: quem tum ille demens laedere se
putabat edictis, ignorans quaecumque falso diceret in
sanctissimum adulescentem, ea vere rec⟨c⟩idere[9] in
memoriam pueritiae suae. Ingressus urbem est quo comitatu
vel potius agmine, cum dextra sinistra, gemente populo
Romano, minaretur dominis, notaret domos, divisurum se
urbem palam suis polliceretur! Rediit ad milites; ibi pesti-
fera illa Tiburi contio. Inde ad urbem cursus; senatus in
Capitolium; parata de circumscribendo adulescente sententia consularis, cum repente—nam Martiam legionem
Albae consedisse sciebat—adfertur ei de quarta nuntius.
Quo perculsus abiecit consilium referendi ad senatum de
Caesare: egressus est non viis, sed tramitibus paludatus.
Eoque ipso die innumerabilia senatus consulta fecit, quae

[8] *corr. Manutius*   [9] *add. SB, cf. 4.10*

[26] Lit. "wearing the *paludamentum*," the (usually) scarlet
cloak of a commanding general.

[27] 28 November. Antony left Rome on the night of 28/29 Nov.,
before daybreak (3.24).

disium intending to march from there on Rome in battle array. He made Suessa, a very thriving town, once of colonists, now of most respectable burghers, run with the blood of terribly brave soldiers. At Brundisium, in the lap of his wife, a woman as cruel as she is greedy to the utmost extent, he slaughtered picked centurions of the Martian Legion. From there in what a blaze of fury he hurried back to Rome, which is to say to the slaughter of the best of her citizens!

Then it was that the immortal gods themselves brought us a totally unforeseen protection. [9] Caesar's amazing, superhuman courage checked the brigand's ferocious, furious onslaughts. Antonius in his delirium thought to damage him with manifestos, unaware that all his slanders of a young man of irreproachable character recoiled as truths upon the memory of his own early life. With what an entourage, or rather regiment on the march, did he enter Rome, while to right and to left, amidst the groans of the Roman people, he threatened householders, noted down houses, and openly promised his followers that he would parcel out the city among them. He returned to his troops. There at Tibur he made that pernicious speech. Back to Rome posthaste; senate called to the Capitol. A consular motion to clip the young man's wings was in readiness, when suddenly—for he already knew that the Martian Legion had stationed itself at Alba—he gets the news about the Fourth. Shocked thereat, he gave up his intention of putting the matter of Caesar before the senate. He left Rome in a general's uniform,[26] not using the highroads but bypaths. And that very day[27] he made countless senatorial

19

quidem omnia ⟨paene⟩[10] citius delata quam scripta sunt.
20 Ex eo non iter, sed cursus et fuga in Galliam. Caesarem
sequi arbitrabatur cum legione Martia, cum quarta, cum
veteranis, quorum ille nomen prae metu ferre non poterat,
eique in Galliam penetranti D. se Brutus obiecit, qui se totius belli fluctibus circumiri quam illum aut regredi aut
progredi maluit Mutinamque illi exsultanti tamquam fre-
nos furoris iniecit. Quam cum operibus munitionibusque
saepsisset nec eum coloniae florentissimae dignitas neque
consulis designati maiestas a parricidio deterreret, tum
me—testor et vos et populum Romanum et omnis deos qui
huic urbi praesident—invito et repugnante legati missi
21 tres consulares ad latronum et gladiatorum ducem. Quis
tam barbarus umquam, tam immanis, tam ferus? Non audivit, non respondit; neque eos solum praesentis sed multo
magis nos a quibus illi erant missi sprevit et pro nihilo
putavit. Postea quod scelus, quod facinus parricida non
edidit? Circumsedet colonos nostros, exercitum populi
Romani, imperatorem, consulem designatum: agros dive-
xat civium optimorum; hostis taeterrimus omnibus bonis
cruces ac tormenta minitatur. [10] Cum hoc, M. Lepide,
pax esse quae potest? Cuius ne supplicio quidem ullo satia-
ri videtur posse res publica.
22 Quod si quis adhuc dubitare potuit quin nulla societas
huic ordini populoque Romano cum illa importunissima
belua posset esse, desinet[11] profecto dubitare his cognitis
litteris quas mihi missas ab Hirtio consule modo accepi.

---

[10] *suppl. SB*
[11] *SB*: desinat *bv*: -ignat *n¹st*

decrees, all of which were deposited almost before they were put in writing. Next, not a march, but a headless 20 flight to (Hither) Gaul. He thought Caesar was in pursuit with the Martian Legion and the Fourth and the veterans, whose name made him quake with fear. As he pushed into Gaul, Decimus Brutus blocked his path, voluntarily letting himself be surrounded by the billows of the whole war rather than let Antonius go backward or forward, and using Mutina to curb his fury like a bridle on a rampant horse. After Antonius had surrounded the town with works and fortifications, and neither the dignity of a flourishing colony nor the majesty of a consul-elect deterred him from his work of treason, at that point, against my will—I call you gentlemen and the Roman people and all the presiding deities of Rome to witness—against my opposition, three consular envoys were sent to this leader of bandits and gladiators. Was there ever such a barbarian, such a mon- 21 ster, such a beast? He did not listen, he did not reply. He treated with scorn and total contempt not only the ambassadors to their faces, but much more us who sent them. Thereafter what crime and villainy has the traitor not perpetrated? He invests our colonists and a Roman army and its imperator, a consul-elect. He ravages the lands of loyal citizens. As a ferocious enemy, he threatens all honest men with crucifixion and torture. [10] What peace can there be with this fellow, Marcus Lepidus? Why, no punishment for him seems harsh enough to satisfy the Republic!

But if anyone could still doubt the impossibility of any 22 sort of fellowship between this body and the Roman people on the one hand and that extremely savage monster on the other, his doubts will certainly cease when he learns the contents of a letter that has just come into my hands,

Eas dum recito dumque de singulis sententiis breviter disputo, velim, patres conscripti, ut adhuc fecistis, me attente
audiatis.

"Antonius Hirtio et Caesari."

Neque se imperatorem neque Hirtium consulem nec
pro praetore Caesarem. Satis hoc quidem scite: deponere
alienum nomen ipse maluit quam illis suum reddere.

"Cognita morte C. Treboni non plus gavisus sum quam
dolui."

Videte quid se 'gavisum,' quid 'doluisse' dicat: facilius
de pace deliberabitis.

"Dedisse poenas sceleratum cineri atque ossibus clarissimi viri et apparuisse numen deorum intra finem anni ver-
tentis aut iam soluto supplicio parricidi aut impendente
laetandum est."

O Spartace! Quem enim te potius appellem, cuius
propter nefanda scelera tolerabilis videtur fuisse Catilina?
'Laetandum esse' ausus es scribere Trebonium 'dedisse
poenas'? 'Sceleratum Trebonium'? Quo scelere, nisi quod
te Idibus Martiis a debita tibi peste seduxit? Age, hoc laeta-
ris: videamus quid moleste feras.

"⟨A senatu⟩[12] iudicatum hostem populi Romani Dolabellam eo quod sicarium occiderit et videri cariorem populo Romano filium scurrae quam C. Caesarem, patriae
parentem, ingemiscendum est."

23

[12] *add. C. F. W. Müller*

sent by the consul Hirtius. While I read it aloud and briefly take issue with it sentence by sentence, may I request you, Members of the Senate, to give me your close attention, as you have done so far?

"Antonius to Hirtius and Caesar."

He neither calls himself imperator, nor Hirtius consul, nor Caesar propraetor. Smart enough, that. Rather than give them their proper titles, he has chosen to drop one that is not rightfully his.

"When I learned of Gaius Trebonius' death, my joy was no greater than my distress."

Mark well what he says 'gave him joy' and what 'gave him distress.' It will be the easier for you to deliberate about peace.

"It is a matter for gladness that a criminal has paid his penalty to the ashes and bones of an illustrious man and that, before a year has elapsed, the will of the gods has made itself manifest since punishment for an act of parricide has already been inflicted or is impending."

Spartacus! What better name to call you by? Your abominable crimes make Catiline look tolerable by contrast in retrospect. Did you dare to write that 'it is a matter for gladness that Trebonius has paid his penalty'? That 'Trebonius was a criminal'? What was his crime, except to draw you away from the destruction you deserved on the Ides of March? Well, this gladdens your heart: let us see 23 what you find hard to bear.

"But it is a matter for lamentation that Dolabella has been declared by the senate an enemy of the Roman people on the ground that he put an assassin to death, and lamentable that the son of a buffoon should seem dearer to the Roman people than Gaius Caesar, the father of the fatherland."

253

Quid 'ingemiscis'? 'Hostem Dolabellam'? Quid? Te non intellegis dilectu tota Italia habito, consulibus missis, Caesare ornato, sagis denique sumptis hostem iudicatum? Quid est autem, scelerate, quod gemas 'hostem Dolabellam iudicatum a senatu'? Quem tu ordinem omnino esse nullum putas, sed eam tibi causam belli gerendi proponis ut senatum funditus deleas, reliqui boni et locupletes omnes summum ordinem subsequantur. At 'scurrae filium' appellat. Quasi vero ignotus nobis fuerit splendidus eques Romanus, Treboni pater. Is autem humilitatem despicere audet cuiusquam qui ex Fadia sustulerit liberos?

24   [11] "Acerbissimum vero est te, A. Hirti, ornatum [esse][13] beneficiis Caesaris et talem ab eo relictum qualem ipse miraris—"

Equidem negare non possum a Caesare Hirtium 'ornatum,' sed illa ornamenta in virtute et industria posita lucent. Tu vero qui te ab eodem Caesare ornatum negare non potes, quid esses, si tibi ille non tam multa tribuisset? Ecquo te tua virtus provexisset, ecquo genus? In lustris, popinis, alea, vino tempus aetatis omne consumpsisses, ut faciebas, cum in gremiis mimarum mentum mentemque deponeres.

"—et te, o puer,—"

'Puerum' appellat quem non modo virum sed etiam fortissimum virum sensit et sentiet. Est istuc quidem no-

---

[13] *del. Gryphius*

---

[28] Done on 4 Feb., by decree of the senate on 2 Feb. (8.6).
[29] Cf. 2.3.
[30] Lit. "chin" (*mentum*). Cicero is fond of alliterative pairs like *mentum mentemque.*

What are you 'lamenting'? 'That Dolabella has been declared a public enemy'? What? Don't you understand that as a result of the holding of a levy all over Italy, the dispatch of the consuls, the recognition given to Caesar, and finally as a result of the donning of military cloaks by the civilian populace,[28] *you* have been declared a public enemy? And why, you criminal, should you 'lament that Dolabella has been declared an enemy by the senate'? You think this body of no account whatsoever, and yet you propose to yourself as your reason for making war the goal of wiping out the senate utterly and of causing all other decent and substantial citizens to go the same way as the leading echelon. But he calls Trebonius 'the son of a buffoon'—as though we had never heard of that distinguished Roman knight, Trebonius' father. And does the father of Fadia's children dare to despise anybody's lowly social origins?[29]

[11] "But the cruelest cut of all is that you, Aulus 24
Hirtius, favored as you were by Caesar's benefactions, left by him in a position at which you yourself marvel—"

To be sure, I cannot deny that Hirtius was 'favored by Caesar,' but such favors shine when they are bestowed on worth and diligence. You, on the contrary, who cannot deny that you were favored by the same Caesar, what would you be today, if Caesar had not conferred so much on you? Would your worth or your lineage have got you anywhere at all? You would have spent your entire life in brothels, gorging, gaming, drinking, as you used to do when you were laying your mouth[30] and mind in the lap of actresses.

"—and you, boy,—"

'Boy,' he calls him; but he has found him and will find him not only a man but a very brave man too. That name

men aetatis, sed ab eo minime usurpandum qui suam amentiam huic puero praebet ad gloriam.

25   "—qui omnia nomini debes—"

'Debet' vero solvitque praeclare. Si enim ille 'patriae parens,' ut tu appellas—ego quid sentiam videro—cur non hic parens verior a quo certe vitam habemus e tuis facinerosissimis manibus ereptam?

    "—id agere ut iure damnatus sit Dolabella—"

Turpem vero actionem, qua defenditur amplissimi auctoritas ordinis contra crudelissimi gladiatoris amentiam!

    "—et ut venefica haec liberetur obsidione—"

'Veneficam' audes appellare eum virum qui tuis veneficiis remedia invenit? Quem ita obsides, nove Hannibal aut si quis acutior imperator fuit, ut te ipse obsideas neque te istinc, si cupias, possis explicare. Recesseris: undique omnes insequentur; manseris: haerebis. Nimirum recte veneficam appellas a quo tibi praesentem pestem vides comparatum.

    "—ut quam potentissimus sit Cassius atque Brutus."

26   Putes Censorinum dicere aut Ventidium aut etiam ipsos Antonios. Cur autem nolint potentis esse non modo optimos et nobilissimos viros sed secum etiam in rei publicae defensione coniunctos?

    "Nimirum eodem modo haec aspicitis ut priora;—"

---

[31] Cf. 4.3.   [32] Above, §23.   [33] Antony writes as though Hirtius and Octavian were responsible for the actions of the senate since without their backing as commanders of military forces counterbalancing those of Antony, it would have been impossible for the senate to pursue their anti-Antonian policies favorable to the tyrannicides.   [34] Lit. "she-poisoner," the feminine gender aggravating the insult.

does indeed go with his age,[31] but it comes very ill from one who makes this boy glorious through his own madness.

"—who owe everything to your name—" 25

Yes, he 'owes,' and splendidly he pays. If Caesar was 'the father of the fatherland,' as you call him[32]—never mind what I think—is not this young man more truly a *father* to whom we assuredly owe our lives which he snatched from your most villainous hands?

"—are making every effort to have Dolabella justly condemned—"[33]

Indeed a disgraceful line of action, by which the authority of this august body is defended against the madness of a ruthless gladiator!

"—and trying to get this viper[34] liberated from a siege—"

You dare call 'viper' the man who found the antidote to your venoms? Yes, you latter-day Hannibal (or any cleverer general, if there was one), you are besieging him in such a way that you are besieging yourself, nor can you extricate yourself from your present situation even if you wish. If you pull back, they will all be after you from every side; if you stay put, you will be stuck in a trap. Doubtless you rightly call 'viper' the contriver of the destruction you see staring you in the face.

"—to give maximum power to Cassius and Brutus."

You would think he was talking about Censorinus or 26 Ventidius or even the Antonii themselves. Why should Hirtius and Caesar begrudge power to men who are not only of the highest merit and birth, but are also linked with them in the defense of the Republic?

"I suppose you look at present circumstances just as you did at those of the past;—"

CICERO

Quae tandem?

"—castra Pompei senatum appellatis."

[12] An vero tua castra potius senatum appellaremus?
In quibus tu es videlicet consularis cuius totus consulatus
est ex omni monumentorum memoria evulsus; duo praetores sine causa diffisi se aliquid habituros—nos enim Caesaris beneficia defendimus—; praetorii Philadelphus Annius
et innocens Gallius; aedilicii, corycus laterum et vocis
meae, Bestia, et fidei patronus, fraudator creditorum, Trebellius, et homo diruptus dirutusque Caelius, columenque
amicorum Antoni, Cotyla Varius, quem Antonius delicia-
rum causa loris in convivio caedi iubebat a s⟨er⟩vis¹⁴ publicis; septemvirales Lento, Nucula, tum deliciae atque
amores populi Romani, L. Antonius; tribuni ⟨plebis⟩¹⁵ duo
designati, primum Tullus Hostilius, qui suo iure in porta
nomen inscripsit qua, cum prodere imperatorem suum
non potuisset, reliquit; alter est designatus Insteius nescio
qui fortis, ut aiunt, latro; quem tamen temperantem fuisse

¹⁴ *corr. Ferrarius*
¹⁵ tribuni ⟨plebis⟩ *SB*: tribunicii *D*

---

35 Julius Caesar's enemies claimed that the "true" senate followed Pompey in 49–48, when he evacuated Italy and fought
Caesar in Greece (2.54; Plut. *Pomp.* 64.3), but Antony's sarcastic
assertion here is that by obeying the senate, Octavian and Hirtius
are in effect treating Pompey's old followers as equivalent to the
senate because that faction was imposing its will on that body.

36 Cf. above, §5.

37 Censorinus and Ventidius, mentioned just above and in §2.

38 Cicero mockingly calls T. Annius Cimber "Brotherly" (Philadelphus, lit. "brother-loving"), in allusion to Annius' alleged
murder of his own brother (11.14).

What circumstances, pray?

"—you call Pompeius' camp 'the senate.'"[35]

[12] Well, were we rather to call *your* camp 'the senate'? You are, it is plain to see, a consular in it, a man whose entire consulate has been struck off every form of record.[36] There are two praetors,[37] who fear without any grounds that they will be left with nothing—for we are upholding Caesar's benefactions. Ex-praetors next: Brotherly[38] Annius and the guiltless Gallius.[39] Ex-aediles: Bestia, the punching-bag on which I exercised my voice and lungs;[40] Trebellius, patron of credit and defrauder of creditors;[41] Caelius, a ruptured wreck of a man; and the mainstay of Antonius' friends, Cotyla Varius, whom Antonius used to have flogged by public slaves at dinner, just for fun. Members of the Board of Seven: Lento, Nucula, and then the Roman people's darling and delight, Lucius Antonius. Two tribunes of the plebs designate: first Tullus Hostilius, who inscribed his name, as he had a right to do, on the gate by which he deserted his imperator, not having succeeded in betraying him;[42] the other designate is one Insteius, said to be a resolute robber, though they report that when he was a bath-attendant in Pisaurum he was a good mixer.[43]

[39] A sarcastic allusion to some notorious crime?

[40] Cicero had defended him six times (11.11).

[41] See 6.11 and 11.14, n. 16.

[42] Nothing is known of this. We can conjecture, however, that the Porta Hostilia was the one on the north side of Mutina, through which the road from Hostilia (mod. Ostiglia, a town *c.* 28 mi. N., on the N. bank of the Po) entered the city (cf. the Porta Ostiensis at Rome). The imperator will, of course, be D. Brutus.

[43] A play on two senses of *temperans*: "mixing" (e.g., hot and

27 ferunt Pisauri balneatorem. Sequuntur alii tribunicii, T.
Plancus in primis: qui ⟨ni⟩si[16] senatum dilexisset, numquam curiam incendisset. Quo scelere damnatus in eam
urbem redi⟨i⟩t[17] armis, ex qua excesserat legibus. Sed hoc
ei commune cum pluribus sui similibus. Illud tamen
⟨non⟩[18] verum in hoc Planco quod proverbi loco dici solet,
perire eum non posse, nisi ei crura fracta essent. Fracta
sunt, et vivit. Hoc tamen, ut alia multa, Aquilae referatur
acceptum. [13] Est etiam ibi Decius, ab illis, ut opinor,
Muribus Deciis; itaque Caesaris munera erosit:[19] Decio-
rum quidem multo intervallo per hunc praeclarum virum
memoria renovata est. Saxam vero Decidium praeterire
qui possum, hominem deductum ex ultimis gentibus ut
eum tribunum plebis videremus quem civem numquam
28 videramus? Est quidem alter Saserna: sed omnes tamen
tantam habent similitudinem inter se ut in eorum praeno-
minibus errem. Nec vero †Extitius†, Philadelphi frater,
quaestor, praetermittendus est, ne, si de clarissimo adulescente siluero, invidisse videar Antonio. Est etiam Asinius
quidam senator voluntarius, lectus ipse a se. Apertam curiam vidit post Caesaris mortem: mutavit calceos; pater

16 *corr. SB*   17 *corr. Poggius*   18 *suppl. Zumpt*
19 *SB*: -ra rosit *b*: numerose (murer- *v*) sit (sed *n*) *nstv*

cold water) and "temperate." Insteius may be the "bathman" of
Att. 14.5.1 (see SB ad loc.).   44 In the rioting after the murder of the demagogue P. Clodius in Jan. 52. Cf. 6.10.

45 The expression is equivalent to "born to be hanged" (see
11.14 and n. 17).   46 See 11.13. This Decius may or may not
have claimed descent from the Decii Mures (*mus* = "mouse" or
"rat"), heroes of the early Republic.

Others, ex-tribunes, follow, headed by Titus Plancus, who   27
would never have set fire to the senate-house,[44] if he had
not had high regard for the senate. Convicted of that
crime, he returned by force of arms to the city from which
he had been expelled by force of law. That, however, he has
in common with many others of the same stamp as himself.
But in the case of this Plancus, the old saying "he can't die
unless his legs are broken"[45] has proved false: they *were*
broken, and still he is alive. But let this, like many other
things, go down to Aquila's credit. [13] Decius too is there,
a scion, I believe, of the well-known Mures Decii,[46] which
accounts for his gnawing up Caesar's gifts. The memory of
the Decii has been revived after a long interval through
this noble fellow. And how can I pass over Saxa Decidius,
fetched from far-off lands[47] for us to behold as a tribune
of the plebs, though we had never seen him as a citizen?
One of the two Sasernae is there, but they are all so much   28
of a muchness that I get their first names muddled. Nor
must we leave out Brotherly's brother, Sextus Titius(?),[48] a
quaestor; if I say nothing about this illustrious young man,
it may be thought I was jealous of Antonius. There is also
a certain Asinius, a self-appointed senator, enrolled on
his own authority. He saw the senate-house open after
Caesar's death. He changed his boots,[49] and all of a sudden

[47] Celtiberia in north-central Spain (11.12).

[48] The restoration of this name for Extitius of the MSS is uncertain. See SB, *Two Studies*2, 23; *MRR* 3.85, s.v. Extitius. This
man will have been the brother (or cousin?) of T. Annius Cimber,
to whom Cicero sarcastically gave the agnomen "Brotherly"
(Philadelphus); see n. 38 above.   [49] Senators wore special
boots with an ivory crescent at the toe.

conscriptus repente factus est. Non novi Sex. Albisium, sed tamen neminem tam maledicum offendi qui illum negaret dignum Antoni senatu. Arbitror me aliquos praeterisse; de eis tamen qui occurrebant tacere non potui.

Hoc igitur fretus senatu Pompeianum senatum despicit, in quo decem fuimus consulares: qui si omnes viverent, bellum omnino hoc non fuisset; auctoritati cessisset auda-
29 cia. Sed quantum praesidi fuerit in ceteris, hinc intellegi potest, quod ego unus relictus ex multis contudi et fregi adiuvantibus vobis exsultantis praedonis audaciam. [14] Quod si non Fortuna nobis modo eripuisset Ser. Sulpicium eiusque collegam ante, ‹M.›[20] Marcellum—quos civis, quos viros!—si duo consules, amicissimos patriae, simul ex Italia eiectos, si L. Afranium, summum ducem, si P. Lentulum, civem cum in ceteris rebus tum in salute mea singularem, si ‹M.›[21] Bibulum, cuius est in rem publicam semper merito laudata constantia, si L. Domitium, praestantissimum civem, si Appium Claudium, pari nobilitate et voluntate praeditum, si P. Scipionem, clarissimum virum maiorumque suorum simillimum, res publica tenere potuisset, certe eis consularibus non esset Pompeianus
30 despiciendus senatus. Utrum igitur aequius, utrum melius rei publicae fuit, Cn. Pompeium an sectorem Cn. Pompei vivere Antonium? Qui vero praetorii! Quorum princeps M. Cato idemque omnium gentium virtute princeps. Quid

[20] *add. Naugerius*
[21] *add. R. Klotz*

---

[50] Spelling uncertain; see SB, *Two Studies*[2], 5 s.v. Sex. Albedius.
[51] Of 49, L. Cornelius Lentulus Crus and C. Claudius Marcellus. Cicero's real opinion of them and the consulars (except

he has become a member. I do not know Sextus Albisius,[50] but I have never met anyone scurrilous enough to deny that he deserves a place in Antonius' senate. I think I have left a few out, but I could not fail to mention those who came to mind.

Relying then upon this senate, he despises the Pompeian senate, which included ten of us consulars. If all of them were alive, this war would never have taken place; audacity would have yielded to authority. How much the others would have contributed to our protection may be inferred from the fact that I, the sole survivor out of many, have crushed and broken the audacity of this rampaging pirate with the help of you gentlemen. [14] But if Fortune had not snatched Servius Sulpicius away from us a little while ago and previously his colleague Marcus Marcellus (what men they were, what Romans!), if the Republic could have kept the two consuls,[51] great patriots both, who were driven out of Italy at the same time, and Lucius Afranius, that fine commander, and Publius Lentulus, an outstanding citizen in general and particularly in the matter of my restoration, and Marcus Bibulus, whose steadfast loyalty to the Republic has always been deservedly praised, and that fine Roman Lucius Domitius, and Appius Claudius, whose patriotism matched his lofty birth, and the illustrious Publius Scipio, the very image of his ancestors—with those consulars assuredly the Pompeian senate would not have been contemptible. Which then better suited and benefited the Republic, that Gnaeus Pompeius live or Gnaeus Pompeius' *sector*,[52] Marcus Antonius? But what of the ex-praetors! Chief among them was Marcus

perhaps for P. Lentulus Spinther) was very much less flattering than he pretends.　　　　[52] See 2.39, n. 37.

reliquos clarissimos viros commemorem? Nostis omnis. Magis vereor ne longum me in enumerando quam ne ingratum in praetereundo putetis. Qui aedilicii, qui tribunicii, qui quaestorii! Quid multa? Talis senatorum et dignitas et multitudo fuit ut magna excusatione opus eis sit qui in illa castra non venerunt.

Nunc reliqua attendite.

[15] "Victum Ciceronem ducem habuistis."

Eo libentius 'ducem' audio quod certe ille dicit invitus; nam de 'victo' nihil laboro. Fatum enim meum est sine re publica nec vinci posse nec vincere.

"Macedoniam munitis exercitibus."

Et quidem fratri tuo qui a vobis nihil degenerat extorsimus.

"Africam commisistis Varo bis capto."

Hic cum Gaio fratre putat se litigare.

"In Syriam Cassium misistis."

Non igitur sentis huic causae orbem terrae patere, te extra munitiones tuas vestigium ubi imprimas non habere?

31   "Cascam tribunatum gerere passi estis."

Quid ergo? Ut Marullum, ut Caesetium a re publica removeremus eum per quem ut neque idem hoc posthac neque multa eius modi accidere possent consecuti sumus?

---

53 By sanctioning the seizure of Macedonia by Marcus Brutus. For the supposed enabling role of Hirtius and Octavian, cf. n. 33 above.   54 Sex. Quinctilius Varus was taken prisoner at Corfinium in 49 and presumably again in Caesar's African campaign in 46.   55 C. Antonius was captured by the Pompeian admiral M. Octavius in 49. News of his second capture in Macedonia in March 43, at the surrender of Apollonia to Marcus Brutus, would by now have reached Rome.   56 Tribunes in 44, arbitrarily dismissed from office by Caesar in late Jan. or Feb.

Cato, chief also in virtue among all mankind. Why should I remind you of the other illustrious figures? You know them all. I am more afraid of your thinking me long-winded in the enumeration than of appearing ungrateful in the omission. What of the ex-aediles, the ex-tribunes of the plebs, the ex-quaestors! In a word, the rank and number of the senators were such that any who did not join that camp are in sore need of an excuse.

Now listen to the rest.

[15] "You have as your leader the vanquished Cicero."

I am the more gratified to hear the word 'leader' because he certainly uses it against his will. As for 'vanquished,' that does not trouble me. It is my fate that apart from the Republic I can neither be vanquished nor vanquish.

"You fortify Macedonia with armies."[53]

Yes, and we have wrenched it away from your brother, who is quite worthy of the rest of your family.

"You have entrusted Africa to Varus, a prisoner twice over."[54]

Antonius thinks he's having a dispute with his brother Gaius.[55]

"You have sent Cassius to Syria."

So don't you perceive that the whole world lies open to this cause of ours, whereas you have nowhere outside your fortifications to set your foot?

"You have allowed Casca to hold the tribunate."   31

And why not? Were we to remove him from public life like Marullus and Caesetius,[56] when we have him to thank that the dismissal of a tribune from office and many similar proceedings cannot occur in future?

"Vectigalia Iulianis Lupercis ademistis."

Lupercorum mentionem facere audet neque illius diei memoriam perhorrescit quo ausus est obrutus vino, unguentis oblitus, nudus gementem populum Romanum ad servitutem cohortari?

"Veteranorum colonias, deductas lege senatus consulto sustulistis."

Nos sustulimus an contra lege comitiis centuriatis lata sanximus? Vide ne tu veteranos, eos tamen qui erant perditi, perdideris in eumque locum deduxeris ex quo ipsi iam sentiunt se numquam exituros.

32 "Massiliensibus iure belli adempta reddituros vos pollicemini."

Nihil disputo de 'iure belli'—magis facilis disputatio est quam necessaria—illud tamen animadvertite, patres conscripti, quam sit huic rei publicae natus hostis Antonius, qui tanto opere eam civitatem oderit quam scit huic rei publicae semper fuisse amicissimam.

[16] "Neminem Pompeianum qui vivat teneri lege Hirtia dictitatis."

Quis, quaeso, iam legis Hirtiae mentionem facit? Cuius non minus arbitror latorem ipsum quam eos de quibus lata est paenitere. Omnino mea quidem sententia legem illam appellare fas non est; et, ut sit lex, non debemus illam Hirti legem putare.

---

57 Caesar added a third college of Luperci to the two previously existing, gave it his name, and set Antony over it (Cass. Dio 45.30.2). The Luperci celebrated the festival of the Lupercalia on 15 Feb., and Antony as Lupercus offered Caesar a crown in 44 (2.84–87).

58 A consular law passed in early 43 (see 10.17) replaced flawed legislation of Antony and sanctioned colonies of veterans settled by Caesar and, after his death, by Antony.

"You have deprived the Julian Luperci of their revenues."

Does he dare make mention of the Luperci?[57] Does he not shudder at the memory of that day when soaked in wine, smeared with unguents, and naked he dared to urge a groaning Roman people into slavery?

"You have abolished by a senatorial decree colonies of veterans legally established."

Have we abolished them, or have we not on the contrary legalized them by a bill passed in the Centuriate Assembly?[58] You had best consider whether *you* have not ruined the veterans (those, it is true, who were ruined already)[59] and brought them into a situation from which they themselves now realize there is no way out.

"You are promising to restore to the Massilians what 32 was taken away from them by the right of war."

I will not debate about 'the right of war' (that would be more easy than needful), but please observe, Members of the Senate, what a born enemy Antonius is to this Republic since he so intensely hates a community that he knows has always been a most devoted friend to this Republic!

[16] "You keep maintaining that no Pompeian now living is bound by the Hirtian law."

Who, I ask you, talks about the Hirtian law[60] any more? I daresay its sponsor disapproves of it no less than do those against whom it was passed. In my opinion, it is not right to call it a law at all; and supposing it to be a law, we ought not to think of it as Hirtius' law.

---

[59] I.e., those who had squandered their bounties from Caesar and looked to Antony to mend their fortunes.

[60] This law penalizing supporters of Pompey may have been carried by Hirtius as tribune, perhaps in 48.

"Apuleiana pecunia Brutum subornastis."

Quid? Si omnibus suis copiis excellentem virum res publica armasset, quem tandem bonum paeniteret? Nec enim sine pecunia exercitum alere nec sine exercitu fratrem tuum capere potuisset.

33 "Securi percussos Petr⟨ae⟩um[22] et Menedemum, civitate donatos et hospites Caesaris, laudastis."

Non 'lauda⟨vi⟩mus'[23] quod ne audivimus quidem. Valde enim nobis in tanta perturbatione rei publicae de duobus nequissimis Graeculis cogitandum fuit!

"Theopompum, nudum, †non†[24] expulsum a Trebonio, confugere Alexandream neglexistis."

Magnum crimen senatus! De Theopompo, summo homine, neglximus, qui ubi terrarum sit, quid agat, vivat denique an mortuus sit, quis aut scit aut curat?

"Ser. Galbam eodem pugione succinctum in castris videtis."

Nihil tibi de Galba respondeo, fortissimo et constantissimo civi: coram aderit; praesens et ipse et ille quem insimulas 'pugio' respondebit.

"Milites aut meos aut veteranos contraxistis tamquam ad exitium eorum qui Caesarem occiderant: et eosdem nec opinantis ad quaestoris sui aut imperatoris aut commilitonum suorum pericula impulistis."

---

[22] *corr. Haupt*   [23] *corr. Lambinus*   [24] vi *Clark: del.* ς

---

[61] Both were men of considerable standing; see Index. It appears that Brutus had them executed.   [62] Possibly Theopompus of Cnidus, a writer on myth and an influential friend of Caesar.   [63] Sc. with which he had stabbed Caesar.

[64] Antony, quaestor in Caesar's army in 51 (cf. 2.50).

"You have furnished Brutus with the money in the care of Apuleius."

What of it? If the Republic had armed that excellent person with all its resources, what honest man, I ask you, would feel disapproval? And he could neither have maintained an army without money nor taken your brother prisoner without an army.

"You have commended the execution of Petraeus and 33 Menedemus, who had been granted Roman citizenship and were guest-friends of Caesar."

We have not 'commended' something we have not even heard of. I suppose we have nothing more important to think about in this national upheaval than a couple of rascally little Greeks![61]

"Theopompus[62] was stripped bare and expelled by Trebonius. He fled to Alexandria. You have done nothing."

Here indeed the senate has committed a serious crime! We have done nothing about the great Theopompus! And where in the world he is, what he is doing, whether he is alive or dead in fact, who either knows or cares?

"You see in your camp Servius Galba still wearing that same dagger."[63]

I make you no answer about our most gallant and resolute fellow countryman Galba. He will be present in person. He himself and the 'dagger,' with which you reproach him, will reply on the spot.

"You have mustered soldiers, either those belonging to me or veterans, as though to destroy Caesar's killers, and you have surprised them into endangering their own (former) quaestor or imperator[64] or their own comrades in arms."

Scilicet verba dedimus, decepimus: ignorabat legio Martia, quarta, nesciebant veterani quid ageretur; non illi senatus auctoritatem, non libertatem populi sequebantur: Caesaris mortem ulcisci volebant, quam omnes fatalem fuisse arbitrabantur; te videlicet salvum, beatum, floren-

34 tem esse cupiebant. [17] O miser cum re, tum hoc ipso quod non sentis quam miser sis!

Sed maximum crimen audite:

"Denique quid non aut probastis aut fecistis quod faciat, si reviviscat—"

Quis? Credo enim, adferet aliquod scelerati hominis exemplum!

"—Cn. Pompeius ipse—"

O nos turpis, si quidem Cn. Pompeium imitati sumus!

"—aut filius eius, si modo possit?"

'Poterit,' mihi crede: nam paucis diebus et in domum et in hortos paternos immigrabit.

"Postremo negatis pacem fieri posse, nisi aut emisero Brutum aut frumento iuvero."

Alii istuc negant: ego vero, ne si ista quidem feceris, umquam tecum pacem huic civitati futuram puto.

"Quid? Hoc placetne veteranis istis quibus adhuc omnia integra sunt,—"

Nihil vidi tam integrum quam ut oppugnare imperatorem incipiant quem tanto studio consensuque ostenderint ⟨quam oderint⟩.[25]

---

25 offenderint *bsv*: ostenderint *t* | *suppl. Lehmann*

Oh, yes indeed, we hoodwinked them, we took them in! The Martian Legion and the Fourth were ignorant of what was going on; the veterans did not know! They were not supporting the authority of the senate and the liberty of the people, they were out to avenge Caesar's death, which they all considered to have been fate-ordained. As for you, naturally they wanted you safe and happy and flourishing! [17] What a miserable creature you are, not only in actuality but from the very fact that you do not realize *how* miserable! 34

But hear the heaviest charge of all:

"To sum up, what have you not approved or done which, if he came back to life, would not be done by—"

By whom? No doubt he will produce some exemplary villain!

"—Gnaeus Pompeius himself—"

We are disgraced indeed if we have made Gnaeus Pompeius our model!

"—or his son, if he but had the power?"

Oh, he will 'have the power,' take my word. In a few days' time he will be moving into his father's house and suburban estate.

"Finally, you say peace cannot be made, unless I let Brutus go or assist him with grain."

Others issue that ultimatum, but for my part, I do not think this community will ever have peace with you, even if you perform those acts.

"Well, does this policy please veterans in your army who as yet are still quite free to choose,—"

Nothing I have seen could be so free as their choice to start attacking a commander for whom they have shown the extent of their hatred with such zeal and unanimity.

35   "—quos iam[26] vos adsentationibus et venenatis muneribus venistis depravatum."

An corrupti sunt quibus persuasum sit foedissimum
hostem iustissimo bello persequi?

"At militibus inclusis opem fertis. Nihil moror eos salvos esse et ire quo libet, si tantum modo patiuntur perire
eum qui meruit."

Quam benigne! ‹Ei›[27] denique usi liberalitate Antoni
milites imperatorem reliquerint[28] et se ad hostem metu
perterriti contulerint[29] per quos si non stetisset, non Dolabella prius imperatori suo quam Antonius etiam collegae
parentasset.

36   "Concordiae factam esse mentionem scribitis in senatu
et legatos esse consularis quinque. Difficile est credere eos
qui me praecipitem egerint, aequissimas condiciones fe-
rentem—et tamen ex his aliquid remittere cogitantem—
putare aliquid moderate aut humane esse facturos. Vix
etiam veri simile est, qui iudicaverint hostem Dolabellam
ob rectissimum facinus, eosdem nobis parcere posse idem
sentientibus."

Parumne videtur omnium facinorum sibi cum Dolabella societatem initam confiteri? Nonne cernitis ex uno fonte
omnia scelera manare? Ipse denique fatetur, hoc quidem
satis acute, non posse eos qui 'hostem Dolabellam iudica-

26 quos iam *Clark*: quoniam *btv*: quem *s*
27 *add. SB*   28 *SB*: -querunt *D*
29 *SB*: -lerunt *D*

65 I.e., but for the troops raised by Octavian and the desertion
of Antony's two legions, he would have seized and put to death his
enemies in the senate (see §37: *supplicia nobis*) as an offering to

"—whom you have now come to pervert by means of 35
flatteries and poisoned gifts?"

Can it be that they have been corrupted because they
have been persuaded to hunt down a most foul enemy in a
most legitimate war?

"You claim you are merely bringing help to the beleaguered troops. I do not mind if they go in safety wherever
they please, so long as they let perish the individual who
has deserved it."

How kind! In a word, by Antonius' generous terms the
soldiers will desert their commander and betake themselves in terror to the enemy, those soldiers but for whose
opposition Dolabella would not have made a grave-offer-
ing to his dead commander prior to Antonius' having made
one to his colleague.[65]

"You write that the subject of reconciliation has been 36
brought up in the senate and that the envoys are five consulars.[66] It is difficult to believe that those who drove me
headlong when I was offering very fair terms—and was
even thinking of making further concessions—to suppose
that they will do anything moderate and reasonable. Also,
it is scarcely probable that the same people who declared
Dolabella a public enemy because of an eminently proper
action can spare me, sharing, as I do, his sentiments."

Is that not a clear admission that he has entered into
partnership with Dolabella for all manner of villainies?
Don't you perceive that all the crimes flow from a single
source? Antonius himself finally admits (quite clever of
him, I must say) that those 'who declared Dolabella a pub-

Caesar's *manes*, even before Dolabella arrived in Asia and killed
Trebonius.   [66] Cf. 12.18.

verint ob rectissimum facinus'—ita enim videtur Anto-
37 nio—sibi 'parcere idem sentienti.' [18] Quid huic facias
qui hoc litteris memoriaeque mandarit, ita sibi convenisse
cum Dolabella ut ille Trebonium et, si posset, etiam Brutum, Cassium, discruciatos necaret, eadem ipse inhiberet
supplicia nobis? O conservandus civis cum tam pio iusto-
que foedere! Is etiam queritur condiciones suas repu-
diatas, aequas quidem et verecundas, ut haberet Galliam
ultimam, aptissimam ad bellum renovandum instruen-
dumque provinciam; ut Alaudae in tertia decuria iudicarent, id est ut perfugium scelerum esset [cum][30] turpissi-
mis rei publicae sordibus; ut acta sua rata essent, cuius
nullum remanet consulatus vestigium. Cavebat etiam L.
Antonio, qui fuerat aequissimus agri privati et publici de-
cempedator, Nucula et Lentone collega.

38   "Quam ob rem vos potius animadvertite utrum sit elegantius et partibus utilius Treboni mortem persequi an
Caesaris, et utrum sit aequius concurrere nos quo facilius reviviscat Pompeianorum causa totiens iugulata an
consentire ne ludibrio simus inimicis—"

Si esset 'iugulata,' numquam exsurgeret: quod tibi
tuisque contingat. 'Utrum,' inquit, 'elegantius.' Atqui hoc
39 bello de elegantia quaeritur! 'Et partibus utilius.' 'Partes,'
furiose, dicuntur in foro, in curia. Bellum contra patriam nefarium suscepisti; oppugnas Mutinam, circumse-

30 del. Garatoni: quam Clark

67 See 1.20.
68 By insisting on the maintenance of assignments of land
made by the Board of Seven, of which Nucula and Lento were
members, and L. Antonius the chairman (cf. 8.26).

lic enemy because of an eminently proper action' (for so it seems to Antonius) 'cannot spare him, sharing, as he does, Dolabella's sentiments.' [18] What are we to do with a man who puts in a letter, for the record, that he had arranged with Dolabella for him to kill Trebonius and, if he could, Brutus and Cassius, first putting them to the torture, while he himself should inflict the same cruelties upon us? Indeed a citizen to be preserved along with so righteous and just a compact! He even complains that his terms were rejected, fair and modest as they were: namely, that he have Outer Gaul, a province ideally suited for resuming the war and supplying its requirements; that the Larks be jurors in the third panel, which is to say that the foulest dregs of the Republic have protection for their crimes;[67] and that his consular acts be valid, although not a trace of his consulship remains. He also looked after the interests of Lucius Antonius, who had been a most equitable surveyor of public and private land, with Nucula and Lento for colleagues.[68]

"Therefore I ask you gentlemen to observe which is in better taste and more expedient for the party, to avenge Trebonius' death or Caesar's; and which is fairer, for us to clash so as to facilitate the revival of the Pompeians' cause, so often put to the slaughter, or to work together, so as not to be a laughingstock to our enemies—"

If the cause had been 'put to the slaughter,' it would never rise again, which is what I wish for you and your followers. 'Which is in better taste?' says he. To be sure, *taste* is what this war is all about! 'And more expedient for the party.' We speak of 'party,' you lunatic, in the Forum and in the senate-house. You have commenced a wicked war against your native land. You are attacking Mutina, be-

37

38

39

des consulem designatum; bellum contra te duo consules
gerunt cumque eis pro praetore Caesar; cuncta contra te
Italia armata est. Istas tu partis potius quam a populo Romano defectionem vocas? Potius Treboni mortem quam
Caesaris persequimur? Treboni satis persecuti sumus
hoste iudicato Dolabella; Caesaris mors facillime defenditur oblivione et silentio. Sed videte quid moliatur: cum
mortem Caesaris ulciscendam putat, mortem proponit
non eis solum qui illam rem gesserunt sed eis etiam si qui
non moleste tulerunt.

40   [19] "—quibus, utri nostrum ceciderint, lucro futurum
est, quod spectaculum adhuc ipsa Fortuna vitavit, ne videret unius corporis duas acies lanista Cicerone dimicantis:
qui usque eo felix est ut isdem ornamentis deceperit vos
quibus deceptum Caesarem gloriatus est."

Pergit in me maledicta, quasi vero ei pulcherrime prio-
ra processerint: quem ego inustum verissimis maledicto-
rum notis tradam hominum memoriae sempiternae. Ego
'lanista'? Et quidem non insipiens: deteriores enim iugula-
ri cupio, meliores vincere. 'Utri ceciderint,' scribit, 'lucro
41 nobis futurum.' O praeclarum lucrum, cum te victore—
quod di omen avertant!—beata mors eorum futura sit qui
e vita excesserint sine tormentis. A me 'deceptos' ait 'isdem ornamentis' Hirtium et Caesarem. Quod, quaeso, ad-

---

69 Here *defendere* must have this meaning (= *ulcisci*), which it
has in juristic texts (*OLD* s.v. 9).

70 The antecedent is "our enemies" (*inimicis*, i.e. anti-Caesar-
ians, like Cicero), which was the last word quoted above by
Cicero, where he interrupted the flow of Antony's thought midway through §38.

71 A *lanista* was a trainer who oversaw a school of gladiators, to

sieging a consul-elect. Two consuls are waging war against you, and the propraetor Caesar with them. All Italy is in arms against you. Do you call your following a 'party' rather than a defection from the Roman people? Is it preferable for us to avenge Trebonius' death instead of Caesar's? We avenged Trebonius' death sufficiently by declaring Dolabella a public enemy; Caesar's is most easily vindicated[69] with silent oblivion. But notice what he is up to. Holding that Caesar's death calls for vengeance, he proposes death not only for those who did the deed but also for any whom it did not displease.

[19] "—for whom[70] it will be a windfall whichever of us go down, a spectacle that thus far Fortune herself has avoided, not caring to see two opposing battle lines drawn from one corps, fighting each other with Cicero as gladiator-trainer.[71] He is lucky enough to have deceived you with the same compliments with which he has boasted of having deceived Caesar."

He goes on flinging insults at me as though his previous efforts in that line had been a brilliant success; but I shall hand him down to everlasting memory, branded with the marks of insults which are true to the letter. So I am a 'gladiator-trainer'? Yes, and I know my job. I want to see the bad ones killed off and the good ones win. 'Whichever go down,' he writes, 'will be a windfall' for us. A fine windfall, when if *you* win—may the gods avert the omen!—happy will be the death of those who have quit their lives without torture. He says that Hirtius and Caesar have been 'deceived' by me 'with the same compliments.' What compli-

40

41

which Antony appears to allude in the word "corps," *corpus* (lit. "body").

huc a me est tributum Hirtio ornamentum? Nam Caesari
plura et maiora debentur. Deceptum autem patrem Caesarem a me dicere audes? Tu, tu, inquam, illum occidisti
Lupercalibus: cuius, homo ingratissime, flamonium cur
reliquisti?

Sed iam videte magni et clari viri admirabilem gravitatem atque constantiam:

42   "Mihi quidem constat nec meam contumeliam nec
meorum ferre, nec deserere partis quas Pompeius odivit
nec veteranos sedibus suis moveri pati nec singulos ad cruciatum trahi nec fallere fidem quam dedi Dolabellae—"

Omitto alia: 'fidem Dolabellae,' sanctissimi viri, deserere homo pius non potest. Quam 'fidem'? An optimi
cuiusque caedis, urbis et Italiae partitionis, vastandarum
diripiendarumque provinciarum? Nam quid erat aliud
quod inter Antonium et Dolabellam, impurissimos parrici-
das, foedere et fide sanciretur?

43   "—nec Lepidi societatem violare, piissimi hominis—"
Tibi cum Lepido 'societas' aut cum ullo, non dicam
bono civi, sicut ille est, sed homine sano? Id agis ut Lepidum aut impium aut insanum existimari velis. Nihil agis—
quamquam adfirmare de altero difficile est—de Lepido
praesertim, quem ego metuam numquam; bene sperabo,
dum licebit. Revocare te a furore Lepidus voluit, non adiutor esse dementiae. Tu porro ne pios quidem, sed 'piis-
simos' quaeris et, quod verbum omnino nullum in lingua

---

[72] By causing such odium against Caesar when Antony offered
him a crown on 15 Feb. 44.   [73] Antony failed to have himself inaugurated priest of the deified Caesar (Divus Iulius): 2.110;
cf. §47 below.   [74] A clear intimation of mistrust, like the
aside in the previous sentence.

ment, pray, have I bestowed on Hirtius up till now? As for Caesar, he deserves more and greater. But do you dare to say that the elder Caesar was deceived by me? You, yes, *you*, I say, killed him at the Lupercalia.[72] And why have you abandoned his priesthood, ingrate?[73]

Now observe the high seriousness and resolution of a great and famous man:

"As for me, I am determined to put up with insult nei-   42
ther to myself nor to my friends, and not to desert the party which Pompeius hated, nor yet to allow the veterans to be evicted from their homes and dragged off to torture one by one, nor yet to break my pledge to Dolabella—"

The rest I leave aside, but as for his not being able, as a man of honor, to prove false to his 'pledge' given to that model of integrity, Dolabella: 'pledge' concerning what? Concerning the massacre of our best citizens, the parceling out of Rome and Italy, the plunder and devastation of the provinces? What else was there to be guaranteed by pact and pledge between those two foul traitors, Antonius and Dolabella?

"—nor yet to violate my alliance with Lepidus, the hon-   43
orablest of men—"

You in 'alliance with Lepidus' or any other—I won't say good citizen, as he is, but sane man? You make it your aim to wish Lepidus to be thought either a traitor or a madman. Especially in Lepidus' case—even though it is difficult to be certain concerning another person—you are wasting your time. I shall never fear Lepidus, and I shall hope well of him as long as I can.[74] Lepidus has wished to recall you from your frenzy, not to be your abettor in folly. And then you seek not merely honorable but 'honorablest' men, im-

Latina est, id propter tuam divinam pietatem novum in-
ducis.

44   "—nec Plancum prodere participem consiliorum."

'Plancum participem'? Cuius memorabilis ac divina
virtus lucem adfert rei publicae—nisi forte eum subsidio
tibi venire arbitraris cum fortissimis legionibus, maximo
equitatu peditatu Gallorum—quique, nisi ante eius adventum rei publicae poenas dederis, ille huius belli feret
principatum. Quamquam enim prima praesidia utiliora rei
publicae sunt, tamen extrema sunt gratiora.

45   [20] Sed iam se colligit et ad extremum incipit philoso-
phari:

"Si me rectis sensibus euntem di immortales, ut spero,
adiuverint, vivam libenter. Sin autem me aliud fatum ma-
net, praecipio gaudia suppliciorum vestrorum. Namque si
victi Pompeiani tam insolentes sunt, victores quales futuri
sint vos potius experiemini."

'Praecipias' licet 'gaudia': non enim tibi cum Pompeianis, sed cum universa re publica bellum est. Omnes te di
homines, summi medii infimi, cives peregrini, viri mulie-
res, liberi servi oderunt. Sensimus hoc nuper falso nuntio;
vero prope diem sentiemus. Quae si tecum ipse recolueris,
aequiore animo et maiore consolatione moriere.

46   "Denique summa iudici mei spectat huc ut meorum
iniurias ferre possim, si aut oblivisci velint ipsi fecisse aut

---

75 The second-century grammarian Caper quoted *piissimus*
("honorablest") from Cicero's own letters according to later testimony (Cic. *Ep. frag.* 17.3 ed. Watt). It is found in many post-Au-
gustan writers.
76 Of Antony's death, presumably.

porting a new word which does not exist at all in the Latin language to gratify your marvelous sense of honor![75]

"—nor yet to betray Plancus, the partner of my coun- 44 sels."

Plancus your 'partner'? Plancus, whose unforgettable, superhuman manliness is a beacon of hope to the Republic—unless, perhaps, you think he is coming to help you with his most brave legions and his host of Gallic horse and foot!—and is one who will take a leading role in this war, unless you pay your penalty to the Republic before he arrives. Though the help that comes first is of greater use to the Republic, nonetheless, the help that comes last earns more gratitude.

[20] But now he takes stock and in conclusion begins to 45 philosophize:

"If the immortal gods help me as I go my way in rectitude of purpose, which I trust they will, I shall live in good cheer. But if a different fate awaits me, I joyfully anticipate what you will suffer. For if the Pompeians are so insolent in defeat, what they will be like in victory you will find out rather than I."

'Joyfully anticipate' you may! You are not at war with Pompeians but with the entire Republic. All gods and men, the highest, the lowest and those in between, citizens and foreigners, men and women, free men and slaves, all hate you. This was proved to us the other day by a false report,[76] and any day now will be proved by a true one. If you reflect on this quietly, you will die with an easier mind and better consolation.

"Finally, the sum of my judgment is to this effect: I can 46 bear the injuries done to me by my friends, if they on their side should be willing to forget that they have done them,

281

ulcisci parati sunt una nobiscum Caesaris mortem."

Hac Antoni sententia cognita dubitaturumne A. Hirtium aut C. Pansam consules putatis quin ad Antonium transeant, Brutum obsideant, Mutinam expugnare cupiant? Quid de Pansa et Hirtio loquor? Caesar, singulari pietate adulescens, poteritne se tenere quin D. Bruti sanguine poenas patrias persequatur? Itaque fecerunt ut his litteris lectis ad munitiones propius accederent. Quo maior adulescens Caesar, maioreque deorum immortalium beneficio rei publicae natus est, qui nulla specie paterni nominis nec pietate abductus umquam est et intellegit maximam pietatem conservatione patriae contineri.

47 Quod si partium certamen esset, quarum omnino nomen exstinctum est, Antoniusne potius et Ventidius partis Caesaris defenderent quam primum Caesar, adulescens summa pietate et memoria parentis sui, deinde Pansa et Hirtius, qui quasi cornua duo tenuerunt Caesaris tum cum illae vere partes vocabantur? Hae vero quae sunt partes, cum alteris senatus auctoritas, populi Romani libertas, rei publicae salus proposita sit, alteris caedes bonorum, urbis Italiaeque partitio?

[21] Veniamus aliquando ad clausulam.

"Legatos venire non credo."

Bene me novit; veniat qui velit,[31] proposito praesertim exemplo Dolabellae. Sanctiore erunt, credo, iure legati

---

[31] *SB*: velim quo venias *b*: quod venias *t*: bellum quod veniat *v*

---

[77] Cicero plays on two meanings of the verb *accedo*: "to draw close" (a) in the sense of achieving a meeting of two minds and (b) physically, as in the movement of troops.

or if they are ready to make common cause with us in avenging Caesar's death."

When they learn this sentiment of Antonius', do you suppose the consuls Aulus Hirtius and Gaius Pansa will hesitate to go over to Antonius and besiege Brutus and be eager to take Mutina by storm? Why do I speak of Hirtius and Pansa? Will Caesar, a young man with a remarkable sense of family duty, be able to restrain himself from seeking vengeance for his father by the blood of Decimus Brutus? And so, after reading this letter, they proceeded to draw closer—to the siege works.[77] Wherefore, greater is young Caesar, and greater is the kindness of the immortal gods in producing for the Republic a man who has never been led astray by the show of his father's name or by filial duty, and who understands that the highest duty of a son lies in the preservation of his native land. But if this were a struggle of parties, the very name of which is extinct, would Antonius and Ventidius be standing up for Caesar's party rather than, in the first place, Caesar, a young man with the highest sense of family duty and devoted to his father's memory, and, in the second place, Pansa and Hirtius, who captained Caesar's two wings, as it were, when that party was truly so called? But what parties are these, when the aim on the one side is the authority of the senate, the freedom of the Roman people, and the survival of the Republic, while the other aims at the massacre of honest men, the parceling out of Rome and Italy?

[21] Let us at length come to the finale:

"I do not believe the envoys are coming."

Well does he know me. Let him go who chooses, especially with Dolabella's example before his eyes. Envoys, no doubt, will be shielded with more sanctity than the two

quam duo consules contra quos arma fert, quam Caesar
cuius patris flamen est, quam consul designatus quem oppugnat, quam Mutina quam obsidet, quam patria cui igni
ferroque minitatur!

48   "Cum venerint, quae postulant cognoscam."

Quin tu abis in malam pestem malumque cruciatum?
Ad te quisquam veniat nisi Ventidi similis? Oriens incendium qui restinguerent summos viros misimus; repudiasti:
nunc in tantam flammam tamque inveteratam mittamus,
cum locum tibi reliquum non modo ad pacem sed ne ad
deditionem quidem feceris?

Hanc ego epistulam, patres conscripti, non quo illum dignum putarem, recitavi, sed ut confessionibus ipsius
49 omnia patefacta eius parricidia videretis. Cum hoc pacem
M. Lepidus, vir ornatissimus omnibus et virtutis et fortunae bonis, si haec audiret,[32] aut vellet ⟨aut⟩[33] denique
fieri posse arbitraretur? "Prius undis flamma," ut ait poeta
nescio quis, prius denique omnia quam aut cum Antoniis
res publica aut cum re publica Antonii redeant in gratiam.
Monstra quaedam ista et portenta sunt et prodigia rei publicae. Moveri sedibus huic urbi melius est atque in alias,
si fieri possit, terras demigrare, unde Antoniorum "nec facta nec nomen audiat," quam illos, Caesaris virtute eiectos,
Bruti retentos, intra haec moenia videre. Optatissimum
est vincere; secundum est nullum casum pro dignitate et
libertate patriae non ferendum putare. Quod reliquum

---

[32] SB (transp. denique ante fieri): videret denique bsv:
denique t
    [33] add. ς

---

[78] See n. 73.   [79] Author unknown. A verb "will mingle"
is understood; cf. Cass. Dio 55.13.1.

consuls, against whom Antonius bears arms, or Caesar, of whose father he is priest,[78] or the consul-elect, whom he is attacking, or Mutina, which he is besieging, or his native land, which he is threatening with fire and sword!

"When they come, I shall learn their demands." 48

To the devil with you! To the rack with you! Would anyone come to you except a fellow like Ventidius? We sent persons of the highest quality to put out the incipient blaze: you rebuffed them. Are we to send now, to a fire that has spread so wide and taken such hold, now that you have left yourself no room for capitulation, let alone peace?

I have read out this letter, Members of the Senate, not because I thought the author of it worthy of being heeded, but to let you see all his treasons laid bare by his own confessions. Would Marcus Lepidus, so richly en- 49 dowed with all the blessings of nature and fortune, wish peace with this man or even think it possible if he were hearing these words of Antonius? "Sooner fire with water," as some poet or other has expressed it,[79] sooner anything in fact, than the Republic will be reconciled with the Antonii or the Antonii with the Republic. They are, as it were, monsters and portents and prodigies of the Republic. It would be better for this city to be moved from her foundations and to migrate to other lands, if that were possible, where she would "hear neither deeds nor name"[80] of the Antonii, than to see once more inside her walls men who were thrown out by Caesar's prowess and held back from returning by Brutus'. Best of all is victory; second-best is to think no misfortune unbearable, if it be for our native

[80] Fragment of an unknown play, several times quoted in Cicero's letters.

est, non est tertium, sed postremum omnium, maximam turpitudinem suscipere vitae cupiditate.

50   Quae cum ita sint, de mandatis litterisque M. Lepidi, viri clarissimi, Servilio adsentior, et hoc amplius censeo:

"Magnum Pompeium, Gnaei filium, pro patris maiorumque suorum animo studioque in rem publicam suaque pristina virtute, industria, voluntate fecisse quod suam eorumque quos secum haberet operam senatui populoque Romano pollicitus esset, eamque rem senatui populoque Romano gratam acceptamque esse, eique honori dignitatique eam rem fore."

Hoc vel coniungi cum hoc senatus consulto licet vel seiungi potest separatimque perscribi, ut proprio senatus consulto Pompeius collaudatus esse videatur.

land's dignity and freedom. That leaves no third-best, only the worst of all, to plumb the lowest depth of dishonor out of a craving for life.

In these circumstances, concerning the message and 50 letter of the illustrious Marcus Lepidus, I agree with Servilius, and I further propose as follows:

"That Magnus Pompeius, son of Gnaeus, acted worthily of the spirit and patriotic zeal of his father and ancestors and of his own former prowess, diligence, and goodwill in that he promised his services and those of his companions to the senate and people of Rome; and that his action is welcome and pleasing to the senate and people of Rome and will redound to his honor and dignity."

This can either be conjoined with the senatorial decree now under discussion or separated and drafted independently, so that Pompeius may be seen to have been commended by a decree of the senate special to himself.

PHILIPPIC 14

INTRODUCTION

On 14 April 43,[1] the forces under the command of the
consul Gaius Pansa, who was marching north along the
Via Aemilia to join the armies of Hirtius and Octavian at
Mutina, were ambushed by Antony near Forum Gallorum,
a town lying *c.* 8 miles southeast of Mutina on the Via
Aemilia. Pansa and his troops quickly found themselves
in grave difficulty, and the wounds that Pansa received
(14.26) caused him to be removed from the battlefield
to the nearby town of Bononia, where he died of those
wounds on 23 April (*Fam.* 11.13.2). Eventually, however,
the engagement on 14 April ended in a major defeat for
Antony at the hands of Hirtius, who, upon learning of the
fighting, hurried from his camp at Mutina to his colleague's
support and arrived on the scene unexpectedly with two
veteran legions (14.27). An eyewitness account of the battle is preserved in Cicero's correspondence (*Fam.* 10.30),
written by Servius Galba, who had been sent by Hirtius to
accompany Pansa on the last 100 miles of his journey.

News of the victory reached Rome on 20 April (14.12,
16) and made all the greater sensation because it followed

[1] The date given for the battle in *Fam.* 10.30.1, 15 Apr. (*a.d.
xvii Kal. Mai.*), appears to have suffered corruption and should be
corrected to 14 Apr. (*a.d. xvii⟨i⟩*) on the evidence of Ovid, *Fast.*
4.625–627 and *ILS* 108.

on a false report of an Antonian victory, which had arrived a day or two earlier and caused temporary panic (14.15, cf. 10).[2] On the 20th, a crowd escorted Cicero in triumph to the Capitol to offer thanks, and back to his house (14.12). On the next day, 21 April (14.14), the senate was summoned to the Temple of Jupiter Optimus Maximus on the Capitoline (14.8, 12, 27) to hear dispatches from the three commanders. That meeting was almost certainly convened by the city praetor M. Caecilius Cornutus, who assumed the duty of presiding over the senate in the absence of the two consuls, as was customary (e.g., *Fam.* 10.12.3; cf. *ad Brut.* 2.5.3), but Cornutus is nowhere directly addressed in Cicero's *Fourteenth Philippic*.

At the meeting on the 21st, the consular Publius Servilius spoke ahead of Cicero and proposed (1) the immediate resumption of civilian dress for that one day only in celebration of the news of Antony's defeat (14.2) and (2) a public thanksgiving (14.11). Servilius' first proposal is briefly countered by Cicero (14.2–3a), while he argues on the basis of Servilius' proposal for a public thanksgiving that Antony should logically and inevitably be formally declared a *hostis* at long last because such a celebration had never before been decreed to mark a victory over fellow citizens (14.6–10). The speech ends with a eulogy of the three republican commanders and their troops (14.24–35), and is capped by a formal motion to provide them with honors (14.36–38).

[2] Doubtless the false report was inspired by the initial defeat of Pansa's forces by Antony, before Hirtius sent reinforcements to reverse the situation (*Fam.* 10.30.3–4).

INTRODUCTION TO PHILIPPIC 14

STRUCTURE

Propositio

(1–10) War must continue
    (1–5) Goal must be the liberation of Decimus Brutus
    (6–10) Antony and his supporters deserve to be declared
    hostes

Argumentatio

(11–24a) Motion of P. Servilius should be modified
    (11–13a) The three commanders deserve the title *imperator*
    (13b–16) Cicero's enemies have failed in their plot against him
    (17–21a) Rivalry for leadership should be driven by patriotism
    (21b–24a) A public thanksgiving can only be celebrated over public enemies

Narratio

(24b–35) Heroism of the victors
    (24b–29a) The three commanders
    (29b–33) The soldiers
    (34–35) The relatives of the fallen soldiers

Sententia

(36–38) Honors for the victors

M. TULLI CICERONIS
IN M. ANTONIUM ORATIO
PHILIPPICA QUARTA DECIMA

1   [1] Si, ut ex litteris quae recitatae sunt, patres conscripti, sceleratissimorum hostium exercitum caesum fusumque cognovi, sic, id quod et omnes maxime optamus ⟨et⟩[1] ex ea victoria quae parta est consecutum arbitramur, D. Brutum egressum iam Mutina esse cognossem, propter cuius periculum ad saga issemus, propter eiusdem salutem redeundum ad pristinum vestitum sine ulla dubitatione censerem. Ante vero quam sit ea res quam avidissime civitas exspectat adlata, laetitia frui satis est maximae praeclarissimaeque pugnae; reditum ad vestitum confectae victoriae reservate. Confectio autem huius belli est D. Bruti salus.

2   Quae autem est ista sententia ut in hodiernum diem vestitus mutetur, deinde cras sagati prodeamus? Nos vero cum semel ad eum quem cupimus optamusque vestitum redierimus, id agamus ut eum in perpetuum retineamus. Nam hoc quidem cum turpe est, tum ne dis quidem im-

---

[1] *suppl. Naugerius*

294

MARCUS TULLIUS CICERO'S FOURTEENTH PHILIPPIC ORATION AGAINST MARCUS ANTONIUS

[1] Members of the Senate, the dispatches which have
been read out have told me that an army of very wicked enemies has been cut to pieces and routed. If those dispatches had also told me that Decimus Brutus has already
been liberated from the siege of Mutina, the goal that we
all especially pray for and believe has been achieved as a
result of the victory gained by our forces, then I would
have no hesitation in moving a return to our previous dress
on account of Brutus' deliverance, since it was on account
of his peril that we put on our military cloaks. But until the
news which the community is so impatiently awaiting arrives, it is enough to enjoy the happy knowledge of a great
and glorious battle. Reserve a return to normal dress for
final victory. And final victory in this war means Decimus
Brutus' rescue.

What sort of proposal do we have here, that we change
our dress only for today and reappear tomorrow in military
cloaks? No, when once we have returned to the dress we
want and pray for, let us make sure we keep it forever. For
it is indeed not only a disgraceful thing but one not even

mortalibus gratum, ab eorum aris, ad quas togati adieri-
3 mus, ad saga sumenda discedere. Atque animadverto, patres conscripti, quosdam huic favere sententiae quorum ea
mens idque consilium est ut, cum videant gloriosissimum
illum D. Bruto futurum diem quo die propter eius salutem
‹ad vestitum›[2] redierimus, hunc ei fructum eripere cupiant, ne memoriae posteritatique prodatur propter unius
civis periculum populum Romanum ad saga isse, propter
eiusdem salutem redisse ad togas. Tollite hanc: nullam tam
pravae sententiae causam reperietis.

Vos vero, patres conscripti, conservate auctoritatem
vestram, manete in sententia, tenete vestra memoria quod
saepe ostendistis, huius totius belli in unius viri fortissimi
4 et maximi vita positum esse discrimen. [2] Ad D. Brutum
liberandum legati missi principes civitatis qui illi hosti ac
parricidae denuntiarent ut a Mutina discederet; eiusdem
D. Bruti conservandi gratia consul sortitu ad bellum profectus A. Hirtius, cuius imbecillitatem valetudinis animi
virtus et spes victoriae confirmavit; Caesar cum exercitu
per se comparato cum prius his[3] pestibus rem publicam li-
berasset, ne quid postea sceleris oreretur, profectus est ad
eundem Brutum liberandum vicitque dolorem aliquem
5 domesticum patriae caritate. Quid C. Pansa egit aliud di-
lectibus habendis, pecuniis comparandis, senatus consul-
tis faciendis gravissimis in Antonium, nobis cohortandis,

---

[2] *add. Orelli*   [3] cum prius his *SB*: cum (eum *v*) primis *D*

---

[1] The text is uncertain: apparently a reference to hastening the
departure of Antony and his followers from Rome in late Nov.
[2] I.e., his grief over the murder of Caesar, his adoptive father,
did not prevent him from aiding D. Brutus, one of the assassins.

pleasing to the immortal gods for us first to approach their altars in togas, only to depart from there to put on our military cloaks again. And I notice, Members of the Senate, 3 that certain persons favor this proposal, whose purpose and plan is the following: since they see that the day we return to normal dress on account of Decimus Brutus' deliverance will be a most glorious day for him, they wish to deprive him of this gratification and not let it be handed down for posterity to remember that the Roman people put on military cloaks because of one citizen's peril and went back to the garb of peace because of the same citizen's rescue. Take away this reason, and you will find no reason at all for so misguided a proposal.

But do you, Members of the Senate, maintain your authority, stand by your opinion, keep fixedly in mind that which you have often made plain: that the decision in this entire war turns on the life of one very great and gallant man. [2] To liberate Decimus Brutus, leaders of the community were sent as envoys to order that enemy and traitor to withdraw from Mutina. To save the same Decimus Brutus, the consul Aulus Hirtius, after drawing lots, set out to war, his bodily infirmity strengthened by a courageous spirit and the prospect of victory. Caesar, as soon as he had liberated the Republic from these evil creatures,[1] set out with the army he had raised by himself to liberate the same Brutus and stop the commission of further crimes, thus overcoming out of his love for his native land some pain he felt for private reasons.[2] What was Gaius Pansa's object in 5 holding levies, raising funds, passing very severe decrees against Antonius, exhorting us, summoning the Roman

populo Romano ad causam libertatis vocando, nisi ut D.
Brutus liberaretur? A quo populus Romanus frequens ita
salutem D. Bruti una voce depoposcit ut eam non solum
commodis suis sed etiam necessitati victus anteferret.
Quod sperare nos quidem debemus, patres conscripti, aut
inibi esse aut iam esse confectum: ‹s›ed[4] spei fructum rei
convenit et evento reservari, ne aut deorum immortalium
beneficium festinatione praeripuisse aut vim Fortunae
stultitia contempsisse videamur.

6   Sed quoniam significatio vestra satis declarat quid hac
de re sentiatis, ad litteras veniam quae sunt a consulibus et
a pro praetore missae, si pauca ante quae ad ipsas litteras
pertineant dixero. [3] Imbuti gladii sunt, patres conscripti,
legionum exercituumque nostrorum vel madefacti potius
duobus duorum consulum, tertio Caesaris proelio. Si hostium fuit ille sanguis, summa militum pietas: nefarium scelus, si civium. Quo usque igitur is qui omnis hostis scelere
superavit nomine hostis carebit? Nisi mucrones etiam nostrorum militum tremere vultis dubitantis utrum in cive an
7   in hoste figantur. Supplicationem decernitis: hostem non
appellatis. Gratae vero nostrae dis immortalibus gratula-
tiones erunt, gratae victimae, cum interfecta sit civium
multitudo! "De improbis," inquit, "et audacibus." Nam sic
eos appellat clarissimus vir: quae sunt urbanarum male-

---

[4] *corr. Manutius*

[3] Presumably an allusion to some threat to Rome's grain
supply.
[4] Details of these three engagements with Antony's forces on
14 April, at Forum Gallorum, are given in §§26–28.

people to the cause of liberty, unless it was to bring about the liberation of Decimus Brutus? From him the Roman people in great numbers with one voice demanded Decimus Brutus' deliverance, putting it not only before their own benefits but also before the very necessity of nourishment.[3] We must hope, Members of the Senate, that it is on the point of achievement or already achieved. But it is fitting to reserve for the actual event the enjoyment of that for which we hope, so that we may not appear to have grasped too hastily at the gift of the immortal gods or, out of foolishness, to have despised the power of Fortune.

But inasmuch as the intimation you gentlemen give 6 sufficiently declares your views on this matter, I shall come to the dispatches sent by the consuls and the propraetor; but first a few words relevant to the dispatches themselves. [3] The swords of our legions and armies have been dipped, Members of the Senate, or rather steeped in blood in two battles fought by the two consuls and a third fought by Caesar.[4] If that blood was the blood of our country's foes, its shedding by our soldiers was the highest patriotism, but an abominable crime if it was the blood of fellow citizens. How long then shall this man, who has outdone in crime all public enemies, go without the name of public enemy? Unless you wish the very blades of our soldiers to waver, uncertain whether they are being plunged into a fellow citizen or into a public enemy. You gentlemen pro- 7 pose a public thanksgiving, but you do not use the word "enemy." Pleasing indeed will be our thanks to the immortal gods, pleasing our sacrificial offerings for the slaughter of a multitude of fellow citizens! "Comprising," as he puts it, "wicked and reckless individuals." This is what the illus-

dicta litium, non in[i]ustae[5] belli internecivi notae. Testamenta, credo, subiciunt aut eiciunt vicinos aut adulescentulos circumscribunt: his enim vitiis adfectos et talibus
8   malos ⟨aut⟩[6] audacis appellare consuetudo solet. Bellum inexpiabile infert quattuor consulibus unus omnium latronum taeterrimus; gerit idem bellum cum senatu populoque Romano; omnibus—quamquam ruit ipse suis cladibus—pestem, vastitatem, cruciatum, tormenta denuntiat: Dolabellae ferum et immane facinus quod nulla barbaria posset agnoscere, id suo consilio factum esse testatur; quaeque esset facturus in hac urbe, nisi eum hic ipse Iuppiter ab hoc templo atque moenibus reppulisset, declaravit in Parmensium calamitate, quos, optimos viros honestissimosque homines, maxime cum auctoritate huius ordinis populique Romani dignitate coniunctos, crudelissimis exemplis interemit propudium illud et portentum, L. Antonius, insigne odium omnium hominum vel, si etiam
9   di oderunt quos oportet, deorum. Refugit animus, patres conscripti, eaque dicere ⟨re⟩formidat[7] quae L. Antonius in Parmensium liberis et coniugibus effecerit. Quas enim turpitudines Antonii libenter cum dedecore subierunt, easdem per vim laetantur aliis se intulisse. Sed vis calamitosa est quam illis obtulerunt: libido flagitiosa qua Antoniorum oblita est vita. Est igitur quisquam qui hostis appellare non audeat quorum scelere crudelitatem Carthaginiensium victam esse fateatur? [4] Qua enim in urbe

---

    [5] *corr. Ferrarius*   [6] *add. Halm*   [7] *corr. Naugerius*

---

  [5] P. Servilius (see §11).   [6] Pointing to the statue of Jupiter Optimus Maximus, in whose temple on the Capitoline the Senate appears to have been meeting (cf. §§12, 27).

trious proposer[5] calls them: terms of abuse appropriate to a city lawsuit, not brands of deadly warfare. They forge wills, no doubt, or expel their neighbors from their property, or defraud young men: those who indulge in these and similar evil ways are customarily called "bad" or "reckless." An inexpiable war is being waged upon four consuls by the most savage bandit under the sun. He also wages war against the senate and people of Rome. He threatens us all—though he himself is collapsing under the weight of his own disasters—with destruction, devastation, and the pains of torture. He testifies that Dolabella's brutal and monstrous act, which no race of barbarians could acknowledge, was carried out on his advice; what he would have done in this city, had not Jupiter here[6] himself thrust him back from this temple and our city's walls, he made plain in the ruin of the inhabitants of Parma, who, very loyal and respectable folk, closely attached to the authority of this body and the dignity of the Roman people, were most cruelly slaughtered to serve as an object lesson at the hands of that vile monster Lucius Antonius, the conspicuous target of all men's hatred, of all gods' too, if the gods hate whom they ought. My mind recoils, Members of the Senate, and shudders to speak of what Lucius Antonius did in the case of the wives and children of the people of Parma. The Antonii delight in having inflicted upon others by violence the degradations to which they themselves have cheerfully and disgracefully submitted. But it is calamitous violence that they made those people suffer; it is scandalous lust that stains the lives of the Antonii. Is there anyone, then, who hesitates to call enemies men whose crimes, he admits, put the cruelty of the Carthaginians into the shade? [4] What city taken by assault did Hannibal treat so sav-

8

9

301

tam immanis Hannibal capta quam in Parma surrepta Antonius? Nisi forte huius coloniae et ceterarum in quas eo-
10 dem est animo non est hostis putandus. Si vero coloniarum
et municipiorum sine ulla dubitatione hostis est, quid tandem huius censetis urbis quam ille ad explendas egestates
latrocini sui concupivit, quam iam peritus metator et calli-
dus decempeda sua Saxa diviserat? Recordamini, per deos
immortalis, patres conscripti, quid hoc biduo timuerimus
a domesticis hostibus [id est qui intra moenia hostes sunt][8]
rumoribus improbissimis dissipatis. Quis liberos, quis
coniugem aspicere poterat sine fletu? Quis domum, quis
tecta, quis larem familiarem? Aut foedissimam mortem
omnes aut miserabilem fugam cogitabant. Haec a quibus
timebantur, eos hostis appellare dubitamus? Gravius si
quis attulerit nomen, libenter adsentiar: hoc vulgari con-
tentus vix sum, leviore non utar.

11 Itaque cum supplicationes iustissimas ex eis litteris
quae recitatae sunt decernere debeamus, Serviliusque de-
creverit, augebo omnino numerum dierum, praesertim
cum non uni, sed tribus ducibus sint decernendae. Sed hoc
primum faciam ut imperatores appellem eos quorum virtute, consilio, felicitate maximis periculis servitutis atque
interitus liberati sumus. Etenim cui viginti his annis supplicatio decreta est ut non imperator appellaretur aut mi-

[8] *del. Ferrarius*

---

[7] Cf. 11.12, where it is said that Saxa had once performed in
Caesar's army the function of a surveyor in laying out camps.

[8] When a false report of a victory by Antony briefly circulated
in Rome (§15).

[9] *"Imperator"* was a title conferred upon a commander after a

agely as Antonius treated Parma, which he took by stealth? Perhaps he is not to be reckoned an enemy of this colony and of others toward which he is similarly disposed! But if 10 without any doubt he is an enemy of the colonies and municipalities, what do you judge him to be with respect to this city, on which he has set greedy eyes as a means of satisfying his impoverished gang and which Saxa, that skilled and crafty surveyor, had already marked out with his ten-foot rule?[7] By the immortal gods, Members of the Senate, remember our alarm these past two days,[8] the product of wicked rumors spread by enemies within the gates. Who could look dry-eyed at his wife and children, or at his house or roof or guardian god of his household? All had a horrible death or a wretched flight in their thoughts. Do we hesitate to call enemies those at whose hands we feared such calamities? If anybody produces a harsher name, I shall gladly agree to it. This ordinary word barely contents me. A milder one I will not use.

Therefore, since pursuant to the dispatches that have 11 been read, we ought to decree public thanksgivings most justly due, and since Servilius has so proposed, I shall increase the number of days, to be sure, especially as they are to be decreed not to one commander but three. First, however, I shall proceed to salute as "imperators"[9] those by whose courage, judgment, and good fortune we have been set free from the gravest perils of slavery and destruction. After all, who in the past twenty years has been decreed a public thanksgiving and not been saluted an imperator at the same time, though his military achievements

significant victory, first by an acclamation from his troops and later confirmed by vote of the senate.

nimis rebus gestis aut plerumque nullis? Quam ob rem aut supplicatio ab eo qui ante dixit decernenda non fuit aut usitatus honos pervulgatusque tribuendus eis quibus etiam novi singularesque debentur. [5] An si quis Hispanorum aut Gallorum aut Thraecum mille aut duo milia occidisset, illum hac consuetudine quae increbruit imperatorem appellaret senatus: tot legionibus caesis, tanta multitudine hostium interfecta—[dico][9] ita, inquam, hostium, quamvis hoc isti hostes domestici nolint—clarissimis ducibus supplicationum honorem tribuemus, imperatorium nomen adimemus? Quanto enim honore, laetitia, gratulatione in hoc templum ingredi debent illi ipsi huius urbis liberatores, cum hesterno die propter eorum res gestas me ovantem et prope triumphantem populus Romanus in Capitolium domo tulerit, domum inde reduxerit! Is enim demum est mea quidem sententia iustus triumphus ac verus, cum bene de re publica meritis testimonium a consensu civitatis datur. Nam sive in communi gaudio populi Romani uni gratulabantur, magnum iudicium, sive uni gratias agebant, eo maius, sive utrumque, nihil magnificentius cogitari potest.

"Tu igitur ipse de te?" dixerit quispiam. Equidem invitus, sed iniuriae dolor facit me praeter consuetudinem gloriosum. Nonne satis est ab hominibus virtutis ignaris

12

13

[9] *del. Garatoni*

[10] Cicero likens the rejoicing to an *ovatio*, which was a triumphal procession, on a lesser scale than a triumph, to honor a successful military commander.
[11] Caused by the false report concerning Cicero's supposed plans to seize power, described in §14. Hence the remark in the

were minimal or often nonexistent? Accordingly, either
the public thanksgiving should not have been proposed by
the previous speaker, or a regular, customary honor should
be accorded to those who deserve even unprecedented
and extraordinary honors. [5] Or can it be that if somebody   12
had killed a thousand or two thousand Spaniards or Gauls
or Thracians, the senate would salute him as imperator,
following what has now become normal practice, whereas
after the cutting to pieces of so many legions and the
slaughter of such a multitude of enemies—*of enemies*, I repeat, however much these enemies within our gates may
dislike that term—shall we accord the honor of public
thanksgivings to our illustrious commanders and take away
the title of imperator? For with what honor, rejoicing, and
congratulation should those liberators of this city enter
this temple in person, when yesterday on account of their
achievements the Roman people bore me from my house
to the Capitol and back again to my house in an ovation,[10]
almost a triumph! For to my mind, a true, genuine triumph   13
is only when those who have deserved well of the Republic
receive the tributes of a united community. If in the shared
joy of the Roman people they were congratulating one individual, that was a great mark of esteem; if they were
thanking one individual, all the greater; if both, no more
splendid compliment can be conceived of.

Someone may say: "Do you, then, indulge in self-ap-
plause?" It is against my will, to be sure, but a sense of
injury[11] makes me vainglorious, contrary to my habit. Is
it not enough that persons ignorant of the meaning of

next sentence: "Is it not enough (i.e. bad enough: leaving aside the
false allegation against him) . . . ?"

CICERO

gratiam bene merentibus non referri? Etiam in eos qui
omnis suas curas in rei publicae salute defigunt, [impe-
14 tus]^10 crimen ‹et›^11 invidia quaeretur? Scitis enim per hos
dies creberrimum fuisse sermonem, me Parilibus, qui dies
hodie est, cum fascibus descensurum. In aliquem credo
hoc gladiatorem aut latronem aut Catilinam esse collatum,
non in eum qui ne quid tale in re publica fieri posset
effecerit. An [ut]^12 ego, qui Catilinam haec molientem
sustulerim, everterim, adflixerim, ipse exstiterim repente
Catilina? Quibus auspiciis istos fascis augur acciperem,
quatenus haberem, cui traderem? Quemquamne fuisse
tam sceleratum qui hoc fingeret, tam furiosum qui crede-
ret?

Unde igitur ista suspicio vel potius unde iste sermo? [6]
15 Cum, ut scitis, hoc triduo vel quadriduo tristis a Mutina
fama manaret, inflati laetitia atque insolentia impii cives
unum se in locum, ad illam curiam furiis potius suis quam
rei publicae infelicem congregabant. Ibi cum consilia ini-
rent de caede nostra partirenturque inter se qui Capitolium, qui rostra, qui urbis portas occuparent, ad me con-

---

^10 *del. Faërnus*   ^11 *add. Clark*   ^12 *del. Faërnus*

---

12 The Parilia or Palilia (Feast of Pales, the shepherds' god) on
21 April, regarded as Rome's "birthday."

13 By taking up this symbol of magisterial power (*imperium*),
Cicero would, in effect, have been proclaiming himself dictator.

14 *Sustulerim* could mean "removed," but the sequence of
ideas in the three verbs appears to be modeled on the successive
stages in the overturning of a statue.

15 Generally supposed to be the Curia Pompeia, where Caesar
was assassinated; but why would the plotters choose to meet in

true worth make no return of gratitude to those who deserve well? Will even those who devote all their care to the preservation of the Republic be targets for backbiting and envy? You know that during the past few days there was a vast amount of talk that on Shepherds' Day,[12] that is today, I would come down to the Forum with the fasces.[13] I suppose that such a rumor has been concocted against a gladiator or a bandit or a Catiline, not against a man who has made sure that nothing of that kind can happen in the Republic. Was it likely that I, who hoisted,[14] overthrew, and dashed down Catiline when he made such an attempt, should suddenly reveal myself a Catiline? With what auspices was I, an augur, to have accepted those fasces, how long was I going to keep them, to whom should I have handed them over? Could anyone have been so wicked as to invent this tale or so mad as to believe it?

So what is the origin of this suspicion, or rather this talk? [6] When, as you know, three or four days ago a sinister report from Mutina was circulating, our traitorous fellow citizens, puffed up with joy and insolence, gathered together in one place, in that senate-house of theirs,[15] a place of ill omen for their own mad designs rather than for the Republic. When they plotted there our massacre and assigned functions among themselves—who would seize the Capitol, who the Rostra, who the city gates—they thought it likely that the community would rally to me,

14

15

such a place? It is more likely that Cicero is speaking figuratively, referring to a private meeting place, perhaps Calenus' house. *Infelicem* may mean no more than "unlucky," i.e. likely to prove so, but probably alludes to something specific in the history of the locality.

cursum futurum civitatis putabant. Quod ut cum invidia
mea fieret et cum vitae etiam periculo, famam istam fascium dissipaverunt; fascis ipsi ad me delaturi fuerunt.
Quod cum esset quasi mea voluntate factum, tum in me
impetus conductorum hominum quasi in tyrannum para-
batur; ex quo caedes esset vestrum omnium consecuta.
Quae res ⟨non⟩[13] patefecit, patres conscripti, sed suo tem-
16   pore totius huius sceleris fons aperietur. Itaque P. Apuleius, tribunus plebis, meorum omnium consiliorum peri-
culorumque iam inde a consulatu meo testis, conscius,
adiutor, dolorem ferre non potuit doloris mei: contionem
habuit maximam populo Romano unum atque idem
sentiente. In qua contione cum me pro summa nostra
coniunctione et familiaritate liberare suspicione fascium
vellet, una voce cuncta contio declaravit nihil esse a me
umquam de re publica nisi optime cogitatum. Post hanc
habitam contionem duabus tribusve horis optatissimi nun-
tii et litterae venerunt: ut idem dies non modo iniquissima
me invidia liberarit sed etiam celeberrima populi Romani
gratulatione auxerit.
17   Haec interposui, patres conscripti, non tam ut pro me
dixerim—male enim mecum ageretur si parum vobis essem sine defensione purgatus—quam ut quosdam nimis
ieiuno animo et angusto monerem, id quod semper ipse

---

[13] *add.* SB

---

16 See n. 13 above.   17 Antony's chief agent (*procura-
tor*) in Rome (12.18), Calenus?
18 On 20 April, the day the news of the victory over Antony arrived (§12, with the statement below).   19 Cf. §12.

and so in order to bring me into odium or even peril of my life when that happened, they spread this rumor about the fasces. They themselves were even going to offer me the fasces,[16] and when this had been done as though at my own wish, an attack upon me by a hired gang was planned, as if upon a despot. From this there would have followed a massacre of all you senators. These plans, Members of the Senate, failed to be revealed by being put into operation, but when the time is ripe the source[17] of all this villainy will be disclosed. And so, the tribune of the plebs Publius Apuleius, who has been witness, confidant, and helper in all my counsels and dangers from my consulship onwards, could not bear the distress he felt for my distress; he held a packed public meeting,[18] at which the Roman people were completely of one mind. And when at that gathering he wanted to exonerate me from the suspicion about the fasces, as our close attachment and friendship made appropriate, the whole meeting declared with one voice that I had never entertained any but the most loyal thoughts concerning the Republic. Two or three hours after the meeting came the messengers and dispatches we were praying for. Thus the same day not only relieved me of a most unjust odium but also exalted me by the rejoicing[19] of the Roman people in vast numbers.

    I have put in these remarks, Members of the Senate, 17 not so much in self-justification—I would be in a bad way if I were not sufficiently exonerated in your eyes without a defense—as to warn, as I personally have always done, certain mean and petty-minded persons that they should

fecissem, uti excellentium civium virtutem imitatione dignam, non invidia putarent. Magnus est in re publica campus, ut sapienter dicere M.[14] Crassus solebat, multis apertus cursus ad laudem. [7] Utinam quidem illi principes viverent qui me post meum consulatum, cum eis ipse cederem, principem non inviti videbant! Hoc vero tempore in tanta inopia constantium et fortium consularium quo me dolore adfici creditis, cum alios male sentire, alios nihil omnino curare videam, alios parum constanter in suscepta causa permanere sententiamque suam non semper utili-

18 tate rei publicae, sed tum spe tum timore moderari? Quod si quis de contentione principatus laborat, quae nulla esse debet, stultissime facit, si vitiis cum virtute contendit; ut enim cursu cursus, sic in viris fortibus virtus virtute superatur. Tu, si ego de re publica optime sentiam, ut me vincas, ipse pessime senties? Aut, si ad me bonorum concursum fieri videbis, ad te improbos invitabis? Nollem, primum rei publicae causa, deinde etiam dignitatis tuae. Sed si principatus ageretur, quem numquam expetivi, quid tandem mihi esset optatius? Ego enim malis sententiis vinci non possum, bonis forsitan possim et libenter.

19 Haec populum Romanum videre, animadvertere, iudicare quidam moleste ferunt. Poteratne fieri ut non proinde homines ‹de›[15] quoque ut quisque mereretur iudicarent? Ut enim de universo senatu populus Romanus verissime

---

[14] dicere M. *Clark*: dicerem *t*: -re *bsv*: -re L. *coni. Halm*
[15] *suppl. Ferrarius*

---

[20] A praenomen is needed to distinguish the orator L. Crassus from M. Crassus, political ally of Caesar and Pompey. The choice is uncertain, but the reading of *t* favors the latter.

regard the merit of outstanding citizens as deserving imitation, not envy. Public life is a broad field, as Marcus Crassus was in the habit of wisely saying,[20] and the path to glory is open to many. [7] I only wish those leaders of the community were still alive who not unwillingly saw me in a position of leadership after my consulship, though I myself gave them prior place. But today, when we are so badly off for brave and resolute consulars, what distress do you think I feel when I see some expressing disloyal sentiments, others totally indifferent, others not persevering resolutely enough in the cause they have embraced and not always regulating their views by reference to the advantage of the Republic but sometimes by hope and sometimes by fear! If, however, anybody is concerned about rivalry for leadership, which ought not to exist, he is acting very foolishly if he competes with merit by means of demerit. As speed is overcome by speed, so, when brave men are rivals, merit is overcome by merit. If I am a good patriot, will you[21] be a bad one in order to get the better of me? Or, if you see decent men rally to me, will you invite wicked men to join you? I wish it were not so, first for the sake of the Republic, and also, secondly, for the sake of your reputation. But if leadership, which I have never sought, were the issue, what, for heaven's sake, would be more desirable from my point of view? I cannot be bested by bad proposals, but perhaps I could by good ones—and gladly.

Some individuals are annoyed that the Roman people see, notice, and judge what goes on. Was it not inevitable that the public judge each of us just as each deserved? Concerning the senate as a whole, the Roman

18

19

[21] Addressing Calenus (cf. 5.25; 7.5).

iudicat nullis rei publicae temporibus hunc ordinem firmi-
orem aut fortiorem fuisse, sic de uno quoque nostrum
et maxime qui hoc loco sententias dicimus sciscitantur
omnes, avent audire quid quisque senserit, ita de quoque
20 ut quemque meritum arbitrantur existimant. Memoria
tenent me ante diem xiii[i][16] Kalendas Ianuarias principem revocandae libertatis fuisse; me ex Kalendis Ianuariis
ad hanc horam invigilasse rei publicae; meam domum
measque auris dies noctesque omnium praeceptis moni-
tisque patuisse; meis litteris, meis nuntiis, meis cohorta-
tionibus omnis qui ubique essent ad patriae praesidium
excitatos; meis sententiis a Kalendis Ianuariis numquam
legatos ad Antonium; semper illum hostem, semper hoc
bellum, ut ego, qui omni tempore verae pacis auctor fuis-
21 sem, huic essem nomini pestiferae pacis inimicus. Idem
Ventidium, cum alii praetorem, ego semper hostem. Has
in sententias meas si consules [designati][17] discessionem
facere voluissent, omnibus istis latronibus auctoritate ipsa
senatus iam pridem de manibus arma cecidissent.

[8] Sed quod tum non licuit, patres conscripti, id hoc
tempore non solum licet verum etiam necesse est, eos qui
re sunt hostes verbis notari, sententiis nostris hostis iudi-
22 cari. Antea cum hostem ac bellum nominassem, semel et
saepius sententiam meam de numero sententiarum sustu-

16 corr. *Budaeus*
17 del. *Manutius*

22 Lit. "in this position," i.e. as ex-consuls. Senators were
called upon to express their views in order of rank by office, the ex-
consuls being polled first (after the consuls-elect in the latter half
of the year: cf. 5.35).

people judge very truly that never in the history of the Republic has this body shown itself braver or more resolute. In the same way, everyone asks questions about each individual senator among us and especially about those who speak in the first rank.[22] They are eager to hear what opinion each of us has expressed, and they estimate each of us as they think he has deserved. They remember that on the twentieth of December I took the lead in the recovery of freedom; that from the first of January up to this hour I have watched over the interests of the Republic; that my house and my ears have been open day and night to the advice and warnings of all; that my letters, my messages, my encouragements roused all and sundry, wherever they might be, to come to the aid of our native land; that ever since the first of January I have never voted for envoys to be sent to Antonius,[23] but always called him an enemy and this conflict a war, so that I, who have at all times striven for true peace, was hostile to this name of a pernicious peace. Likewise I always called Ventidius an enemy, while others called him a praetor. If the consuls had been willing to hold a vote on these proposals of mine, the authority of the senate would of itself long ago have caused the weapons to drop from all those brigands' hands.

[8] But that which was not permitted then, Members of the Senate, not only is permissible but is even necessary at this time: those who are enemies in fact must be branded such in words, declared enemies by our votes. Previously when I used the terms "enemy" and "war," they repeatedly removed my motion from the list of motions to be put to a

[23] Contradicted by his admission in 12.1 that he was duped into voting for the second peace embassy.

lerunt: quod in hac causa fieri iam non potest. Ex litteris
enim C. Pansae A. Hirti consulum, C. Caesaris pro praetore, de honore dis immortalibus habendo sententias dicimus. Supplicationem modo qui decrevit, idem imprudens
hostis iudicavit; numquam enim in civili bello supplicatio
decreta est. Decretam dico? Ne victoris quidem litteris
23 postulata est. Civile bellum consul Sulla gessit, legionibus
in urbem adductis quos voluit expulit, quos potuit occidit:
supplicationis mentio nulla. Grave bellum Octavianum in-
secutum est: supplicatio nulla victori. Cinnae victoriam
imperator ultus est Sulla: nulla supplicatio decreta a senatu. Ad te ipsum, P. Servili, num misit ullas collega litteras
de illa calamitosissima pugna Pharsalia? Num te de supplicatione voluit referre? Profecto noluit. At misit postea
de Alexandria, de Pharnace: Pharsaliae vero pugnae ne
triumphum quidem egit. Eos enim civis pugna illa sustule-
rat quibus non modo vivis sed etiam victoribus incolumis
24 et florens civitas esse posset. Quod idem contigerat supe-
rioribus bellis civilibus. Nam mihi consuli supplicatio nullis armis sumptis non ob caedem hostium, sed ob conserva-
tionem civium novo et inaudito genere decreta est. Quam
ob rem aut supplicatio re publica pulcherrime gesta postu-
lantibus nostris imperatoribus deneganda est, quod prae-

24 P. Servilius (§11).

25 Cicero conveniently overlooks the *supplicatio* voted to
Caesar in 45 (see n. 33 below).

26 Caesar and Servilius were consuls in 48.

27 His victories in 47, in Egypt and later over Pharnaces, at the
Battle of Zela in Pontus.

28 On 3 December 63 (cf. 2.13).

vote; that cannot now be done in the present case. Pursuant to dispatches from the consuls Gaius Pansa and Aulus Hirtius and propraetor Gaius Caesar, we are voicing our proposals concerning the payment of honor to the immortal gods. The senator who just proposed a public thanksgiving[24] has in so doing, and unbeknown to himself, declared them enemies; for no public thanksgiving has ever been voted in a civil war.[25] "Voted," did I say? Indeed, none has ever been asked for in a victor's dispatch. Sulla as consul fought a civil war; he marched his legions into Rome, banished whom he chose, killed whom he could: no mention of a public thanksgiving. A major war, the war of Octavius, came next: no public thanksgiving for the victor. Sulla as imperator avenged Cinna's victory: no public thanksgiving voted by the senate. To you yourself, Publius Servilius, surely your colleague[26] did not send any dispatch concerning the disastrous Battle of Pharsalia, did he? Nor did he want you to consult the senate concerning a public thanksgiving, did he? Of course he didn't. But he sent one subsequently concerning Alexandria and another concerning Pharnaces.[27] For the Battle of Pharsalia he did not celebrate a triumph either. For if those citizens whom that battle took away had not only lived but been victorious, the community could have survived and prospered. That was likewise the case in previous civil wars. For to me as consul a public thanksgiving of a new and unheard of sort was decreed,[28] without there being any resort to arms, voted not on account of the slaughter of enemies but of the preservation of citizens. Therefore, either you must refuse a public thanksgiving to our commanders for their splendid successes on behalf of the Republic when they are asking for it, something that has never happened to anybody except

ter A. Gabinium contigit nemini, aut supplicatione decernenda hostis eos de quibus decernitis iudicetis necesse est.

[9] Quod ergo ille re, id ego etiam verbo, cum imperatores eos appello: hoc ipso nomine et eos qui iam devicti sunt et eos qui supersunt hostis iudico [cum victores appello imperatores].[18] Quo modo enim potius Pansam appellem, etsi habet honoris nomen amplissimi; quo Hirtium? Est ille quidem consul, sed alterum nomen benefici populi Romani est, alterum virtutis atque victoriae. Quid? Caesarem, deorum beneficio rei publicae procreatum, dubitemne appellare imperatorem? Qui primus Antoni immanem et foedam crudelitatem non solum a iugulis nostris sed etiam a membris et visceribus avertit.

Unius autem diei quot et quantae virtutes, di immortales, fuerunt! Princeps enim omnium Pansa proeli faciendi et cum Antonio confligendi fuit; dignus imperator legione Martia, digna legio imperatore. Cuius si acerrimum impetum cohibere Pansa potuisset, uno proelio confecta res esset. Sed cum libertatis avida legio effrenatius in aciem hostium irrupisset ipseque in primis Pansa pugnaret, duobus periculosis vulneribus acceptis sublatus e proelio rei publicae vitam reservavit. Ego vero hunc non solum imperatorem sed etiam clarissimum imperatorem iudico, qui, cum aut morte aut victoria se satis facturum rei publicae spopondisset, alterum fecit, alterius di immortales omen avertant!

[18] *del. Ferrarius*

[29] In May 56, but not the only refusal, despite Cicero's assertion. At least one other is known: T. Albucius in *c.* 104 (*MRR* 1.560). [30] Pansa, however, did die of his wounds soon after this speech was delivered (*Fam.* 10.33.4; Suet. *Aug.* 11).

Aulus Gabinius,[29] or by decreeing a public thanksgiving you necessarily declare enemies those to whom your decree refers.

[9] Therefore, when I salute our commanders as "imperators," I am expressing in words what Servilius is expressing in fact: by this very title I declare enemies both those already thoroughly vanquished and those who remain. How better should I address Pansa, though he bears 25 the title of our highest public office? Or Hirtius? He is consul, to be sure, but that title came as the gift of the Roman people, while this one is conferred by valor and victory. What of Caesar, him who was engendered for the sake of the Republic by the favor of the Gods? Am I to hesitate to salute him as imperator—Caesar, who was the first to turn Antonius' foul, monstrous cruelty aside not only from our throats, but also from our limbs and vitals?

Immortal gods, how many and how great were the deeds of valor that a single day brought forth! Pansa was 26 first among them all to join battle and clash with Antonius: a commander worthy of the Martian Legion, as the legion is worthy of its commander. And if Pansa had been able to restrain their passionate onslaught, the issue would have been settled in a single engagement. But when in their eagerness for freedom the legion broke too impetuously into the enemy's lines and Pansa himself was fighting among the foremost, he received two dangerous wounds and was removed from the field to reserve his life for the Republic. I declare him not only imperator but also a most illustrious imperator, who having pledged himself to do his duty to the Republic by either death or victory, has achieved the one and as for the other, may the immortal gods avert the omen![30]

27   [10] Quid dicam de Hirtio? Qui re audita e castris duas
legiones eduxit incredibili studio atque virtute, quartam
illam quae relicto Antonio se olim cum Martia legione con-
iunxit, et septimam quae constituta ex veteranis docuit hoc
proelio militibus eis qui Caesaris beneficia servassent senatus populique Romani carum nomen esse. His viginti
cohortibus, nullo equitatu, Hirtius ipse aquilam quartae
legionis cum inferret, qua nullius pulchriorem speciem
imperatoris accepimus, cum tribus Antoni legionibus
equitatuque conflixit, hostisque nefarios, huic Iovi‹s Optimi›[19] Maximi ceterisque deorum immortalium templis,
urbis tectis, libertati populi Romani, nostrae vitae sangui-
nique imminentis prostravit, fudit, occidit, ut cum ad-
modum paucis, nocte tectus, metu perterritus, princeps
latronum duxque fugerit. O solem ipsum beatissimum qui,
ante quam se abderet, stratis cadaveribus parricidarum
cum paucis fugientem vidit Antonium!

28   An vero quisquam dubitabit appellare Caesarem imperatorem? Aetas eius certe ab hac sententia neminem de-
terrebit, quando quidem virtute superavit aetatem. Ac
mihi semper eo maiora beneficia C. Caesaris visa sunt quo
minus erant ab aetate illa postulanda: cui cum imperium
dabamus, eodem tempore etiam spem eius nominis defe-
rebamus; quod cum es‹se›t[20] consecutus, auctoritatem
decreti nostri rebus gestis suis comprobavit. Hic ergo adu-

---

19 *suppl. Muretus*   20 *coni. Halm*

---

31 In contrast with veterans who squandered their bounties
and joined Antony in the hope of repairing their fortunes (11.37;
13.3).   32 *Imperium* ("command") as propraetor, granted on
Cicero's motion on 1 Jan. (5.45), not the title *imperator*.

[10] What am I to say of Hirtius? When the report   27
reached him, he led two legions out of camp with remarkable zeal and energy: the Fourth, which having abandoned
Antonius previously joined the Martian Legion, and the
Seventh, which was composed of veterans and showed in
this battle that those soldiers who had properly looked after their bounties from Caesar[31] hold dear the name of the
senate and people of Rome. With these twenty cohorts and
no cavalry, Hirtius, himself bearing forward the eagle of
the Fourth Legion—history has no finer picture of an imperator to show—clashed with the three legions and cavalry of Antonius and laid low, routed, slew those wicked
enemies, who were threatening this Temple of Jupiter
Best and Greatest and the other temples of the immortal
gods, the roofs of Rome, the liberty of the Roman people,
and our lives and lifeblood. Consequently, the chief and
leader of the bandits fled in a panic, under cover of dark-
ness, with a very few companions. Oh happiest of days!
The sun of that day, before it set, beheld Antonius and a
few others in flight over a field strewn with the carcasses of
traitors.

Or will anyone hesitate to salute Caesar as imperator?   28
Assuredly his age will deter no one from this proposal,
since he has indeed surpassed his age with his valor. I have
always rated what we owe to Gaius Caesar all the higher,
the less it was to be expected from one of his years. When
we were giving him military command, we were at the
same time holding out to him the prospect of that title, and
having obtained it,[32] he confirmed the authority of our decree by his own exploits. This young man of the highest

lescens maximi animi, ut verissime scribit Hirtius, castra
multarum legionum paucis cohortibus tutatus est secun-
dumque proelium fecit. Ita trium imperatorum virtute,
consilio, felicitate uno die locis pluribus res publica est
29 conservata. [11] Decerno igitur eorum trium nomine
quinquaginta dierum supplicationes: causas, ut honorifi-
centissimis verbis consequi potuero, complectar ipsa sententia.

Est autem fidei pietatisque nostrae declarare fortissimis militibus quam memores simus quamque grati. Quam
ob rem promissa nostra atque ea quae legionibus bello
confecto tributuros nos spopondimus hodierno senatus
consulto renovanda censeo; aequum est enim militum, ta-
30 lium praesertim, honorem coniungi. Atque utinam, patres
conscripti, protinus[21] omnibus solvere nobis praemia lice-
ret! Quamquam nos ea quae promisimus studiose cumula-
ta reddemus. Sed id quidem restat, ut spero, victoribus,
quibus senatus fides praestabitur: quam quoniam difficillimo rei publicae tempore secuti sunt, eos numquam opor-
tebit consili sui paenitere. Sed facile est bene agere cum
eis a quibus etiam tacentibus flagitari videmur: illud admi-
rabilius et maius maximeque proprium senatus sapientis est, grata eorum virtutem memoria prosequi qui pro pa-
31 tria vitam profuderunt. Quorum de honore utinam mihi
plura in mentem venirent! Duo certe non praeteribo quae
maxime occurrunt: quorum alterum pertinet ad virorum

---

21 *coni. SB*: civibus *D*

---

33 A celebration of this exceptional length had been granted
only once previously, to Caesar for his final victory in the Civil
War, at Munda in 45 (Cass. Dio 43.42.2).

spirit, as Hirtius most truly writes, defended a camp of many legions with a few cohorts and fought a successful engagement. Thus by the courage, judgment, and good fortune of three imperators, in the course of a single day and in multiple places, the Republic was preserved. [11] Therefore I move public thanksgivings lasting fifty days in the name of the three.[33] The grounds I shall embrace in my motion, in the most laudatory terms I can command.

Further, it is a matter of good faith and of dutifulness on our part to declare to these terribly brave soldiers how mindful and how sensible we are of what we owe them. For this reason I propose that our promises and all we ourselves pledged to do for the legions after the conclusion of hostilities be renewed in today's senatorial decree. It is only fair that the soldiers, especially such soldiers as these, be honored along with their commanders. I only wish, Members of the Senate, that we could pay rewards to all of them straightaway; to be sure, we shall zealously discharge the promises we have made, and with interest. But that indeed awaits the victors, I hope, to whom the senate will keep its word, and inasmuch as the soldiers trusted that word in a very grave crisis of the Republic, they must never regret their decision. But it is easy to deal fairly with men who seem to demand such treatment even though their voices are silenced. It is a more admirable and more generous and especially fitting thing for a wise senate to accompany with grateful memory the valor of those who have laid down their lives for their native land. I only wish I could think of more ways to do them honor. At least I shall not omit the two ways which most readily occur to me. One of them relates to the everlasting glory of these outstandingly

29

30

31

fortissimorum gloriam sempiternam, alterum ad lenien-
dum maerorem et luctum proximorum.

[12] Placet igitur mihi, patres conscripti, legionis Martiae militibus et eis qui una pugnantes occiderint monumentum fieri quam amplissimum.

Magna atque incredibilia sunt in rem publicam huius
merita legionis. Haec se prima latrocinio abrupit Antoni;
haec tenuit Albam; haec se ad Caesarem contulit; hanc
imitata quarta legio parem virtutis gloriam consecuta est.
Quarta victrix desiderat neminem: ex Martia non nulli in
ipsa victoria conciderunt. O fortunata mors quae naturae

32   debita pro patria est potissimum reddita! Vos vero patriae
natos iudico; quorum etiam nomen a Marte est, ut idem
deus urbem hanc gentibus, vos huic urbi genuisse videatur. In fuga foeda mors est; in victoria gloriosa. Etenim
Mars ipse ex acie fortissimum quemque pignerari solet. Illi
igitur impii quos cecidistis etiam ad inferos poenas parricidi luent; vos vero qui extremum spiritum in victoria ef-
fudistis piorum estis sedem et locum consecuti. Brevis a
natura vita nobis data est; at memoria bene redditae vitae
sempiterna. Quae si non esset longior quam haec vita, quis
esset tam amens qui maximis laboribus et periculis ad
summam laudem gloriamque contenderet?

33   Actum igitur praeclare vobiscum, fortissimi, dum vixis-
tis, nunc vero etiam sanctissimi milites, quod vestra virtus
neque oblivione eorum qui nunc sunt nec reticentia poste-
rorum sepulta esse poterit, cum vobis immortale monu-

brave men, the other to alleviating the grief and lamentation of their relations.

[12] Therefore, Members of the Senate, I recommend the erection of a monument on the grandest possible scale to the soldiers of the Martian Legion and to those who fell fighting at their side.

Great and extraordinary are the services of this legion to the Republic. This legion was the first to sever itself from Antonius' banditry; this held Alba; this went over to Caesar. Following its example, the Fourth Legion won equal glory for its manly conduct. The conquering Fourth has not lost a man. Of the Martian, some fell in the hour of victory. Death, our debt to nature, is fortunate indeed when it is paid for the sake of one's native land. But you, I declare, were born for your native land, you whose very name is from Mars, so that the same god may appear to have given birth to this city for the world and to you for this city. Death in flight is shameful, in victory glorious. Mars himself customarily appropriates as his own the bravest in the battle line. Those traitors whom you killed will pay for their crime of treason even in the world below; whereas you who breathed your last in victory have gained the dwelling place of pious souls. Brief is the life granted us by nature, but the memory of a life nobly sacrificed is eternal. And if that memory lasted no longer than this life of ours, who would be so mad as to strive after highest praise and glory at the cost of most grievous toils and perils?

Therefore, it has gone well with you, most valiant soldiers while you lived and now also most revered because your valor will be able to be buried neither in the oblivion of the present generation nor in the silence of posterity, since the senate and people of Rome will raise for you, I

32

33

mentum suis paene manibus senatus populusque Romanus exstruxerit. Multi saepe exercitus Punicis, Gallicis,
Italicis bellis clari et magni fuerunt, nec tamen ullis tale
genus honoris tributum est. Atque utinam maiora possemus, quando quidem a vobis maxima accepimus! Vos ab
urbe furentem Antonium avertistis; vos redire molientem
reppulistis. Erit igitur exstructa moles opere magnifico
incisaeque litterae, divinae virtutis testes sempiternae,
numquamque de vobis eorum qui aut videbunt vestrum
monumentum aut audient gratissimus sermo conticescet.
Ita pro mortali condicione vitae immortalitatem estis
consecuti.

34   [13] Sed quoniam, patres conscripti, gloriae munus optimis et fortissimis civibus monumenti honore persolvitur,
consolemur eorum proximos, quibus optima est haec quidem consolatio: parentibus, quod tanta rei publicae praesidia genuerunt; liberis, quod habebunt domestica exempla
virtutis; coniugibus, quod eis viris carebunt, quos laudare
quam lugere praestabit; fratribus, quod in se ut corporum,
sic virtutis similitudinem esse confident. Atque utinam his
omnibus abstergere fletum sententiis nostris consultisque
possemus, vel aliqua talis eis adhiberi publice posset oratio
qua deponerent maerorem atque luctum gauderentque
potius, cum multa et varia impenderent hominibus genera
mortis, id genus quod esset pulcherrimum suis obtigisse
eosque nec inhumatos esse nec desertos, quod tamen ipsum pro patria non miserandum putatur, nec dispersis
bustis humili sepultura crematos, sed contectos publicis

might almost say with their own hands, an immortal memorial. Often many armies were great and famous in the Punic, Gallic, and Italian wars, and yet to none was paid an honor of this kind. If only we could do more, since from you we have received so much! You turned Antonius in his fury away from Rome. You repelled him as he was getting ready to return. Therefore, a magnificent structure will be raised and incised with an inscription that will bear eternal witness to your godlike valor; and the tongues of those who shall see or hear of your monument shall never cease to talk of you in profound gratitude. Thus in return for mortal life you have won immortality.

[13] But, Members of the Senate, inasmuch as their 34 due gift of glory is paid to our most loyal and valiant countrymen by the honor of a monument, let us offer solace to their relations, for whom the following is indeed the best solace: for their parents, that they gave birth to such bulwarks of the Republic; for their children, that they will have examples of courage in their own families; for their wives, that they will be parted from husbands whom it will be more fitting to praise than to mourn; for their brothers, that they will be confident of resembling them in valor as well as in bodily appearance. Would that we could wipe away the tears of all of these by our motions and decrees, or that a public oration could be made to them such as might persuade them to lay aside lamentation and mourning and rather rejoice that while many different kinds of death hang over men's heads, the fairest kind of all has befallen their kinsfolk; that their loved ones are not unburied and forsaken—though even that is accounted no pitiable fate if it is for the sake of one's native land—nor yet burnt with humble funeral rites and placed in scattered graves;

operibus atque muneribus eaque exstructione quae sit ad
35 memoriam aeternitatis ara Virtutis. Quam ob rem maximum quidem solacium ⟨erit⟩[22] propinquorum eodem monumento declarari et virtutem suorum et populi Romani
pietatem et senatus fidem et crudelissimi memoriam belli:
in quo nisi tanta militum virtus exstitisset, parricidio M.
Antoni nomen populi Romani occidisset.

Atque etiam censeo, patres conscripti, quae praemia
militibus promisimus nos re publica recuperata tributuros,
ea vivis victoribusque cumulate, cum tempus venerit, per-
solvenda; qui autem ex eis quibus illa promissa sunt pro
patria occiderunt, eorum parentibus, liberis, coniugibus,
fratribus eadem tribuenda censeo.
36 [14] Sed ut ⟨omnia⟩[23] aliquando sententia complectar,
ita censeo:

"Cum C. Pansa consul, imperator, initium cum hostibus confligendi fecerit, quo proelio legio Martia admirabili
incredibilique virtute libertatem populi Romani defenderit, quod idem legiones tironum fecerint; ipseque C. Pansa
consul, imperator, cum inter media hostium tela versare-
tur, vulnera acceperit; cumque A. Hirtius consul, imperator, proelio audito, re cognita, fortissimo praestantissi-
moque animo exercitum castris eduxerit impetumque in
M. Antonium exercitumque hostium fecerit eiusque copias occidione occiderit, suo exercitu ita incolumi ut ne
37 unum quidem militem desiderarit; cumque C. Caesar
⟨pro praetore⟩,[24] imperator, consilio diligentiaque sua cas-

[22] *add. Poggius*
[23] *add. SB*
[24] *add. P. Laetus*

that, instead, they will lie beneath a publicly raised monument, a structure that to all eternity shall be an altar of Valor. Therefore it will be the relatives' greatest consolation that by the same monument is declared the valor of their kin, the respectfulness of the Roman people, the good faith of the senate, and the memory of a most brutal war, a war in which, if there had not existed the signal valor of our soldiers, the name of the Roman people would have perished by Marcus Antonius' treason.

I further move, Members of the Senate, that the rewards which we promised to bestow upon the soldiers after the Republic had been set on its feet again are to be paid to them, living and victorious, with interest when the time comes. To the parents, children, wives, and brothers of those to whom those promises were made and who have died for their country, I move that the same be paid.

[14] But to embrace, finally, all this in a proposal, I move as follows:

"Whereas Gaius Pansa, consul and imperator, did commence an engagement with the enemy, in which battle the Martian Legion defended the freedom of the Roman people with wonderful and incredible valor, as did also the legions of new recruits; and Gaius Pansa, consul and imperator, did himself receive wounds when he was engaged in the thick of the enemies' missiles; and whereas Aulus Hirtius, consul and imperator, when he heard of the battle and learned the situation, did with exceptional courage lead out his army from camp and attack Marcus Antonius and his army composed of enemies and did cut Antonius' forces to pieces without the loss of a single man from his own ranks; and whereas Gaius Caesar, propraetor and imperator, by skillful and prudent generalship did success-

CICERO

tra feliciter defenderit copiasque hostium quae ad castra
accesserant profligarit, occiderit: ob eas res senatum existimare et iudicare eorum trium imperatorum virtute, imperio, consilio, gravitate, constantia, magnitudine animi, felicitate populum Romanum foedissima crudelissimaque
servitute liberatum.

Cumque rem publicam, urbem, templa deorum immortalium, bona fortunasque omnium liberosque conser-
varint dimicatione et periculo vitae suae: uti ob eas res
bene, fortiter feliciterque gestas C. Pansa A. Hirtius consules, imperatores, alter ambove, aut si aberunt, M. Cornutus, praetor urbanus, supplicationes per dies quinquaginta ad omnia pulvinaria constituat.

38   Cumque virtus legionum digna clarissimis imperatoribus exstiterit: senatum, quae sit antea pollicitus legionibus
exercitibusque nostris, ea summo studio re publica recuperata persoluturum.

Cumque legio Martia princeps cum hostibus conflixe-
rit, atque ita cum maiore numero hostium contenderit ut
plurimos caederent, caderent non nulli; cumque sine ulla
retractatione pro patria vitam profuderint; cumque simili
virtute reliquarum legionum milites pro salute et libertate
populi Romani mortem oppetiverint: senatui placere ut C.
Pansa A. Hirtius consules, imperatores, alter ambove, si

34 This first part of Cicero's motion confers the title *imperator*
on the three commanders (cf. §11).

35 Lit. "at all the *pulvinaria* ("sacred couches")" placed outside
the various temples (cf. 2.110, n. 138).

328

fully defend his camp, putting to rout and slaughter such enemy forces as had approached his camp: I move that in recognition of these achievements the senate judges and pronounces that by the courage, ordinance, skill, stead-fastness, resolution, devotion, and fortune of the three said commanders the Roman people has been freed from most cruel and degrading servitude.[34]

Next, whereas in combat and hazard of their lives they have preserved the Republic, the city of Rome, the temples of the immortal gods, and the property, estates, and children of us all, I move that in honor of these courageous and successful actions, Gaius Pansa and Aulus Hirtius, consuls and imperators, either one or both, or in their absence Marcus Cornutus, the city praetor, shall institute public thanksgivings for a period of fifty days, in every place of worship.[35]

Next, whereas the valor of the legions has been shown   38
worthy of their illustrious commanders, I move that the senate, upon the restoration of public order, shall discharge with all zeal the promises previously made to our legions and armies.

Next, whereas the Martian Legion took the lead in engaging the enemy, and, fighting against odds, lost certain of their own number while inflicting heavy losses on their adversaries, sacrificing their lives for their own country with no backward thought; and whereas the soldiers of the remaining legions encountered death no less valiantly for the safety and liberty of the Roman people: I move that it is the senate's decision that Gaius Pansa and Aulus Hirtius, consuls and imperators, either one or both, if they see fit, make provision and contract for the erection of a monument on

eis videatur, eis qui sanguinem pro vita, libertate, fortunis
populi Romani, pro urbe, templis deorum immortalium
profudissent monumentum quam amplissimum locandum
faciendumque ⟨curent, quaestoresque⟩[25] urbanos ad eam
rem pecuniam dare, attribuere, solvere iubeant, ut exstet
ad memoriam posteritatis sempiternam scelus crudelissi-
morum hostium militumque divina virtus: utique, quae
praemia senatus militibus ante constituit, ea solvantur eorum qui hoc bello pro patria occiderunt parentibus, liberis, coniugibus, fratribus, eisque tribuantur quae militibus
ipsis tribui oporteret, si vivi vicissent qui morte vicerunt."

[25] *suppl. Ferrarius et A. Augustinus et Garatoni*

the grandest possible scale to those who have shed their blood for the life, liberty, and estate of the Roman people, for the city of Rome, and for the temples of the immortal gods; and further that those same officials shall direct the city quaestors to give, assign, and pay monies for the said monument, to the end that there may be down through the ages an eternal record of our savage foes' wickedness and of our own soldiers' noble valor. Further, I move that the rewards previously authorized by the senate for the soldiers be paid to the parents, children, wives, or brothers of those who died for their native land in this war; and that they, the survivors, receive what the men themselves should have received, had they lived victorious who for victory died."

FRAGMENTA M. TULLI CICERONIS ORATIONIBUS PHILIPPICIS ASCRIPTA

[*Oratio Philippica* IV]

1 Quid? Hoc senatus consultum facit clam te ex urbe proieceris?

(*Non., p. 373.34–35M = 595L*: Proiectum, subtractum. M. Tullius in *Philippicarum* lib. IV: 'Quid? . . .')

[*Oratio Philippica* XIV]

2 titubare, haesitare, quo se verteret nescire

(*Non., p. 182.8–10M = 267L*: Titubare, trepidare. M. Tullius *Philippicarum* lib. XIIII: 'titubare . . .')

---

[1] Not found in the extant oration; reminiscent of Cicero's description of Antony's flight from Rome in Jan. 49 after the

FRAGMENTS ATTRIBUTED TO MARCUS TULLIUS CICERO'S PHILIPPIC ORATIONS

[*Fourth Philippic*][1]

1 What? Does this decree of the senate cause you to re-move yourself from the city in secret?

(*Nonius Marcellus*: "Cast out" means "removed." ‹For example:› Marcus Tullius says in the *Fourth Philippic*: 'What? . . .')

[*Fourteenth Philippic*][2]

2 to falter, to hesitate, not to know where he was to turn

(*Nonius Marcellus*: "To totter" means "to falter." ‹For example:› Marcus Tullius in the *Fourteenth Philippic*: 'to . . .')

passage of the *senatus consultum ultimum* (2.52).
   [2] Not found in the extant oration.

CICERO

Oratio Philippica XVI

3 Latere⟨n⟩sis ne vestigium quidem deflexit.

(*Arus., Gramm. Lat. VII, p. 467.15–16K:* Deflexit de proposito, Cic. *Philipp.* XVI: 'latere . . . ')

Oratio Philippica XVII

4 Non est illa dissensio disceptata bello.

(*Arus., Gramm. Lat. VII, p. 467.17–18K:* Disceptata lis est, Cic. *Philipp.* XVII: 'Non . . .')

Orationes Philippicae incertae

5 mulionem Ventidium

(*Schol. Bob. ad Cic. Mil. 29, p. 120.24–26St:* Quamvis et in *Philippicis* mulionem Ventidium dixerit eapropter, quod de publico redemerat iumentorum praebitionem quae est aput exercitum necessaria. — *Schol. ad Iuv. 7.199:* Ventidius ex mulione Caesaris dictator ⟨is praetor⟩ fuit, ut Tullius in epistolis et in *Philippicis* loquitur. — *Plin. NH 7.135:* P. Ventidium . . . auctor est . . . Cicero mulionem castrensis furnariae fuisse . . .)

6 Cara est cuiquam salus quam aut dare aut eripere potest Antonius?

(*Sen. Suas. 7.5:* Tuis utar, Cicero, verbis: 'Cara . . .')

---

3 On '*Phil.* 16' and '*Phil.* 17' see Introduction (in vol. a).

4 Perhaps M. Iuventius Laterensis, who served as a legate in the army of M. Aemilius Lepidus in 43.

5 Cicero nowhere uses the term 'muleteer' (*mulio*) in the extant *Philippics*. In the letters, it is found only in one written to Cicero by L. Munatius Plancus (*Fam.* 10.18.3 of 15 May 43).

FRAGMENTS

Sixteenth Philippic[3]

3 Laterensis[4] turned aside by not even a step.

(*Arusianus Messius*: He turned aside from something intended, ⟨for example:⟩ Cicero in the *Sixteenth Philippic*: 'Laterensis . . .')

Seventeenth Philippic

4 That disagreement has not been decided by war.

(*Arusianus Messius*: A dispute has been decided, ⟨for example:⟩ Cicero in the *Seventeenth Philippic*: 'That . . .')

Unspecified *Philippics*

5 the muleteer[5] Ventidius

(*Bobbio Scholiast on Cicero's Speech on behalf of Milo*: Although he referred to Ventidius as a muleteer even in the *Philippics* for the reason that Ventidius had previously entered into contracts with the government to furnish beasts of burden that were needed by the army. — *Scholion on Juvenal*: Ventidius was a praetor, having previously been a muleteer of the dictator Caesar, as Tullius says both in the letters and in the *Philippics*. — *Pliny the Elder*: . . . Cicero states that P. Ventidius was a muleteer for an army bakery . . .)

6 Does anyone hold dear preservation that can be given or snatched away by Antony?[6]

(*Seneca the Elder* [*reporting Pompeius Silo*]: Let me quote your own words, Cicero: 'Does . . .')

---

[6] These words, although not directly assigned to the *Philippics* and not found in the extant orations, may have been concocted from snatches of 2.5 and 2.60.

INDEX

References to the *Philippic Orations* are by speech number and numbered sections (numbers in the margins of the text and translation). Proper names are given in their Latin form, and names of persons are arranged alphabetically by *nomina gentilicia,* with cross-references provided for common *cognomina.* After each person's name is given the relevant *RE* number (Pauly-Wissowa) and an indication of political office(s) held and role(s) relevant to the *Philippics.* All dates are B.C. unless otherwise stated. Repetition of a name within a given section is not indicated. Parentheses enclose entire entries for persons and places not explicitly named in the text but signified by such descriptions as, e.g., *consul, uxor* or *municipium;* likewise, parentheses enclose numbered sections where oblique reference is made to persons/ places directly named elsewhere. Angle brackets enclose references to sections where a name is restored to the Latin text. Place names marked with an asterisk will be found on the maps.

The following abbreviations are employed: br. = brother; cos. = consul; cos. suff. = suffect consul; mag. eq. = Master of the Horse; mod. = modern place name; nr. = near; qu. = quaestor; pr. = praetor; pr. urb. = urban praetor; procos. = proconsul; s.v. = consult entry for this item elsewhere in this index; tr. pl. = tribune of the plebs

Brutus: *see* Iunius

Byllis (town in Epirus): 11.26

Caecilia et Didia lex (of 98; required advance promulgation of proposed laws): 5.8

Caecilius Bassus, Q. (*RE* 36; former Pompeian, fled to Syria after Pompey's defeat and later established himself at Apamea): 11.32

Caecilius Cornutus, M. (*RE* 45; pr. urb. 43): 14.37

Caecilii Metelli: 8.15

(Caecilius Metellus, M. [*RE* 77; cos. 115]: 8.14)

(Caecilius Metellus Baliaricus, Q. [*RE* 82; cos. 123]: 8.14)

(Caecilius Metellus Caprarius, C. [*RE* 84; cos. 113]: 8.14)

(Caecilius Metellus Diadematus, L. [*RE* 93; cos. 117]: 8.14)

Caecilius Metellus Macedonicus, Q. (*RE* 94; cos. 143): 8.14

Caecilius Metellus Pius Scipio, Q. (*RE* 99; cos. 52; Pompey's father-in-law): 2.109; 5.19; 13.29

Caelius (or Coelius), Q.? (*RE* 14; gaming companion of M. Antonius): 13.3, 26

Caepio: *see* Iunius Brutus, M.

Caesar: *see* Iulius

Caesennius Lento (*RE* 6; one of the Board of Seven, *see* septemviri): 11.13; 12.20, 23; 13.2, 26, 37

Caesetius Flavus, L. (*RE* 4; tr. pl. 44, removed from office by Caesar): 13.31

Cafo (not in *RE;* centurion before 43; Antonian in 44–43): 8.9 (Cafones), 26; 10.22; 11.12, 37; 12.20

Calenus: *see* Fufius

Cales (mod. Calvi, town in northern *Campania): 12.27

Calpurnius Bestia, L. (*RE* 25; candidate for the praetorship in *c.* 56; convicted and exiled in a sixth trial after five successful defenses by Cic.; recalled by Caesar, he became an Antonian): 11.11; 12.20; 13.2, 26

Calpurnius Bibulus, M. (*RE* 28; cos. 59; die-hard adversary of Caesar): 2.23; 11.34–35; 13.29

Calpurnius Piso, C. (*RE* 63; cos. 67): 2.12

Calpurnius Piso, L. (*RE* 73a; legate of C. Antonius, br. of the triumvir): 10.13

Calpurnius (or Pupius?) Piso, M. (not in *RE*): *see* Pupius Piso

Calpurnius Piso Caesoninus, L. (*RE* 90; cos. 58 and Caesar's father-in-law; on 1 Aug. 44, made a courageous speech attacking M. Antonius in the senate, but later supported com-

*Fidenae (small town in *Latium, slightly NE of *Rome): 9.4

Fides: *see* Trebellius

Figulus: *see* Marcius

Firmani (people of Firmum, mod. Fermo, a town on the Adriatic coast, SE of Ancona): 7.23

*Flaminia via (road NE from *Rome to Adriatic and then N to *Cisalpine Gaul): 12.22–23

Flamininus: *see* Quinctius

Formianum (Pompey's villa nr. Formiae, mod. Formia, a coastal town in southern *Latium): 13.11

Fortuna: 2.88; 11.5; 13.10, 12, 16, 29, 40; 14.5

forum (Romanum): 1.5, 25, 30; 2.21, 49, 56, 85, 107, 112; 3.24, 30, 32; 5.8–9, 18, 41; 6.13, 17; 7.7, 22; 13.39

(*Forum Gallorum [village between *Mutina and *Bononia in *Cisalpine Gaul near which Pansa engaged in battle with M. Antonius and was fatally wounded on 14 Mar. 43]: 14.26)

Fregellana (from *Fregellae, a town in *Latium *c.* 60 mi. SE of *Rome): 3.17

Fufius, Q. (*RE* 7; a Roman knight and half-brother, or cousin(?), of L. Rubrius, s.v.): 2.41

(Fufius [son of the preceding]: 2.41)

(Fufius [Calenus, Q.] [*RE* 9; father of the following]: 8.13)

Fufius Calenus, Q. (*RE* 10; cos. 47; after Caesar's death, M. Antonius' chief supporter in the senate; father-in-law of the cos. Pansa; "enemy" of Cic.): (3.20; 5.1, 25; 7.5); 8.11–12, 15–16, 18–19; 10.3, 5–6; 11.15; 12.(1), 3–4, 18; (14.15, 18)

(Fufius Calenus, Q. [*RE* 11; son of the preceding]: 10.4–5)

Fulcinius, C. (*RE* 1; envoy in 438 to Latin town of *Fidenae, s.v.): 9.(4), 5, (7)

(Fulvia [*RE* Fulvius 113; M. Antonius' second wife, previously married in turn to P. Clodius Pulcher and C. Scribonius Curio]: 1.33; 2.11, 48, 77, 93, 95, 113, 115; 3.4, 16; 5.11, 22; 6.4; 12.1–2; 13.18)

Fulvius Bambalio, M. (*RE* 40; father of the preceding): 2.90; 3.16

Fulvius Flaccus, M. (*RE* 58; cos. 125; important supporter of C. Gracchus, with whom he was killed in 121): 8.14

(Fulvius Flaccus, M. [not in *RE*;

elder son of the preceding]: 8.14)

(Fulvius Flaccus, Q. [*RE* 62; younger br. of the preceding]: 8.14)

Gabinius, A. (*RE* 11; cos. 58): 2.48; 14.24

Galba: *see* Sulpicius

Gallia: 2.76; 3.8; 3.12–13, 31–32, 34, 38; 4.8–9; 5.24, 26, 28, 31, 36–37, 46; 6.3, 5, 8–9; 7.11, 21, 24–26; 8.5, 21; 10.10, 21; 11.4; 12.9–10; 13.20

  Gallia citerior: 3.38; 7.3

  Gallia comata: 8.27

  Gallia togata: 8.27

  Gallia ultima: 2.48, (49); 5.5, 37; 7.3; 12.13; 13.37

  Galliae provinciae: 1.8

  Galli (Gauls): 3.20; 5.6; 13.33, 44; 14.12; *see also* Transpadani, Transalpinae gentes

  Gallica bella: 14.13

  Gallicus tumultus: 5.53; 8.3

Gallius, M. (*RE* 5; pr. 44?): <3.26?>; 13.26

Germani (tribes living E of Rhine): 5.6

  Germanus (pun on *germanus,* meaning "full brother"): 11.14

Glabrio: *see* Acilius

Glaucia: *see* Servilius

Gnatho (character in Terence's *Eunuchus*): 2.15

Gortynius iudex (a judge from

the town of *Gortyn in *Crete, here referring to Cydas, s.v.): 5.13

Gracchi (-us): *see* Sempronii (-ius)

Graecia: 1.7; 10.9–11, 14, 25–26; 11.26

  Graeci (referring to M. Antonius' new jurors): 5.12

  Graeci comites (referring to Mithridates of Pergamum, s.v., and other Greek followers of Caesar): 2.94

  Graeculi (referring to Menedemus and Petraeus, s.vv.): 13.33

  Graeculus iudex (referring to Lysiades, s.v.): 5.14

  Graecum verbum: 1.1. (amnestia); 11.14 (Lysidicus)

Hannibal (*RE* 8; Carthaginian general and inveterate enemy of *Rome): 1.11; 5.25, 27; 6.4, 6; 13.25; 14.9

Helena (*RE* 3; wife of Spartan king Menelaos): 2.55

Hernici (a people in *Latium): 6.13

Hippias (*RE* 10; freedman, friend of M. Antonius): 2.62–63

Hirtia lex (de Pompeianis, of 48 or 46): 13.32

Hirtius, A. (*RE* 2; cos. 43; died

10, 36; 2.28, 30–31, 97;
8.27; 10 *passim;* 11.26–27,
36; 13.26, 32, 37

Iunius Brutus Albinus, D. (*RE*
55a in Suppl. V; cos. desig.
43; leading assassin of
Caesar despite benefits
received from him; in
early April 44 departed
from *Rome to govern
*Cisalpine Gaul, which he
refused to hand over to
M. Antonius in Dec.; later
supported by the senate
and besieged in *Mutina
by Antonius; killed in 43):
3.1, 8–9, 11–12, 14, 34,
37–38; 4.7–9; 5.24, 26, 28,
35–37, 51; 6.3, 6–7, 9;
7.11, (20), 22, 24, 26; 8.5–
6, 17, 21, (24), 27, 33;
10.(4), 10, 15–17, 23; 11.4,
11, (21), 22, 24, 36, 38;
12.3, 9, 11, 22; 13.11, 16,
20, (25), 34, 46, 49; 14.1,
3–5

Iunius Silanus, D. (*RE* 163; cos.
62): 2.12

Iuppiter: 2.32, 110; 5.7–8;
11.11, 28; 13.7; 14.8
——Optimus Maximus:
13.12; 14.(8), 27
——Stator, temple of (at the
foot of the N slope of the
Palatine Hill in *Rome):
2.64

Iuventius Laterensis, M. (*RE*
16; pr. 51; legate in 43 to

M. Lepidus, s.v., loyal to
senate): fr. 3?

Kalendae
——Apriles: 2.93
——Decembres: 3.19, 20
——Februariae: 5.34
——Ianuariae: 1.6; 2.51, 76,
79, 83, 99; 3.1–2, 12, 13,
37; 5.1, 28, 31; 6.1–2;
10.3, 23; 14.20
——Iuniae: 1.6; 2.100,
108
——Maiae: 3.27
——Octobres: 5.19
——Septembres: 5.19
——Sextiles: 1.7, 8, 10, 14

Laco: *see* Abuttius
Laelius, C. (*RE* 2; cos. 190):
11.17
Laelius Sapiens, C. (*RE* 3; cos.
140; son of the preceding;
close friend of Scipio
Aemilianus, s.v.): 2.83;
11.17
Larks (legion): *see* legio V
Alaudae
Lars: *see* Tolumnius
Laterensis: *see* Iuventius
Latina lingua: 13.43
 Latine: 5.13; 7.17
Laudicea (Syrian port nr. *An-
tioch): 9.4
leges annales (laws specifying
qualifications for candi-
dates for political office):
5.47

cos. suff. 38; son of the preceding; opposed M. Antonius' allotment of praetorian provinces in Nov. 44): 3.25

Marcius Tremulus, Q. (*RE* 106; cos. 306, 288; conquered the Hernici): 6.13

Marius, C. (*RE* 14; cos. 107, 104–100, 86; great general, political opponent of Sulla, s.v.): 1.5; 8.15; 11.1; 13.1, 9

Marius, C. (*RE* 15; cos. 82; son of the preceding): 8.7; 13.1

("Marius, C." [Pseudomarius] [*RE* 16; supposititious son of the preceding; executed by M. Antonius in Apr. 44]: 1.5)

Marrucini (a people of east-central Italy): 7.23

Mars: 2.110; (4.5); 14.32

    Mars communis (the uncertain fortune of war): 10.20

    Martia: *see* legio Martia

    Martiales: *see* legio Martia

    Martialis flamen (priest of Mars): 11.18

    Martius campus (the plain formed by the bend in the Tiber, NW of the Capitoline Hill in *Rome): 6.14

Marsi (a people of *Latium): 12.27

Marsicum bellum (revolt of *Rome's Italian allies in 91–87, the Social War): 8.31

Marullus: *see* Epidius Marullus

*Massilia (mod. Marseilles): 8.18; 13.13

    Massilienses (the people of M.): 2.94; 8.18; 13.32

Mela: *see* Pontius

Menedemus (*RE* 16; a prominent Greek supporter of Caesar in western Macedonia in 48): 13.33

Metelli: *see* Caecilii

Metellus: *see* Caecilius

Milo: *see* Annius

Minucia porticus (in the campus Martius, s.v.): 2.84

Minucius Basilus, L. (M. Satrius, *RE* 1, before adoption; *patronus* of Picenum): 2.107

Minucius Thermus, Q. (*RE* 67; envoy sent by the senate in 43 to Sex. Pompeius in Massilia; proscribed in 43, but escaped to join Sex. Pompeius and later M. Antonius): 13.13

*Misenum (a town on the north headland of the Bay of *Naples, here referring to M. Antonius' villa there): 2.48, 73

(Mithridates of Pergamum [*RE* 15; contributed to Caesar's success in the Al-

Patavini (people of *Patavium,
  mod. Padua, a city in
  *Cisalpine Gaul): 12.10
Paullus: *see* Aemilius
Petraeus (a prominent Greek
  supporter of Caesar in
  Thessaly in 48): 13.33
Petusius (*RE* 1; Antonian from
  Urbinum, a town in
  Umbria; M. Antonius
  promised him Cic.'s pos-
  sessions): 12.19; 13.3
Phaedrus (*RE* Phaidros 8; well-
  known Epicurean philoso-
  pher): 5.13
Pharnaces (*RE* Pharnakes 2; son
  of Mithridates the Great;
  defeated by Caesar in 47
  and driven from Pontus):
  14.23
Pharsalia (of or connected with
  the Thessalian town
  *Pharsalus, near which
  Caesar defeated Pompey
  in Aug. 48): 2.39 (fuga);
  2.71 (Pharsalica acies);
  14.23 (pugna)
Philadelphus: *see* Annius
  Cimber
Philippus (V, king of Macedonia; *RE* 10): 11.17
Philippus: *see* Marcius
*Phoenice (Phoenicia): 11.35
Phormio (character in a comedy
  of that title by Terence):
  2.15
Picenus ager (region in NE Italy bordering on the Adriatic): 5.44

*Pisaurum (mod. Pesaro, town
  on Adriatic coast south of
  *Ariminum): 13.26
Piso: *see* Calpurnius; Pupius
Plancus: *see* Munatius
Poenus / Poeni (Carthaginian /
  -s): 5.27; 11.9
Pollentia (mod. Pollenza, town
  in Liguria in SW
  *Cisalpine Gaul): 11.14
Pompeia lex (iudiciaria of 55):
  1.20
Pompeius, Sex. (*RE* 17; father
  of the cos. of 89,
  Pompeius Strabo): 12.27
Pompeius, Sex. (*RE* 18; br. of
  the cos. of 89, Pompeius
  Strabo): 12.27
Pompeius Magnus, Cn. (*RE* 31;
  Pompey the Great, cos.
  70, 55, 52): 1.18, 36; 2.4,
  12, 23–24, 37–38, 54, 62,
  64–65, 67, (69), 73, 75,
  109; 5.39, 41, 43–44;
  11.18, 34; 13.2, 8–12, 26,
  30, 34, 42, 50
  Pompeianae possessiones
    (properties owned by P.):
    13.11
  Pompeiani (Pompeians):
    13.38, 45; 13.32 (-us);
    13.28–29 (-us senatus)
(Pompeius Magnus, Cn. [*RE*
  32; elder son of the preceding; killed in Spain after the Battle of *Munda
  in Mar. 45]: 2.75; 5.39;
  12.23)
Pompeius Magnus, Sex. (*RE* 33;

INDEX

INDEX

*Saxa Rubra (town just N of
*Rome): 2.77
Scaevola: *see* Mucius
Scaevolae: *see* Mucii
Scauri: *see* Aemilii
Scipio: *see* Cornelius Scipio,
Caecilius Metellus Pius
Scipio
Scribonius Curio, C. (*RE* 10;
general and orator, cos.
76, died in 53): 2.12, 45–
46
Scribonius Curio, C. (*RE* 11; tr.
pl. 50; son of the preceding, killed in 49, while
leading Caesarian forces
in Africa; previous hus-
band of M. Antonius' wife
Fulvia, s.v.): 2.3–4, 11,
44–46, (50); (5.11)
Seius Mustela (*RE* 3; Antonian
from the town of Anagnia
and leader of Antonius'
personal bodyguard): 2.8,
106; 5.18; 8.26; 12.14;
13.3
Semproniae leges (of C.
Gracchus in 123, 122):
1.18
Sempronii Gracchi (the two
brothers immediately be-
low): 7.17
Sempronius Gracchus, C. (*RE*
47; tr. pl. 123, 122): 1.18;
8.14
Sempronius Gracchus, Ti. (*RE*
54; tr. pl. 133): 8.13
Sempronius Tuditanus (*RE* 89;
maternal grandfather of

M. Antonius' wife Fulvia,
s.v.): 3.16
Semurium (piece of land close
to *Rome): 6.14
septemviri (the Board of Seven
appointed in 44 to admin-
ister M. Antonius' *lex
agraria*): 5.21, 33; 6.14;
8.26
septemviratus: 2.99
septemviralis: 12.23; 13.26
Sergius (*RE* 2; a mime, friend
of M. Antonius): 2.62
Sergius Catilina, L. (*RE* 23; pr.
68, leader of failed uprising in 63): 2.1, 118; 4.15;
8.15; 13.22; 14.14
Sertorianum bellum (uprising in
Spain led by fugitive Q.
Sertorius [*RE* 3; pr. 83
and supporter of L.
Cinna, cos. 87, s.v.];
crushed in 72): 11.18
Servilius, M. (*RE* 21; tr. pl. 43):
4.16
Servilius Ahala, C. (*RE* 32; mag.
eq. 439, slew Sp. Maelius,
s.v.): 2.26–27
Servilius Caepio Brutus, Q.: *see*
Iunius Brutus, M.
Servilii Cascae (here referring
to the following and a
brother): 2.27
Servilius Casca Longus, P. (*RE*
53; tr. pl. 43, one of the
assassins of Caesar): 2.27;
13.30
Servilius Glaucia, C. (*RE* 65; pr.
100; killed after passage of

361